*Exams #1-5 must pass w/ an 80% or better —
Contact Dr. Vance Cortez-Rucker
he will ~~contact~~ prepare & send certificate!*

Principal Tool Kit

2017 2nd Edition

*Lamar Univ. EPP
Dimples.Jones@lamar.edu*

Principal Tool Kit

2017 2nd Edition

Compiled by:

Dr. Vance Cortez-Rucker
Dr. Sandy Cortez-Rucker

Copyright© 2017 CR Educational Services, LLC

All rights are reserved. No part of the material protected by this copyright notice may be reproduced or utilized in any form or by any means, electronic or mechanical, including photocopying, recording or by any information storage and retrievable system, without express written permission from the copyright holder.

To obtain permission to use the material from this work for any purpose including workshops or seminars, please submit a written request to:

CR Educational Services, LLC
P O Box 547
Kountze, TX 77625

Library of Congress Cataloging-in Publication Data

    Cortez-Rucker, Vance
    Cortez-Rucker, Sandy
    TExES Principal Tool Kit 2017 2nd Edition
    ISBN: 978-1-387-22905-5
    Principal 068

Trademarks: All brand names and product names used in this book are trade names, service marks, trademarks, or registered trademarks of their respective owners. CRES nor the authors are associated.

LIMIT OF LIABILITY.DISCLAIMER OF WARRANTY: Author and publisher have used their best efforts in preparing this book. CRES makes no representations or warranties with respect to the accuracy or completeness of the contents of this book and specifically disclaim any implied warranties of merchantability or fitness for a particular purpose. There are no warranties which extend beyond the descriptions contained in this paragraph. No warranty may be created or extended by sales representatives or written sales materials. The accuracy and completeness of the information provided herein and the opinions stated herein are not guaranteed or warranted to produce any particular results and the advice and strategies contained herein may not be suitable for every individual. Neither CRES nor the author shall be liable for any loss of profit or income or any other damages, including but not limited to special, incidental or consequential.

The opinions, remarks and comments expressed in this publication are the sole work of CRES and were created independently from the National Education Association, Educational Testing Service, or any State Department of Education, Nationals Evaluation Systems or other testing affiliates.

Vance Cortez-Rucker, Ph.D.

Sandy Cortez-Rucker, Ed.D.

Answers@TExESCertifications.com

Website: TExESCert.com

TABLE OF CONTENTS

Introduction to the Principal Tool Kit xiii
What is the TExES Exam? xv
How Do I Study for the TExES? xvii
The Interview xix
Professional Reading List that are represented on the TExES Exam xx

TExES Principal Toolkit and Study Guide 1
Domains and Competencies 2
TExES Security 5
State and National Standards 7
Powers and Duties of the Principal 11
      Code of Ethics and Standard Practices for Texas Educators 14

Study Materials by Subject (alphabetical) 17
Accountability Ratings 2017 18
Affirmative Action Officer (AAO Officer) 21
Attendance Officer 23
Building a Professional Culture – Challenges of the Modern Principal 24
Bullying Prevention – Policies and Procedures 25
      Additional Documentation – Off Campus Bullying/Harassment Situations 26
Bullying and OCR 27
Campus Behavior Coordinator 28
Community Resource Management 29
Contracts and the Modern Principal 30
Contract and At-Will Employment 32
Co-Teaching and the Principal 34
Co-Teaching – A Model for Classroom Management 36
Co-Teaching and Special Education 37
Copyright: Fair Use 38
Crisis Management Plan (CMP) and Crisis Intervention Plan (CIP) 40
Curriculum – Instructional Program 42
Cyberbullying and Student First Amendment Rights 43
Cyber Security 44
Data Driven School Improvement 46
Death – Dealing with Crisis at the School 48

Campus Emergency Plan – Large ISD	48
Campus Emergency Plan – Rural ISD	49
Notifications and Announcement Procedures	49
If Death occurs while school is in session	50
Parent Notification	50
Determine Degree of Trauma	50
Roles for School Personnel	50
Principal Role	51
What if Death was a Suicide?	51
Disciplinary Alternative Education (DAEP) Placement	52
Discipline a Student with Disabilities	53
Documentation	56
Documentation – Why?	57
Effective Texas Classroom Environment	58
ELL and the Modern Principal	60
ELL Strategies	62
Emergency Management	63
Emergency Planning for Drill and Exercises	65
Fire/Evacuation	65
Lockdown	65
Tornado/Severe Weather	66
Shelter-in-Place	66
Reverse Evacuation	67
Emotional and Behavioral Assessment	68
Equity in the Interview	69
Evaluation and the Modern Principal – PDAS until changed by TEA to T-TESS	70
FERPA and the Modern Principal	72
Can a list of Student's Health Issues be Distributed to the Teachers and/or Staff?	72
Food Services	74
Grading Policy and Acceleration of Grades	76
Grievances and the Modern Principal	77
Homeless Students (McKinney-Veto)	80
Legal/Illegal Interview Questions	82
Leadership	85
Leadership (Situational Leadership)	86
Leadership (Transformational)	88
Management Overview – TEA Module #14	89
No Pass, No Play (UIL)	93

Novice Teacher and the Effective School Administrator 95

Parental Rights and the Modern Principal 97

Professional Learning Communities (PLC) 99

Records 100

Response to Intervention: School Building Level 101

Safe Routes to School Programs 103

Scenario Strategies – Technical Reading 105

Sexual Harassment Investigations 108

Technology and the Principal's Role 109

Transportation 111

Transportation of Students 112

Language Proficiency Assessment Committee (LPAC) 113

    LPAC and Assessment Committee 114

    LPAC and Placement 116

    LPAC Meeting 118

        Membership 118

        Responsibility 118

        Exiting the Program 119

Site-Based Decision Making (SBDM) 121

    SBDM Manual– An Overview 122

    SBDM – State Requirements 124

    SBDM – Membership as Described by TEC 11.251 and 11.252 129

    SBDM – Schoolwide Program Implementation 133

    SBDM – Campus Improvement Plan (CIP) 134

    School Health Advisory Council (SHAC) 136

    Site-Based Decision Making (SBDM) and the Modern Principal 139

        SBDM – Principal Responsibilities 139

        SBDM – Structure and Its Impact on a Campus 140

        SBDM – Mental Picture of the First-Year Administrator 141

    SBDM – Planning Cycle – Impact of Data 143

    SBDM - TAPR – Understanding Data Charts 144

SBDM Budgeting 147

    SBDM Budgeting 148

    Objective Budgeting 149

    Budget Process Overview 149

    Budgetary Approaches 150

    Site Based Budgeting 150

    Annual Budget Responsibilities and Guidelines 151

Roles and Responsibilities 151

Development of Campus Budget 151

SBDM Budget – Budget Code (Example) 152

Site Based Budgeting and the Principal 154

Campus Budget and the Modern Principal 155

Function 10 – Instructions & Instructional Related Services 156

Function 20 – Instructional & School Leadership 157

Function 30 – Student Support Services 157

SBDM Budget – Budget Redirection on the Campus 160

SBDM Budget – Rural and Low-Income School Programs 162

Year Long Budget Process 163

SBDM – Activity Fund and the Modern Principal 164

Special Education 167

Special Education, ARD and the Responsibilities of the Modern Principal 168

Basic Questions for the Principal 168

Participants of the ARD Meeting 168

Discipline-related School Removals 169

Special Education–ARD Committee Decision Making Process for the Texas Assessment Program 170

Special Education and Change of Placement 172

Special Education – IEP Changes 173

Special Education – Extended School Year (ESY) 174

Special Education – Timelines 175

Title Grants 177

Title Grants and the School Principal 178

Title I, Part A – Improving Basic Programs 180

Title II and Teacher Professional Development 182

Title III, Part A 184

Title IV, Part A 186

Title VII, Part A 187

Title IX Proportionality 188

Acronyms for Principals 193

Budget Acronyms 194

LPAC Acronyms 194

NCLB Acronyms 194

PDAS Acronyms 195

SBDM Acronyms 196

References 198

Introduction to the Principal Tool Kit

Best Practice and the Principal Tool Kit:

What do you need to know as a first-year administrator? How do you know you have the knowledge base of a first-year administrator? Importantly, how do you attain the above goals?

The Principal Tool Kit is designed to help examinees prepare for the TExES certification exam. The Principal Tool Kit has been created to offer the examinee the content validity of the beginning educator. The critical indicators of the formative year of the profession are shown and explained. The information is based on the state and national standards along with the principal standards.

As the lead professor, my team has identified the state mandated content. I have a high degree of confidence research has produced a document that successfully outlines the first year's standards of a school administrator. The construct and content of this document have a validity level that successfully meets both CAEP and SAC requirements. Both national agencies are now focusing on "program completers" as the hallmark of a successful program.

The TExES measures the content and professional knowledge required of an entry-level principal or assistant principal in Texas public schools (068 State Manual, 2015). The exam is a criterion-referenced exam designed to measure the knowledge (school policy, procedures, and law) of the examinee and, more importantly, the "application" of the knowledge. The exam is developed around large scenario driven story lines based on real-world situations faced by the current school administrator.

The Principal Tool Kit does not incorporate the process of "strategies" on its pages. The creator of the book has over thirty years of public school service and chose to create the book along the lines of, "what a beginning administrator should know," and not just to establish a book of testing strategies.

The challenge of the TExES is the ability to read technically. The scenarios are lengthy and full of data. It must be the skill of the reader to seek out (without becoming bogged down in the details) the required information of the test writer and pair that with the proper answer. This is difficult for many examinees.

Finally, it is extremely beneficial for the examinees to have in their possession the many manuals, journals and other professional writing offered by TEA/SBEC. If the examinees wish to understand, "Where do the questions come from?" The review of the manuals and other state documents will make it very clear.

What is the TExES Exam?

The TExES Principal Exam:

The Texas Examination of Educator Standards (TExES) measures the content and application of your present administrative knowledge. This content and application are based on the state and national standards of the Educational Leadership Profession and clearly establishes what TEA/SBEC discerns as the "entry-level" knowledge and application base for K-12 school administrators.

Organization of the TExES:

The framework for this exam is based on the State of Texas Certification Standards for SchoolAdministrators. The content covers broad areas called domains and competencies.

Time and the TExES:

The present framework of the TExES is very fluid. Due to the nature of our profession, there are continual changes in school policy, procedures, and law. As such, the nature of the exam alters to meet these changing needs. The best testing strategy is to review, prepare and take the TExES as soon as you complete all of your Universities prerequisites. Time, with this exam, is not your friend.

Not Your Grandmothers Exam:

The ability of the present TExES to alter to meet the changes of our profession have also morphed the exam into a vital highly specific testing instrument. The exam has moved from the lower end of the Bloom's Taxonomy - Knowledge, Comprehension, and Application- to the more robust and difficult areas of test evaluation determined by - Analysis, Synthesis, and Evaluation.

The move to the higher order of skills has impacted many candidates seeking the Principal Certification, in Texas. The determination of success on the TExES can't be indicated by the present system of grades, within our programs. While multiple students will clearly have high GPA scores, it is abundantly clear this is not an indicator of success in this highly-evolved exam.

The TExES has now enjoined itself with the many other professional exams, in our state. The legal profession requires passing "the Bar" before the actual practice of that profession may begin. Even though the candidate has completed all the higher educational challenges, the "final exam" is given, and the candidate must meet state and federal certification requirements.

The Certified Public Account profession also requires passing of a certificated exam to begin the practice of the candidate's profession. The number of professional organizations is now limitless as to those requiring the passing of a "final exam" given outside the higher education field and based on the application of knowledge learned. So historically, the TExES has moved into this rarified field.

Your Higher Education Program does NOT cover it All:

Students are thinking that the present higher education programs - such as Educational Leadership – will cover all the knowledge needed to pass the TExES exam are very mistaken. The very nature of our profession (if allowed to use this phrase) is continuously changing, and other than the "basic" knowledge the "progressive" knowledge is learned by the candidate through active reading, seminar and webcast participation of changing education events and interactive networking with professionals in the field.

All professionals seek to enhance continually their knowledge base through the interactive process of learning. None of us wish to go to a doctor who has not reviewed his or her profession in a decade or two. Nor would we wish to turn over our tax challenges to a CPA, who has not reviewed state and federal tax changes in a decade or two. Such is also the nature of the educational professional.

NOTE: This information is gathered from TEA/ETS/SBEC.

> *"The difference between a successful person and others is not a lack of strength, not a lack of knowledge, but rather a lack of will."*
> - Vince Lombardi

How Do I Study for the TExES?

There are several mistakes a student will make while reviewing for the TExES. The first is the idea there are code words or phrases within the scenarios that will "point" the student in the right direction. That is false. Many years this process for test taking was taught. The TExES is a professional exam designed around the student's ability to "apply" actual school policy, procedure, and law. As the state increases the exam to focus on decentralized (SBDM) government within the public-school system. The actual focus is on the application of the present TEC and TAC statutes. As such, code words and phrases within the scenarios are not commonly created by the test writers.

Once a student takes and fails the TExES for the first time, the student will immediately review their TEA grade report. Assuming the documentation will help point to specific areas of weakness the assumption is false. The TExES's grade report indicates in "general terms" weakness below the actual Domains of 1,2 and 3. The numerical numbers within the actual competencies are not strong indicators of weakness in those competencies. Most students will review the TExES report and then "focus" their time on reviewing the competency areas showing the – as they think – actual weakness. The student must remember the actual TExES exam is a computer generate exam. A computer-generated exam means the total number of actual competency based questions will vary, and the "points" for those individual competency questions will vary. Therefore, to review just the indicated competency weakness shown on the TExES grade report most often will lead to unsatisfactory progress for the next exam.

Domain II	Educational Leadership	First Try	Second Try	Third Try
	Total Questions 45		Total Questions	Total Questions
	Competency 4	14 questions	9 questions	12 questions
	Competency 5	8 questions	14 questions	10 questions
	Competency 6	14 questions	11 questions	14 questions
	Competency 7	9 questions	10 questions	9 questions

Looking at the table shown above it can be seen, from exam to exam the number of questions per competency changes, and the actual questions points will change. This being said it is better to review for each Domain rather than individual competencies.

The present TExES exam is separated into several parts. Usually, approximately 50% of the exam is related to the SBDM and the application of procedural policy within the SBDM manual. Other portions of the exam are separated into specific areas in which questions are formulated. These groups of questions will make up approximately 25% each of the exam. Questions will focus on all the other major areas of first-year principal responsibility. Such as LPAC, ARD, School Personnel, Emergency Procedures, Budget and others. Focusing the review on specific areas of weakness, from a past TExES exam is assuming that specific area type of question will be on the next exam is mathematically very remote.

Assuming the test format will be the same from test to test will create a false sense of success. The exam is a living instrument and as such alters as the test writers, which are many, decide. If the student understands the knowledge of a first-year administrator (policy, procedure, and law) "how" the exam asks the questions within a scenario should not be a concern, the student must read for understanding and apply this knowledge.

Further areas that create a weakness for the students would be the assumption that what they have learned in their present Educational Leadership Programs will suffice them to pass the TExES. That is also a fallacy as the TExES is a living testing instrument. As such, it is continuously changing as school policy, procedures and law change with each new legislative session and court case decision. The exam is made up of 120 questions, of which 20 are always "piloted" question to be used in the next test iterations. Present Educational Leadership Programs cannot stay up fully with the ever-changing world of Education in Texas, and therefore ALL professional educators must have a proactive professional reading regiment. To do less weakens your ability to pass the TExES exam and allows an individual to become further behind in their chosen profession.

A University grade point average is not an indicator of the ability to pass the TExES. Present statistical data of over 8,000 students who have taken the TExES exam, clearly indicate success on the TExES exam had no relation to a high G.P.A.

Finally, an individual must read and understand at a technical level. An individual must understand present school policy, procedures, and law. An individual must go through the testing process with a firm understanding of knowledge and responsibility of a first-year administrator. To do less will likely produce a negative result on the TExES.

Ultimately it is up to the individual to study the state manuals and articles to prepare themselves for this arduous TExES exam. The EPP's programs are but a portion of the overall process of acquiring the knowledge to succeed in the challenging field of school administration. The Texas Education Agency is very clear on the responsibilities of a first-year administrator. The TEA manuals, reports, and surveys clearly share first-year administrative responsibilities with those willing to review them.

NOTE: This information has been gleaned through experience and hard work with students and professors for the TExES Principal Exam.

> *"Teaching is not a lost art, but the regard for it is a lost tradition."*
> - Jacques Barzun

The Interview

Before you go in:

- Know who you'll meet. Find out if you will be speaking with a principal or a panel of teachers, administrators, and parents.
- Do your homework
- Checkup on the campus AEIS or TARP
- Read the walls of the school when you get there!
- Be prepared to show what you know.

Possible "themes" to questions:
Theme questions have a far reaching and global question. Be energetic and positive.

- What special talents do you bring to our school?
- Could you start a needed program?
- What can you add to the school community?
- How do you communicate with parents?
- Describe projects you've designed.
- What strategies have you used to reach all learners?
- What strategies are you aware to support the range of learning styles and differences?
- Recall an experience that went poorly. What would you do differently?
- What are you reading professionally?
- Describe a modern effective classroom.
- How do you know students are learning when you do a walk-through?

Other areas that will be approached during an interview:

Vision: Schools want an administrator to address daily issues and concerns, but also have an overarching view or motive for participating in the school community. Possible questions might ask you to articulate your primary goals; for example, instruction development, community visibility or technological development.

Discipline: Administrators know that little can be accomplished without competent discipline management and procedures in place, so interview questions will possibly address classroom management philosophy or discipline experience.

Relationships: Administrators serve as liaisons between students, parents, teachers, administration, the school board and community members, interview questions will focus on relationship development. Possible questions might measure how administrators might handle disgruntled teachers, concerned parents or disengaged students. Administrators can play up communication skills, articulate compassion and patience or highlight previous experience negotiating positive outcomes in high-stakes or conflicted situations.

Professional Readings that are represented on the TExES

Here are but a few of the professional readings that are used on the TExES:

- TEA Management Guide #14
- TEA Budget Guide #14
- ELL Handbook - 2014 edition
- ARD Handbook - 2014 edition
- Special Education Handbook - 2014 edition
- FERPA Handbook - 2014 edition
- SBDM Handbook
- PDAS Handbook
- Texas School Law - 2014 edition (all new policy and procedures approved by TEA)
- Texas School Personnel Law -2014 edition (all new procedures approved by TEA and Texas Courts).
- Sexual Harassment & Bullying Manual-TEA
- TEPSA website - read the latest news as it impacts the TExES
- TEPSA Instructional Leader -- read the latest news as it impacts the TExES
- TASSP - Texas Study magazine--read the latest news as it impacts the TExES
- NCLB Manual
- LPAC Manual
- Co-Teaching and the Texas Principal
- Affirmative Action
- Campus Improvement
- Crisis Management Manual
- Copyright Law Articles (UT-website)
- New Vison for Texas Schools-TEA Article
- No Pass and NO play Policy Review
- OCR Bulletin: stopbullying.gov also located on the TEA website.
- Parental Rights for student records –TEA Policy

Organization Support for the Modern Texas Administrator

Texas Elementary Principals and Supervisors Association
www.tepsa.org/

Texas Association of Secondary School Principals
www.tassp.org/

Texas Association of School Administrators
www.tasanet.org/page/259

Professional Resources and Support Texas School Administrators' Legal Digest
www.legaldigest.com/

Final Thoughts about the TExES:

I always tell students, "Do not depend on others to prepare you for this exam". I strongly suggest an interactive, participatory approach to the learning, understanding, and applying of the Analytical, Synthesis, and Evaluation processes of this profession.

As a future administrator, keep your professional readings up-to-date and do not allow the day-to-day activities to keep you from this important task. Always review what is happening on your professional websites, journals, and your state's educational departments' sites and manuals.

NOTE: Additional links for furthur reading can be found on our website: http://TExESCert.com/Links

> "Well, if it can be thought, it can be done, a problem can be overcome."
> - E. A. Bucchianeri

TEXES PRINCIPAL TOOL KIT and STUDY GUIDE

CR Educational Services, LLC
PRINCIPAL'S TOOLKIT and STUDY GUIDE
COMPILED and ASSEMBLED by
DR. VANCE CORTEZ-RUCKER and DR. SANDY CORTEZ-RUCKER

Domains and Competencies

The TExES (Texas Examination of Educator Standards) is the state certification or Licensure exam that measures the content and professional knowledge required of a new and aspiring leader in Texas public schools. The test is based on the content of **state and national standards**. The state and national standards are separated into three Domains, which are defined by competencies and further defined by descriptive statements of those competencies.

Let me take a moment here and describe what a whole school community means to the test writers. The total school community is all of the many parts of the living breathing dynamics of the modern public school. That includes but not limited to business, groups, organizations, government entities, parental and labor groups, individual parents, student and student groups, as well as all of the staff both certificated and non-certified inside and outside the walls of the schoolhouse. The state and national standards directly affect this living community. **The TExES assumes the new principal understand this and its implications**.

Domain One: *School Community Leadership* is based on the state and national content standards that best describe the capability of the administrator. The content standards focus on the business school community, parental school community, the professional collegial community within the building, and communication requirements. The new administrator will be able to focus his or her total school community on the cultural, vision, and mission of the school and school district. The administrator should be able to focus his total school community by building consensus about the school's needs and should develop positive and interactive communication strategies to support and move success forward. The administrator should always model professional ethical behavior and apply all state laws and school district policy and procedures.

Domain Two: *Instructional Leadership* is based on the state and national content standards that best describe the knowledge of the administrator. The content standards are focused on the "action" of the administrator. The administrator will know how to facilitate, design and implement the challenges of Domain Two. In this domain, the principal should be able to impact, curriculum, and collaborative district planning; implementation and monitoring are important in this domain. The administrator will be able to advocate, nurture and sustain the instructional program and develop and implement strategies to strengthen the success of the students and professional staff. The administrator must be able to analyze for possible needs both curricula and budgetary. The evaluation of programs and professional staff, needs assessment, implementation, and staff development is also key elements in this domain.

Domain Three: *Administrative Leadership* is based on the state and national content standards that best describe the knowledge of the administrator. The content standards focus on the management process of the administrator. Budget, allocation of human resources, material, and financial resources according to policy and procedures is crucial. Time management, the management of the school physical plant, equipment and support systems, must be done efficiently and effectively.

Domain I: School Community Leadership

Competency 1: The principal knows how to shape campus culture by facilitating the development, articulation, implementation, and stewardship of a vision of learning that is shared and supported by the school community.

- SBDM Handbook
- Principal Tool Kit - AAO

Competency 2: The principal knows how to communicate and collaborate with all members of the school community, respond to diverse interests and needs, and mobilize resources to promote student success.

- SBDM Handbook
- Principal Tool Kit – Community Resource Management
- Principal Tool Kit – Homeless Students (McKinney-Vento)

Competency 3: The principal knows how to act with integrity, fairness, and in an ethical and legal manner.

- SBDM Handbook
- Principal Tool Kit - Powers and Duties TEC 11.202
- Principal Tool Kit – Code of Ethics
- Principal Tool Kit – Parental Rights and the Modern Principal
- Principal Tool Kit – No pass, No play
- Principal Tool Kit – Legal/Illegal Interview Questions
- Principal Tool Kit – Equity in the interview
- FERPA Handbook
- Principal Tool Kit – Food Services

Domain II: Instructional Leadership

Competency 4: The principal knows how to facilitate the design and implementation of curricula and strategic plans that enhance teaching and learning; ensure alignment of curriculum, instruction, resources, and assessment; and promote the use of varied assessments to measure student performance.

- Principal Tool Kit – Curriculum/Instructional Program
- Principal Tool Kit – Co-Teaching
- Texas Co-Teaching Handbook
- Texas ARD Handbook
- Texas ELL Handbook
- Texas LPAC Handbook
- Principal Tool Kit – Modern Effective Texas Classroom Environment

Competency 5: The principal knows how to advocate, nurture, and sustain an instructional program and a campus culture that are conducive to student learning and staff professional growth.

- PDAS Manual
- Principal Tool Kit- Co-Teaching and the Modern Principal
- FERPA Manual

Competency 6: The principal knows how to implement a staff evaluation and development system to improve the performance of all staff members, select and implement appropriate models for supervision and staff development, and apply the legal requirements for personnel management.

- Principal Tool Kit – Extended School year
- Principal Tool Kit – Evaluation and the Modern Principal
- PDAS Manual
- Principal Tool Kit – Leadership (Situational)

Competency 7: The principal knows how to apply organizational, decision-making, and problem-solving skills to ensure an effective learning environment.

- Principal Tool Kit – copyright: fair use
- Principal Tool Kit – Co-Teaching and the Modern Principal
- Principal Tool Kit – Co-Teaching and Special Education

Domain III: Administrative Leadership

Competency 8: The principal knows how to apply principles of effective leadership and management in relation to campus budgeting, personnel, resource utilization, financial management, and technology use.

- SBDM Handbook
- Principal Tool Kit – Budgeting
- TEA Budget Guide #14
- TEA Management Guide #14
- TEA Overview of Management

Competency 9: The principal knows how to apply principles of leadership and management of the campus physical plant and support systems to ensure a safe and effective learning environment.

- Principal Tool Kit – Crisis management Plan and crisis intervention plans
- Principal Tool Kit - Cyberbullying and student first amendment rights
- Principal Tool Kit- Cyber security
- Principal Tool Kit - Dealing with the crisis at the school
- Principal Tool Kit – Emergency management
- Principal Tool Kit – Sexual Harassment Investigation

TExES SECURITY

Brief Instructions about the TExES
Computer Administered Test (CAT)

Starting with September 1, 2015, and finalized on December 31, 2015, the candidate for certification may now test a total of five times. Once the candidate reaches the fifth try on the exam a series of hurdles must be completed by the candidate and sent to TEA. **It is strongly advised that the candidate should understand the testing and retesting process**. Consult your EPP (University) for further information.

The TExES is not like any other exam you have taken during your career. The exam is not developed around knowledge or comprehension based questions. The application of theory or the memorizing list will not work. The exam is a living testing instrument based on the "latest" challenges and changes to school policy, procedure, and law. The exam uses application of analysis, determination through synthesis and ultimately asks the tester to use evaluation skills in any given scenario and/or group of questions. So, in essence, the exam asks you to "apply" what you know. Not from "experience" **but from the state's point of view (policy, procedure, and law)**. Also, it is obvious that "time" is not a friend of the student. The longer you wait, the less prepared you are for the exam.

What to Bring to the Test Center?
1. An admission ticket for the test you are taking
2. If you do not bring your admission ticket, you may not be permitted to test
3. Valid and acceptable identification document(s) with a name, signature, and photograph
4. Your ID will be checked before you are admitted

Security:
1. You are not allowed to bring cell phones, smartphones (e.g., Android™, Blackberry®, iPhone®), tablets, personal digital assistants (PDAs) and other electronic, listening, recording, scanning or photographic devices into the test center.
2. If you are found to be in possession of or using any of these devices before, during or after the test administration (including breaks), your device may be inspected and/or confiscated and you will be dismissed from the test. Your test fees will be forfeited, and your scores will be canceled, even if the dismissal is not enforced on the day of the test.
3. Test administrators are not permitted to hold cell phones or other devices for anyone.
4. Some types of watches (e.g., calculator, computing, digital, watches with alarms, smart watches, and stopwatches) are not allowed in the test room. You may be asked to remove your watch and store it during the administration.

General Information:
1. You have a total of five hours to take the test.
2. During the test, you may take one optional break. If you wish to take a break, you should raise your hand.
3. Time will not stop for this break; it is recommended that the break not exceeds 15 minutes.
4. You may use the scratch paper provided to work out answers.
5. All scratch paper must be turned in to the test administrator at the end of the testing session.

Computer-Administered Tests:
1. This test consists entirely of multiple- choice questions.
2. All questions will be presented via the computer, and you will select responses using the computer.

3. Read the directions carefully. You are responsible for reading and understanding the directions before beginning the test.
4. No oral instructions will be provided.
5. The time you take to read the directions is not considered part of the testing time.
6. It is recommended that you spend no more than fifteen minutes reading the directions.
7. Avoid spending too much time on one question
8. Carefully follow the directions to avoid wasting time.
9. Do Not Panic. Concentrate on the current question only, and do not think about how you answered other questions
10. Understand the details of the question. Understanding the details of a question may help you find the answer.
11. Don't make questions more difficult than they are. Don't read for hidden meanings or tricks.
12. Avoid spending too much time on one question.
13. Leave no questions unanswered. Nothing is subtracted from a score if you answer a question incorrectly.
14. Pace yourself, so you have enough time to answer every question. Be aware of the time limit for each section and task.

> *"Beautiful souls are shaped by ugly experiences."*
> — Matshona Dhliwayo

State and National Standards

*A good Principal Program will apply the following standards as their guides.

NAESP's Standards:

Standard 1: Lead student and adult learning
Standard 2: Lead diverse communities
Standard 3: Lead 21st century learning
Standard 4: Lead continuous improvement
Standard 5: Lead using knowledge and data
Standard 6: Lead parent, family, and community engagement

National Board of Professional Teaching Standards (for Principals):

Advances student learning and engagement.
Recruits and retains the best teachers.
Improves teacher and school performance.

Educational Constituencies Council (ELCC) National Standards:

Standard 1.0: Graduates are educational leaders who have the knowledge, skills, and abilities to promote the success of all students by facilitating the articulation, formulation, and dissemination of a school or district vision of learning supported by the school community.

Standard 2.0: Graduates are educational leaders who have the knowledge and ability to support the success of all students by promoting and maintaining a positive school culture for learning, by promoting effective instructional programs, by applying best practices to student learning, and by designing and implementing comprehensive professional growth plans for staff.

Standard 3.0: Graduates are educational leaders who have the knowledge and ability to promote the success of all students by managing the organization, operations, and resources in a way that promotes a safe, efficient, and effective learning environment.

Standard 4.0: Graduates are educational leaders who have the knowledge and ability to promote the success of all students by collaborating with families and other community members, responding to diverse community interests and needs, and mobilizing community resources.

Standard 5.0: Graduates are educational leaders who have the knowledge and ability to promote the success of all students by demonstrating a respect for the rights of others and by acting responsibly.

Standard 6.0: Graduates are educational leaders who have the knowledge and ability to promote the success of all students by articulating, analyzing and describing, and communicating the larger political, social, economic, legal, and cultural context and advocating for all students

Standard 7.0: Graduates are educational leaders who have the ability and experience to promote the success of all students by completing an internship that provides significant opportunities for synthesizing and applying knowledge and practicing the skills identified in

(a) Principal Certificate Standards. The knowledge and skills identified in this section must be used by an educator preparation program in the development of curricula and coursework and by the State Board for Educator Certification as the basis for developing the examinations required to obtain the standard Principal Certificate. The standards also serve as the foundation for the individual assessment, professional growth plan, and continuing professional education activities required by §241.30 of this title (relating to Requirements to Renew the Standard Principal Certificate).

(b) Learner-Centered Values and Ethics of Leadership. A principal is an educational leader who promotes the success of all students by acting with integrity and fairness and in an ethical manner. At the campus level, a principal understands, values, and is able to:

   (1) model and promote the highest standard of conduct, ethical principles, and integrity in decision making, actions, and behaviors;

   (2) implement policies and procedures that encourage all campus personnel to comply with Chapter 247 of this title (relating to Educators' Code of Ethics);

   (3) model and promote the continuous and appropriate development of all learners in the campus community;

   (4) promote awareness of learning differences, multicultural awareness, gender sensitivity, and ethnic appreciation in the campus community; and

   (5) articulate the importance of education in a free democratic society.

(c) Learner-Centered Leadership and Campus Culture. A principal is an educational leader who promotes the success of all students and shapes campus culture by facilitating the development, articulation, implementation, and stewardship of a vision of learning that is shared and supported by the school community. At the campus level, a principal understands, values, and is able to:

   (1) create a campus culture that sets high expectations, promotes learning, and provides intellectual stimulation for self, students, and staff;

   (2) ensure that parents and other members of the community are an integral part of the campus culture;

   (3) use strategies to ensure the development of collegial relationships and effective collaboration of campus staff;

   (4) respond appropriately to the diverse needs of individuals within the community in shaping the campus culture;

   (5) use emerging issues, trends, demographic data, knowledge of systems, campus climate inventories, student learning data, and other information to develop a campus vision and plan to implement the vision;

   (6) facilitate the collaborative development of a shared campus vision that focuses on teaching and learning;

   (7) facilitate the collaborative development of a plan in which objectives and strategies to implement the campus vision are clearly articulated;

   (8) align financial, human, and material resources to support the implementation of the campus vision;

   (9) establish processes to assess and modify the plan of implementation to ensure achievement of the campus vision;

   (10) support innovative thinking and risk-taking efforts of everyone within the school community and view unsuccessful experiences as learning opportunities; and

   (11) acknowledge, recognize, and celebrate the contributions of students, staff, parents, and community members toward the realization of the campus vision.

(d) Learner-Centered Human Resources Leadership and Management. A principal is an educational leader who promotes the success of all students by implementing a staff evaluation and development system to improve the performance of all staff members, selects and implements appropriate models for supervision and staff development, and applies the legal requirements for personnel management. At the campus level, a principal understands, values, and is able to:

  (1) collaboratively develop, implement, and revise a comprehensive and on-going plan for professional development of campus staff that addresses staff needs and aligns professional development with identified goals;

  (2) facilitate the application of adult learning and motivation theory to all campus professional development, including the use of appropriate content, processes, and contexts;

  (3) ensure the effective implementation of the professional development plan by allocation of appropriate time, funding, and other needed resources;

  (4) implement effective, legal, and appropriate strategies for the recruitment, selection, assignment, and induction of campus staff;

  (5) use formative and summative evaluation processes appropriate to the position held to further develop the knowledge and skills of campus staff;

  (6) diagnose and improve campus organizational health and morale through the implementation of strategies designed to provide on-going support to campus staff members; and

  (7) engage in on-going, meaningful, and professional growth activities to further develop necessary knowledge and skills and to model lifelong learning.

(e) Learner-Centered Communications and Community Relations. A principal is an educational leader who promotes the success of all students by collaborating with families and community members, responding to diverse community interests and needs, and mobilizing community resources. At the campus level, a principal understands, values, and is able to:

  (1) demonstrate effective communication through oral, written, auditory, and nonverbal expression;

  (2) use effective conflict management and group consensus building skills;

  (3) implement effective strategies to systematically gather input from all campus stakeholders;

  (4) develop and implement strategies for effective internal and external communications;

  (5) develop and implement a comprehensive program of community relations, which uses strategies that will effectively involve and inform multiple constituencies, including the media;

  (6) provide varied and meaningful opportunities for parents to be engaged in the education of their children;

  (7) establish partnerships with parents, businesses, and other groups in the community to strengthen programs and support campus goals; and

  (8) respond to pertinent political, social, and economic issues that exist in the internal and external environment.

(f) Learner-Centered Organizational Leadership and Management. A principal is an educational leader who promotes the success of all students through leadership and management of the organization, operations, and resources for a safe, efficient, and effective learning environment. At the campus level, a principal understands, values, and is able to:

  (1) implement appropriate management techniques and group processes to define roles, assign functions, delegate authority, and determine accountability for campus goal attainment;

  (2) gather and organize information from a variety of sources for use in creative and effective campus decision making;

  (3) frame, analyze, and creatively resolve campus problems using effective problem-solving techniques to make timely, high-quality decisions;

  (4) develop, implement, and evaluate change processes for organizational effectiveness;

(5) implement strategies that enable the physical plant, equipment, and support systems to operate safely, efficiently, and effectively to maintain a conducive learning environment;

(6) apply local, state, and federal laws and policies to support sound decisions while considering implications related to all school operations and programs;

(7) acquire, allocate, and manage human, material, and financial resources according to school district policies and campus priorities;

(8) collaboratively plan and effectively manage the campus budget;

(9) use technology to enhance school management; and

(10) use effective planning, time management, and organization of work to maximize attainment of school district and campus goals.

"Failing over and over again is how you learn to succeed over and over again."
- Matshona Dhliwayo

Powers and Duties
TEC: Sec. 11.202. PRINCIPALS

Sec. 11.202. PRINCIPALS.
1. The principal of a school is the instructional leader of the school and shall be provided with adequate training and personnel assistance to assume that role.

<u>Each principal shall:</u> — *It will be done*

   (1) approve all teacher and staff appointments for that principal's campus from a pool of applicants selected by the district or of applicants who meet the hiring requirements established by the district, based on criteria developed by the principal after informal consultation with the faculty;

   (2) set specific education objectives for the principal's campus, through the planning process under Section <u>11.253;</u>

Sec. 11.253. (SBDM)

CAMPUS PLANNING AND SITE-BASED DECISION-MAKING.
   (a) Each school district shall maintain current policies and procedures to ensure that effective planning and site-based decision-making occur **at each campus** to direct and support the improvement of student performance for all students.

Each school year, the principal of each school campus, with the assistance of the campus-level committee, shall develop, review, and revise the <u>campus improvement plan</u> for the purpose of <u>improving student performance for all student populations, including students in special education programs.</u>

<u>Campus improvement plan must:</u>
1. **Assess** the academic achievement for each student in the school using the student achievement indicator system as described by Section *TAPR*
2. **Set** the campus performance objectives based on the student achievement indicator system, including objectives for special needs populations, including students in special education programs under Subchapter A, Chapter 29; *TAPR*
3. **Identify** how the campus goals will be met for each student; *Campus Strategies*
4. **Determine** the resources needed to implement the plan; *Principal & Budget committee*
5. **Identify** staff needed to implement the plan; *Principal & Staffing committee*
6. **Set** timelines for reaching the goals; *Principal & SBDM*
7. **Measure** progress toward the performance objectives periodically to ensure that the plan is resulting in academic improvement; *Daily, weekly & 6 weeks grades*
8. **Include** goals and methods for violence prevention and intervention on campus; *SHAC*
9. **Provide** for a program to encourage parental involvement at the campus; and *SBDM*
10. If the campus is an elementary, middle, or junior high school, set goals **and objectives for the coordinated health program** at the campus based on: *SHAC*

School Health Advisory Council (SHAC):

1. Student fitness assessment data, including any data from research-based assessments such as the school health index assessment and planning tool created by the Federal Centers for Disease Control and Prevention.
2. Student academic performance data
3. Student attendance rates
4. The percentage of students who are educationally disadvantaged.
5. The use and success of any method to ensure that students participate in moderate to vigorous physical activity as required by Section **28.002(l)**.
6. Any other indicators recommended by the local school health advisory council.

Campus procedures must be established to ensure that **systematic communications** measures are in place to periodically obtain broad-based community, parent, and staff input, and to provide information to those persons regarding the recommendations of the campus-level committees.

A principal shall regularly consult the campus-level committee in:

1. Planning
2. Budgeting
3. Curriculum
4. Staffing patterns
5. Staff development - this area MUST be approved by the SBDM through the CIP
6. School organization
7. Operation
8. Supervision
9. Evaluation of the campus educational program

Sec. 11.251. PLANNING AND DECISION-MAKING PROCESS:

(a) The board of trustees of each independent school district shall ensure that a district improvement plan **and improvement plans for each campus** are **developed, reviewed, and revised annually** for the purpose of improving the performance of all students. The board shall annually approve district and campus performance objectives and shall ensure that the district **and campus plans:**

1. Are mutually supportive to accomplish the identified objectives
2. At a minimum, support the state goals and objectives
3. Will involve the professional staff of the district, parents, and community members in establishing and reviewing the district's and campuses' educational plans, goals, performance objectives, and major classroom instructional programs. Shall establish a procedure under which meetings are held regularly by district- and campus-level planning and decision-making committees that include representative professional staff, including, if practicable, at least one representative with the primary responsibility for educating students with disabilities, parents of students enrolled in the district, business representatives, and community members. The committees shall include a business representative without regard to whether the representative resides in the district or whether the business the person represents is located in the district. The board, or the board's designee, shall periodically meet with the district-level committee to review the district-level committee's deliberations.

(b) For purposes of establishing the composition of committees under this section:

1. A person who stands in parental relation to a student is considered a parent;
2. A parent who is an employee of the school district is not <u>considered a parent representative</u> on the committee;
3. A parent is not considered a representative of community members on the committee; and community members must reside in the district and must be at least 18 years of age.

Code of Ethics and Standard Practices for Texas Educators

All Texas educators are responsible for knowing the Texas Administrative Code that defines the Educators' Code of Ethics rules.
ENFORCEABLE STANDARDS
Modified 6/23/2011

I. Professional Ethical Conduct, Practices and Performance.

Standard 1.1: The educator shall not intentionally, knowingly, or recklessly engage in deceptive practices regarding official policies of the school district, educational institution, educator preparation program, the Texas Education Agency, or the State Board for Educator Certification (SBEC) and its certification process.

Standard 1.2: The educator shall not knowingly misappropriate, divert or use monies, personnel, property or equipment committed to his or her charge for personal gain or advantage.

Standard 1.3: The educator shall not submit fraudulent requests for reimbursement, expenses or pay.

Standard 1.4: The educator shall not use institutional or professional privileges for personal or partisan advantage.

Standard 1.5: The educator shall neither accept nor offer gratuities, gifts, or favors that impair professional judgment or to obtain special advantage. This standard shall not restrict the acceptance of gifts or tokens offered and accepted openly from students, parents of students or other persons or organizations in recognition or appreciation of service.

Standard 1.6: The educator shall not falsify records, or direct or coerce others to do so.

Standard 1.7: The educator shall comply with state regulations, written local school board policies and other state and federal laws.

Standard 1.8: The educator shall apply for, accept, offer, or assign a position or a responsibility on the basis of professional qualifications.

Standard 1.9: The educator shall not make threats of violence against school district employees, school board members, students or parents of students.

Standard 1.10: The educator shall be of good moral character and demonstrate that he or she is worthy to instruct or supervise the youth of this state.

Standard 1.11: The educator shall not intentionally or knowingly misrepresent the circumstances of his or her prior employment, criminal history, and/or disciplinary record when applying for subsequent employment.

Standard 1.12: The educator shall refrain from the illegal use or distribution of controlled substances and/or abuse of prescription drugs and toxic inhalants.

Standard 1.13: The educator shall not consume alcoholic beverages on school property or during school activities when students are present.

II. Ethical Conduct Toward Professional Colleagues.

Standard 2.1: The educator shall not reveal confidential health or personnel information concerning colleagues unless disclosure serves lawful professional purposes or is required by law.

Standard 2.2: The educator shall not harm others by knowingly or recklessly making false statements about a colleague or the school system.

Standard 2.3: The educator shall adhere to written local school board policies and state and federal laws regarding the hiring, evaluation, and dismissal of personnel.

Standard 2.4: The educator shall not interfere with a colleague's exercise of political, professional or citizenship rights and responsibilities.

Standard 2.5: The educator shall not discriminate against or coerce a colleague on the basis of race, color, religion, national origin, age, gender, disability, family status, or sexual orientation.

Standard 2.6: The educator shall not use coercive means or promise of special treatment in order to influence professional decisions or colleagues.

Standard 2.7: The educator shall not retaliate against any individual who has filed a complaint with the SBEC or who provides information for a disciplinary investigation or proceeding under this chapter.

III. Ethical Conduct toward Students.

Standard 3.1: The educator shall not reveal confidential information concerning students unless disclosure serves lawful professional purposes or is required by law.

Standard 3.2: The educator shall not intentionally, knowingly, recklessly, or negligently treat a student or minor in a manner that adversely affects or endangers the learning, physical health, mental health or safety of the student or minor.

Standard 3.3: The educator shall not intentionally, knowingly, or recklessly misrepresent facts regarding a student.

Standard 3.4: The educator shall not exclude a student from participation in a program, deny benefits to a student, or grant an advantage to a student on the basis of race, color, gender, disability, national origin, religion, family status, or sexual orientation.

Standard 3.5: The educator shall not intentionally, knowingly, or recklessly engage in physical mistreatment, neglect, or abuse of a student or minor.

Standard 3.6: The educator shall not solicit or engage in sexual conduct or a romantic relationship with a student or minor.

Standard 3.7: The educator shall not furnish alcohol or illegal / unauthorized drugs to any person under 21 years of age or knowingly allow any person under 21 years of age to consume alcohol or illegal / unauthorized drugs in the presence of the educator.

Standard 3.8: The educator shall maintain appropriate professional educator-student relationships and boundaries based on a reasonably prudent educator standard.

Standard 3.9: The educator shall refrain from inappropriate communication with a student or minor, including, but not limited to, electronic communication such as cell phone, text messaging, email, instant messaging, blogging, or other social network communication. Factors that may be considered in assessing whether the communication is inappropriate include, but are not limited to:

i. The nature, purpose, timing, and amount of the communication
ii. The subject matter of the communication
iii. Whether the communication was made openly or the educator attempted to conceal the communication
iv. Whether the communication could be reasonably interpreted as soliciting sexual contact or a romantic relationship
v. Whether the communication was sexually explicit
vi. Whether the communication involved discussion(s) of the physical or sexual attractiveness or the sexual history, activities, preferences, or fantasies of either the educator or the student

Please see the Texas Education Agency website if you have any questions.

> *"An individual has not started living until he can rise above the narrow confines of his individualistic concerns to the broader concerns of all humanity."*
> — Martin Luther King, Jr.

TEXES STUDY MATERIAL

BY SUBJECT

Accountability Ratings 2017

Index's and the Need to Meet Certain Ratings

The **2017 Accountability Manual** describes the 2017 accountability system and explains how information from different sources is used to assign accountability ratings and award distinction designations.

In 2017, one of the following ratings is assigned to each district and <u>campus based on its performance on the required indices</u>. Unless otherwise noted, the term districts include open-enrollment charters. Met Standard indicates acceptable performance and is assigned to districts and campuses that meet the targets on all required indices for which they have performance data.

Met Alternative Standard indicates acceptable performance and is assigned to eligible charter districts and alternative education campuses (AECs) that are evaluated by alternative education accountability (AEA) provisions. To receive this rating, eligible charter districts and AECs must meet modified targets on all required indices for which they have performance data.

Improvement Required indicates unacceptable performance and is assigned to districts and campuses, including charter districts and AECs evaluated under AEA provisions, that do not meet the targets on all required indices for which they have performance data.

Each index has a <u>specific target,</u> <u>and districts/campuses must meet and index's target</u> to show acceptable performance for that index.

2017 Accountability Performance Index Targets for Non-AEA Districts and Campuses

Target	Index 1	Index 2	Index 3	Index 4	
	Student Achievement Target	Student Progress Target	Closing Performance Gap Target	All Components	STAAR Component Only
Districts	60	22	28	60	13
Campuses					
Elementary	60	32	28	n/a	12
Middle		30	26	n/a	13
High School/K–12 and Elementary/Secondary		17	30	60	21

AEA means Alternative Education Accountability

To **receive a Met Standard or Met Alternative Standard rating**, a district **or campus** must meet the performance index target on the following indices <u>for which it has performance data</u>:

Index 1 OR Index 2 **AND** Index 3 AND Index 4

For example, a campus with performance data for all four indices must meet the target on either Index 1 or Index 2 and the targets on Index 3 and Index 4. A campus with performance data for Index 1, Index 3, and Index 4 must meet the target on all three of those. A campus with performance data for only Index 1 and Index 3 must meet the target on both indices. A campus with performance data for only Index 1 and Index 2 needs only to meet the target on either one.

Every campus is labeled as one of four school types according to its grade span based on 2016–17 enrollment data reported in the fall Public Education Information Management System (PEIMS) submission.

The four types are:
- Elementary
- Middle School
- Elementary/Secondary (also referred to as K–12)
- High School

EXAMPLE:

Texas Education Agency

Department of Assessment and Accountability

Division of Performance Reporting

2016 Accountability Ratings as of August 15, 2016

District/Campus Name	District/Campus Number	2016 Accountability Rating*	Index 1 Student Achievement			Index 2 Student Progress			Index 3 Closing Performance Gaps			Index 4 Postsecondary Readiness		
			Index Score	Index Target	Index Met	Index Score	Index Target	Index Met	Index Score	Index Target	Index Met	Index Score	Index Target	Index Met
LAKE TRAVIS H S	001	Met Standard	92	60	Y	29	17	Y	49	30	Y	88	60	Y
LAKE TRAVIS MIDDLE	041	Met Standard	95	60	Y	47	30	Y	62	26	Y	76	13	Y
HUDSON BEND MIDDLE	042	Met Standard	92	60	Y	46	30	Y	59	26	Y	76	13	Y
LAKE TRAVIS EL	101	Met Standard	86	60	Y	43	32	Y	45	28	Y	49	12	Y
LAKEWAY EL	102	Met Standard	93	60	Y	52	32	Y	62	28	Y	74	12	Y
BEE CAVE EL	103	Met Standard	92	60	Y	47	32	Y	49	28	Y	56	12	Y
LAKE POINTE EL	104	Met Standard	95	60	Y	53	32	Y	66	28	Y	71	12	Y
SERENE HILLS EL	105	Met Standard	92	60	Y	51	32	Y	46	28	Y	67	12	Y
WEST CYPRESS HILLS EL	106	Met Standard	92	60	Y	53	32	Y	55	28	Y	60	12	Y

Hudson Bend Middle School: Review the Target numbers for each Index.

1. Index 1 (STUDENT ACHIEVMENT) target is 60 the middle school index for 2016 was 92 so they MET Standards
2. Index 2 (STUDENT PROGRESS) target is 30 the middle school index for 2016 was 46 so they MET Standards
3. Index 3 (CLOSING THE GAP) target is 26 the middle school index for 2016 was 59 so they MET Standards
4. Index 4 (POSTSECONDARY READINESS) target is 13 middle school indices for 2016 was 76 so they MET Standards

The KEY is to understand that each "INDEX" is a label for a specific area for student growth!

So, if you wish to see "overall student growth-total scores- in academics THAT is Index 1. If you want to view "overall student progress toward academic achievement-numerical comparisons" THAT is index 2. If you want to view a statistical number indication student growth in overall achievement of those who had NOT met passing THAT is Index 3. If you want to see growth of students toward reaching that next level of post-secondary academic growth THAT is Index 4.

Know the index scores for each of the campus levels. From this point you can then compare and determine (when viewing data) what campus may or may not have MET Standards.

Affirmative Action Officer

While this is relatively new to Texas, the Affirmative Action Officers may also be identified as the district's Title IX Coordinator or building principal.

The responsibilities of this position include but are not limited to coordinating and implementation of the district's efforts to comply with the state and federal affirmative action regulations.

Why this new position? **On March 24, 2014**, new federal regulations impact all government and state entities that accept federal funds for schools this would be the Title monies and others. The school districts must make every effort to hire veterans and the disabled by establishing benchmarks. It is important to note that "benchmarks" must not be seen or responded to as a quota, which are expressly forbidden.

Although a specific job description is difficult to identify, there are some basic concepts that seem to apply to this new position, in our state.

The AAO (Affirmative Action Officer) will:
- **Oversee the implementation of the district's affirmative action plan to increase minorities in the district.**
- **Oversee the development and implementation of the district's comprehensive equity plan.**
- **Monitors implementation of the plan and related strategies for improvement.**
- **Maintains communication with staff, students, and community.**
- **Coordinates and provides mandated in-service trainings for all certified and non-certified staff.**
- **Understands and has full knowledge of the district grievance procedures and employment policies, and can be identified as the "point person" for students and staff filing grievance procedures.**
- **Assures that the district maintains fair and impartial hiring practices; frequently sits in on interviews.**
- **Performs other duties as necessary.**

Basic Topics for in-service by the AAO:
- **Bullying**
- **Cultural Diversity**
- **Sexual Harassment**
- **Multicultural curriculum and activities**
- **Discrimination and bias awareness**

Other areas where the AAO might have some responsibility:
- **Textbook selection** and ensuring criteria reflecting sensitivity to discrimination and bias.
- **Monitoring employment goals** and policy.
- Serving on screening and interviewing committees—where appropriate.
- Serve as support to building principals to review:
- **Course descriptions** for language and compliance.

- Student classroom assignments to meet gender "balance."
- Review work study placement for gender "balance."
- Review club participation for gender "balance."
- Conduct a student survey every three years to identify student sports interest.

Attendance Officer

The role of principal has changed dramatically over the past couple of decades (Levine 2005). It wasn't too long ago that a principal's primary tasks were limited to making sure that the buses ran on time, ordering supplies, and addressing personnel issues (Usdan, McCloud, & Podmostko, 2000). Nowadays, a principal's main responsibility is student learning (The Wallace Foundation, 2012; Usdan, McCloud, & Podmostko, 2000). Since the administrative and building management duties have not disappeared, the average principal now puts in over 10 hours a day (Usdan, McCloud, & Podmostko, 2000).

In Texas, children between the ages of 6 and 18, depending on when the child's birthday falls, are required to attend school unless otherwise exempted by law. School employees investigate and report violations of the state compulsory attendance law. At the beginning of the school year all parents will be notified in writing of the state attendance requirements. Under the law, if the student is absent from school on 10 or more days or parts of days within a six-month period in the same school year or on three or more days or parts of days within a four-week period: (1) Student's parent/guardian is subject to prosecution under Texas Education Code Section 25.093 (2) Student is subject to prosecution under Texas Education Code Section 25.094 Excessive absences will result in loss of credit unless the student makes up the missed work in an acceptable alternative manner including but not limited to: Saturday School, Summer School, or after school hours. An unusual extenuating circumstance is a basis for appeal to the principal. (Go to the TEA website and Ask for Student Attendance Accounting Handbook – You can download the most current version from there.)

The principal of each campus is responsible for reviewing his or her respective Campus Summary Reports for completeness and accuracy. A principal should compare reports from the TEA, which reflect Public Education Information Management System (PEIMS) data, to locally produced reports for reasonableness and accuracy. By signing the Campus Summary Report—or, in the case of a paperless attendance accounting system, by indicating his or her approval of data electronically—a principal affirms that he or she has checked, or caused to be checked, the accuracy and authenticity of the attendance data. (Student Attendance Accounting Handbook, 2016).

Record Requirements for Enrollment

Section 25.002 requires that a child's prior school district or the person enrolling the child provide certain records. The required records are 1) a birth certificate or other proof of identity, 2) the child's records from the school most recently attended, and 3) immunization records. [66] These are the only records statutorily required for enrollment. Student social security numbers are used for purposes of the Public Education Information Management System; however, a district or open-enrollment charter will assign the student a state-approved alternative student identification number if the student's social security number is not provided. (Go to TEA website and search for Attendance, Admission, Enrollment Records, and Tuition. Look for the most current year and the regulations.)

Texas Education Code 25.091 - **Powers and Duties of Attendance Officers** (Go to TEA website and search for Briefing Book on Public Education Legislation, then search for TEA Code 25.091.)

Designation of School Attendance Officer

Under §25.088, the governing body of a school district or of an open-enrollment charter school may select an attendance officer to enforce the attendance of students. If an open-enrollment charter school does not select an attendance officer, §25.090 requires the county peace officers to perform the duties of an attendance officer with respect to students in the open-enrollment charter school.

Duties of School Attendance Officer

Section 25.091 lists the duties of a school attendance officer. The section lists separately the duties of attendance officers who are peace officers and the duties of those who are not peace officers. Please note that the statute authorizes an attendance officer to refer a student to truancy court only for "unexcused absences." Excused absences are not included in the number of absences required for a referral or complaint. In addition to enrolled students with unexcused absences, a school attendance officer's duties extend to persons within compulsory attendance age who are not exempt from compulsory attendance and are not enrolled in school.

Section 25.091(b-1) authorizes a peace officer who has probable cause to believe that a child is in violation of the compulsory school attendance law under §25.085 to take the child into custody for the purpose of returning the child to the child's school campus.

An attendance officer is required to apply truancy prevention measures adopted by the district under §25.0915 and may make a referral to truancy court under §25.091 only if the truancy prevention measures fail to meaningfully address the student's conduct. Each referral must specify whether the student is eligible for or receives special education services and must be accompanied by a statement from the student's school certifying that the school applied the truancy prevention measures and the measures failed to meaningfully address the student's school attendance.

Truancy Prevention Measures

A school district is required to adopt truancy prevention measures under §25.0915. If a student has three or more unexcused absences for three or more days or parts of days within a four-week period but less than 10 or more days or parts of days within a six-month period, the district shall initiate truancy prevention measures. If the school determines that the student's absences are the result of pregnancy, being in the state foster program, homelessness, or being the principal income earner for the student's family, the district shall offer additional counseling to the student and may not refer the student to a truancy court. A district shall employ a truancy prevention facilitator or juvenile case manager to implement the truancy prevention measures. At least annually, the truancy prevention facilitator shall meet to discuss effective truancy prevention measures with a case manager or other individual designated by a truancy court to provide services to students of the district.

Section 25.095 requires school districts and open-enrollment charter schools to notify parents of attendance requirements at the beginning of the school year. An additional notice is required after a student has a certain number of unexcused absences. Tardies are generally not considered absences for purposes of compulsory attendance enforcement.

Note: For additional details go to the TEA website and search for Attendance, Admission, Enrollment Records, and Tuition

Building a Professional Culture: Challenge of the Modern Principal

1. A modern principal will commit to a high standard for all students to close the achievement gap.

- Researches all data and identifies the achievement gap across the campus population.
- Develops plans with the SBDM to reduce the achievement gap.

2. Creates a culture of high expectations for all faculty, staff and students.

- **A modern principal will guide** the application of all state standards to meet the learning needs of all students.
- **Analyzes all** teaching strategies and situations through a series of walk-throughs and yearly evaluations, in search of appropriate teaching and learning practices.
- **Develops** along with recommendations from the SBDM a process to support teachers' growth and development, to meet the need to reduce the learning gap.

3. **A modern principal will actively** create relationships, procedures and structures that provide time and resource for a collaborative teaching and learning environment.

- Supports collaborative teaching and learning opportunities.
- Supports mutual distribution of responsibility, accountability and benefits among the faculty and staff.
- Involves students, when appropriate in school improvement teams.

4. **A modern principal will provide** opportunities for a safe educationally rich environment.

- Supports and environment to express educational beliefs and ideas.
- Supports opportunities to seek teaching and learning improvement through innovation.

5. A modern principal will provide continuous constructive and positive feedback to the educational professional.

- Support a process to provide positive feedback through:
    - Walkthroughs
    - Co-teaching
    - Peer coaching
    - Student performance
- Supports an effective data analysis through:
    - Student performance data
    - Disaggregation of test scores
    - Yearly evaluations and comparison to student data

Bullying Prevention Policies and Procedures

Texas Education Code: 37.0832

It is vital that educators can distinguish between the typical conflicts that take place every day in school and those that rise to the level of bullying and harassment. Knowing the definitions as they are set out in the law is critical to the decision-making process.

Your first response to possible bullying and/or harassment is to consult the school district policy manual and the student code of conduct!

1. Definition of Bullying:

Engaging in the written or verbal expression, expression through electronic means, or physical conduct that occurs on school property, at a school-sponsored or school-related activity, or in a vehicle operated by the district. (This definition does not necessarily include bullying that occurs on campus.)

2. To constitute bullying the **conduct must meet two elements**:

- Must have the effect or will have the effect of **physically harming a student, damaging a student's property, or placing a student in reasonable fear of harm to the student's person or property.**
- **Be sufficiently severe, persistent, and pervasive enough that the action or threat creates an intimidating, threatening, or abusive educational environment for a student.**

3. In addition, the conduct described above must also:

- Exploit an imbalance of power between the student perpetrator and the student victim through written or verbal expression or physical conduct.
- Interfere with a student's education or substantially disrupt the operation of a school.

DOCUMENTATION IS THE KEY:

1. When conducting a bullying investigation, it is absolutely critical that thorough documentation is showing:

- The exact nature of the complaints
- The action that was taken
- Any training provided to teachers
- All measures to educate students and parents about the problem

2. The Complaining party should write a statement and sign it.

3. Disciplinary records of the alleged harasser should be acquired and placed in the documentation.

4. Witness statements from students, teachers, and staff.

5. All video surveillance

NOTE: Always follow district policy and procedures. I recommend a person new to the field of administration join a professional organization and become a member of the Texas School Legal Digest for all up-to-date district and school legal information!

Data extracted from Texas School Administrator Legal Digest and West Law.

ADDITIONAL DOCUMENTATION USED FOR OFF-CAMPUS BULLYING/HARASSMENT SITUATION:

If the situation involves off-campus use of social media, the campus/district must show the impact that the event had on the operations of the school or that officials reasonably believed that a material and substantial disruption was likely to occur.

Without the following the school may be in violation of the students First Amendment rights.

1. Impact on classes including teacher statements.
2. Time and effort spent in the investigation.
3. Computer records are showing off-campus computer used in relation to the event.
4. The need for meetings with teachers, staff, parents and local law enforcement.
5. The need for counseling services for students are impacted.
6. Any time spent with the media.
7. Potential for ongoing disruptions.
8. All disciplinary action took—**and its ALIGNMENT** to district policy and student code of conduct.
9. All efforts to provide due process.
10. Efforts to provide training for student, staff, parents and teachers on anti-bullying and cyberbullying BEFORE and AFTER the event.

NOTE: Keep in mind this is an emerging area of school law. Administrators must keep informed of new legal developments in this area and, when in doubt, consult your superintendent and school attorney BEFORE imposing discipline of a student for off-campus speech or behavior.

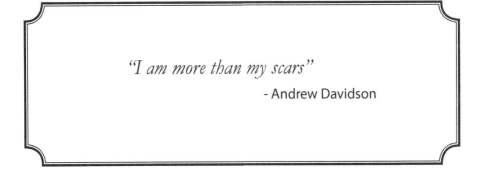

"I am more than my scars"
- Andrew Davidson

Bullying and OCR

As a way of reminder, the ninth circuit court case in Missouri gave us the judge's ruling (2009) that changed the nature of 504. This judge used OCR language in explaining the many nuances of the case and thus added a new level of legalese to our discussion and description.

With that in mind, the Texas courts along with the Office of Civil Rights (OCR) has issued a new guidance on bullying of students with disabilities--it is a must read for ALL administrators and those wishing to be administrators. Even more importantly, you WILL see this information on the TExES, in the future.

Everyone must be attuned to the idea the TExES is a living testing instruments and as such continually changes to meet the challenges of today's educational world.

Top bullets of the Guidance from TEA:
- Students with disabilities are at a higher risk of being singled out by bullies!
- **Courts will show <u>little tolerance</u> for school districts that fail to take appropriate action to stop the harassment!**
- The findings of a court to "deliberate indifference" are devastating in public relations and financial, to a school district!

Avoiding deliberate indifference:
- discipline the alleged bullies -- **document**
- open communication with students, parents about the concerns. – **document**
- training for student, staff and parents about bully programs and how to recognize the actions – **document**
- training for student, staff and parents about bullying and how to stop it – **document**

All of the above information can be located in the newest OCR bulletin: stopbullying.gov also the latest on the TEA website!

> *"I've learned ... That opportunities are never lost; someone will take the ones you miss."*
> – Andy Rooney

Campus Behavior Coordinator

SB 107

A person at each campus must be designated to serve as the campus behavior coordinator. This person may be the building principal and or any other campus administrator selected by the principal.

The CBC is primarily responsible for maintaining student discipline.

Duties of the CBC:

1. **Must <u>promptly notify</u> a student's parent or guardian if the student is placed into in-school or out-of-school suspension, placed in a disciplinary alternative education program, expelled, or placed in a juvenile justice alternative educational program or is taken into custody by a law enforcement officer.**
   a) Prompt Notification:
   - IF the parent has not been notified (telephone or in person) by 5:00 of the first business day after the action to the student.
   - The CBC shall mail written notice of the action to the parent or guardian.

2. The CBC shall respond to a teacher sending a student to the campus CBC by:
   - Employing appropriate discipline management techniques consistent with the student code of conduct; that can reasonably be expected to improve the student's behavior before returning the student to the classroom.
   - If the student's behavior does not improve, the CBC shall employ alternative discipline management techniques, including any progressive interventions designated as the responsibility of the campus CBC in the student code of conduct.

NOTE: SB 107 is the source of this information

IMPORTANT!

Document, Document, Document –

Remember!! If it is NOT on paper, it is Vapor!!

Community Resource Management

1. **A modern principal will actively** collaborate with:

   - **Community and county health services**
   - **Community and county social services**
   - **Community and county police and fire services**

2. **A modern principal will develop** mutually beneficial relationships with:

   - Community business organizations
   - Community religious organizations
   - Community political and service organizations.

     a. The principal will identify and document the relationship and ensure equitable and open access for all groups as required by District policy.

3. **A modern principal will effectively** employ all community resources that will support student learning.

   - The principal will identify, evaluate and document successful community resource usage and allocation.

4. **A modern principal will** develop sustainable community resources to support student learning.

   - Document and provide positive information to the community about resource benefits.
   - Clearly identify and communicate resource needs from the community.
   - Develop a sustainable resource allocation process.

[Handwritten note: FERPA - I cannot give the reports out until they are "cleaned" up with getting names blacked out, etc.]

> "You are never too old to set another goal or to dream a new dream"
>
> — C. S. Lewis

Contracts and the Modern Principal

Probationary Contracts

A probationary contract is offered to a teacher new to a district, and a teacher who was previously employed by a district who returns to the district after a two-year lapse. A new teacher can work on a probationary contract for up to five years. A teacher who has taught five years of the last eight will be offered a term contract after one year.

- A district may employ an experienced teacher or principal on a term contract. For brand new teachers, the probationary period can actually last up to four years. For a teacher who has taught in five of the last eight school years, the probationary period can only last one year.
- After the probationary period, the school district must place the employee on a term or continuing contract, or else dismiss the employee.

Rights of the probationary contracts. On a day-to-day basis, a probationary contract teacher is entitled to all the rights and privileges of employment of all teachers:

- State minimum salary schedule and any applicable local schedules
- 30-minute duty-free lunch
- Five days of personal leave and any applicable local leave
- 450 minutes of planning and prep time every two weeks
- Entitled to the same subchapter F hearing that a term and continuing contract teacher receive

Term Contracts

Most Texas school districts offer term contracts. A term contract is for a time certain, usually 1 or 2 years. On a day-to-day basis, a term contract teacher is entitled to all the rights and privileges of employment of all teachers:

- State minimum salary schedule and any applicable local schedules
- 30-minute duty-free lunch
- Five days of personal leave and any applicable local leave
- 450 minutes of planning and prep time every two weeks
- Entitled to the same subchapter F hearing that a term and continuing contract teacher receive

Continuing Contracts

A continuing contract is as close to K-12 tenure as we have in Texas.

- State minimum salary schedule and any applicable local schedules
- 30-minute duty-free lunch
- Five days of personal leave and any applicable local leave
- 450 minutes of planning and prep time every two weeks

- Entitled to the same subchapter F hearing that a term and continuing contract teacher receive
- A continuing contract ceases to exist only if the employee resigns, retires, or is lawfully dismissed

The Non-Renewal Timeline:

- Always set a schedule for contract decisions and actions.
- Work backwards from the 10th day before the last day of instruction to create your action plans.
- Make sure you have documentation for all decisions and concerns.
- Make sure your documentation has been reviewed by the central office before you move forward with decisions. Always listen to legal counsel.
- It is wise to make decision sometime in March. This allows time for the school board to meet in April for final decisions.
- Be prepared for the unexpected!
- Always DOCUMENT and NEVER wait until the last minute.

Note from Dr. Sandy Cortez-Rucker:

As a Principal, you hold the key to assisting teachers to become all they can be. But remember, you are there to cheer them on and inspire them to do their best. For those teachers that do not go the extra mile or give all they can, you have a responsibility as the Administrator to remove. Above all else, remember Kids Come First. Non-renewal and/or immediate removal is not pleasant or easy on the nerves to do. Just remember, Kids come first! That is the reason we are there to educate and assist the kids to gain hope and confidence and the best education we can afford them.

> *"Optimism is the faith that leads to achievement. Nothing can be done without hope and confidence."*
> - Helen Keller

Contract and At-Will Employment

In Texas, most workers are hired at-will, meaning they are employed at the will of the employer, and they may quit or be fired at any time. In Texas school districts, however, most professional employees, including all full-time classroom teachers, are employed by written employment contracts. The following are resources related to contracts, including contracts governed by Texas Education Code chapter 21; at-will employment; and ending employment, including contract nonrenewal, termination, suspension, reduction in force, and resignation.

Contracts
Related Policies

Your local school board policy manual contains TASB's (LEGAL) reference policies and board-adopted (LOCAL) policies. Your district may also have relevant administrative regulations. For more information on contracts, see district policy and regulations at the following codes:

DC	Employment Practices
DCA	Probationary Contracts
DCB	Term Contracts
DCC	Continuing Contracts
DCE	Other Types of Contracts

TASB Resources

- TASB Legal Services developed and maintains Model School District Educator Contracts for term, probationary, and noncertified employees. These contracts are available to members of HR Services in the **HR Library** and to subscribers of the **Legal Research Library** behind myTASB at no additional charge.

- The TASB **HR Library**, available behind myTASB for members of HR Services, collects information and resources on contracts and assignments.

- For information relating to superintendent contracts, see eSource at **Governance – Superintendent**.

At-Will Employment
Related Policies

For more information on at-will employment, see district policy and regulations at the following codes:

DC	Employment Practices
DCD	At-Will Employment
DPB	Substitute, Temporary, and Part-Time Positions

TASB Resources
The TASB **HR Library**, available behind myTASB for members of HR Services, collects information and resources on at-will employment under the heading Employment, including information on noncontract/at-will employment, substitute teachers, and independent contractors.

Other Resources
The Texas Workforce Commission **Especially for Texas Employers** Website provides general information for employers in Texas about employment at-will.

Related Policies

Ending Employment

For more information on ending employment, see district policy and regulations at the following codes:

DF	Termination of Employment
DFAA	Suspension/Termination During Probationary Contract
DFAB	Termination at End of Probationary Year
DFAC	Return To Probationary Status
DFBA	Suspension/Termination During Term Contract
DFBB	Nonrenewal of Term Contract
DFCA	Suspension/Termination During Continuing Contract
DFD	Hearings Before Hearing Examiner
DFE	Resignation
DFF	Reduction in Force
DFFA	Financial Exigency
DFFB	Program Change
DFFC	Continuing Contracts

TASB Resources

- TASB Legal Services' article **Reductions in Force** provides a basic overview of the legal and policy concerns pertaining to reductions in force.

- TASB Legal Services' **Exit Incentives—Points to Consider** provides an overview of legal issues relating to early resignation notice incentives and standard exit incentives, including a form for early resignation notice incentives.

- TASB Legal Services' article **Resignations by Certified Personnel** explains the legal principles governing resignations of contract employees and explains when and how a resignation can be withdrawn.

- For subscribers, the TASB Legal Services' **Legal Research Library** behind myTASB contains a number of relevant resources, including a Good Cause Index, information on TEA's independent hearing examiners, and an archive of commissioner decisions dating back to 1995.

Other Resources

- The Texas Education Agency (TEA) Office of Legal Services **Teacher FAQs** document answers questions about resignation and nonrenewal.

- The TEA Office of Legal Services **Hearings and Appeals** Website provides information about local hearings before hearing examiners, appeals to the commissioner, and judicial appeals.

- The TEA **Local Hearing Decisions** Website provides a searchable database of local hearing examiner decisions.

- The TEA **Superintendent Reporting—FAQs** Website answers questions about the requirement that superintendents report educator misconduct that results in termination or resignation.

- The Texas Workforce Commission (TWC) **Especially for Texas Employers** Website provides general information for employers in Texas about employee termination and post-employment issues.

- The TWC **Rapid Response Program** Website provides information to assist laid-off employees.

NOTE: Texas Association of School Boards website under School Law, Personnel, Contract and At Will Employment is where this information is Compiled.

Co-Teaching and the Principal

Co-Teaching:

Administrators must be held accountable for the effectiveness of co-teaching on their campuses, including how successful they have been in implementing, monitoring, and evaluating co-teaching.

Co-teaching is a learning environment in which two or more certified professionals **share the responsibility:**
- Lesson planning
- Delivery of instruction
- Progress monitoring for their students

As a team, they share:
- Physical classroom space
- Instructional decisions
- Student accountability

Purpose of Co-Teaching is to allow professional educators the opportunity to **share their**:
- Diverse range of abilities
- Expertise in designing rigorous learning experiences tailored to meet the unique needs of all students
- Curriculum and instruction
- Classroom management
- Knowledge of typical students
- Instructional pacing
- Differentiating instruction
- Monitoring progress
- Understanding learning processes
- Teaching for mastery

The Target Population can be:
- Students with IEPs
- Limited English Proficient (LEP)
- Migrant
- 504 students
- Students with behavioral challenges
- Students with severe cognitive impairments
- Students who are identified as Gifted/Talented

Campus administrators are responsible for:
- Overseeing day-to-day implementation
- Addressing program challenges
- Evaluating co-teach partners by conducting
- Walk-throughs
- Formal appraisals

To facilitate efficient professional development, the building principal must:
- Develop pre-planning packets that
- Provide training on building a collaborative campus culture
- Develop a shared understanding of co-teaching
- Build a collaborative relationship

NOTE: *Co-Teaching: A How to Guide* – We recommend you download the document from the internet and keep a copy on your desk for easy reference.

> *"Defeat is not the worst of failures, not to have tried is the true failure."*
> - George Woodberry, American Literary Critic

Co-Teaching: A Model for Classroom Management

Why Co-Teach?

Co-teaching provides a structure for special and general educators to work together to educate students with disabilities in the general education classroom. According to special education law (PL 94-142), students with disabilities should be served in the "least restrictive environment" – in most cases an environment that allows students with disabilities to be educated alongside their non-disabled peers. Over time, the least restrictive environment has been interpreted as more than a particular location: The conception has broadened to include an educational approach that minimizes social restriction and provides students with disabilities access to the general education curriculum (*Lenz & Deschler, 2004*). Thus, students with disabilities are moving into general education classrooms. Co-teaching facilitates this placement by enabling specialized social and academic support.

Who Is Responsible for Students with Disabilities?

Although students with disabilities typically spend the majority of their time in general education classrooms, there has been some confusion about who is responsible for their education (*Maheady, Harper, & Mallette, 2001*). Special education students have been considered primarily or solely the responsibility of special education teachers. However, funding for all students who receive instruction from general educators, including those with disabilities, is allocated to general education, implying that general educators are responsible for the education of all students within their classrooms--with or without disabilities. These funds are used to pay budget items including salaries for general education teachers and supplies for the general education classroom (*Office of the Federal Register, 2005*).

Research studies have shown that co-teaching can be very effective for students with special needs, especially those with milder disabilities such as learning disabilities. When implemented correctly, co-teaching can be a very successful way to teach all students in a classroom setting

Benefits of Co-teaching:

- Access to the general education curriculum and general education setting
- Students with disabilities will still receive specialized instruction
- Differentiated instruction
- Collegial sharing of scope, expertise and teaching capacity

Models of Co-teaching:

(*FRIEND AND COOK, 2004*)

1. **One teach, one observe:** one teacher delivers instruction while the other observes student learning and assesses student understanding and academic functioning
2. **One teach, one assist:** one teacher will take the lead in providing instruction while the other moves around the classroom and assists students who may be struggling
3. **Parallel Teaching:** The class is divided in half, and the same material is presented at the same time by both teachers (teacher to student ratio becomes more manageable)
4. **Station Teaching:** Both teachers are actively involved in instruction and the students rotate from one station to the next, learning new material
5. **Alternative Teaching:** One teacher takes a small group of students and provides instruction that is different than what the large group is receiving
6. **Team Teaching:** Both teachers instruct on the same lesson with all students present

Co-Teaching and Special Education

Many considerations for beginning a campus co-teaching program must be considered. Issues will arise that will be specific to the camps and caution and skill must be applied to stay within the special education guidelines.

Personnel Paring:

It is essential that the administrator carefully consider to the paring of personnel for the co-teaching assignment. First, all staff members and personnel must understand that co-teaching will be the expected standard of practice. Staff and personnel must be willing to plan and work together. The professionals selected must understand they need to attend professional development together. A plan for resolving professional and personal disagreements must be created and in place. Conflict management and follow-up resources must be available to co-teaching partners. The administrator must be a viable and trained individual in resolving conflicts.

Personnel Paring-Strengths:

The goal of co-teaching is to blend the strengths of the professional individuals. The results are the paring will create an atmosphere of learning from each other. The ultimate result is student achievement.

Keeping within the special education laws:

Using the students' IEPs, identify required special education support services by student and content area (i.e. mainstream with no special education support, inclusion support such as itinerant and/or co-teach support, content mastery, resource, self-contained, etc.).

1. Review current staff for various class arrangements to determine who is available to provide inclusion support services.
2. Decide a ratio for general **education students to students with disabilities**, based on the students' needs. This ratio may vary from classroom to classroom based on student composition and teacher scheduling in the classroom. There is no state-required ratio; this is a locally determined decision.
3. Build the master schedule for general education and special education teacher assignments (*schedule students with disabilities into classrooms before scheduling of non-disabled peers*), ensuring that **student needs drive master schedule**. This is especially important at the secondary level because your ratio may determine a need for special education support in multiple sections of the same course.

NOTE: Co-Teaching Handbook, pg. 32 – Administrative Scheduling of the Co-Teaching Classroom

Copyright: Fair Use

The short excerpt below is but a small fraction of the extensive copyright law, for educators. I would strongly suggest you go to the URL site below for further review. Fair use is a legal principle that defines the limitations on the exclusive rights of copyright holders.

While there is no simple test to determine what is fair use, the Copyright Act (Section 107) sets forth four fair use factors which should be considered, to determine whether a use is a "fair use":

1. Purpose and character of use, including whether such use is of a commercial nature or is for nonprofit educational purposes
2. Nature of the copyrighted work
3. Amount and substantiality of the portion used in relation to the copyrighted work as a whole
4. Effect of the use upon the potential market for or value of the copyrighted work

PERMITTED USES OF EDUCATIONAL MULTIMEDIA PROGRAMS

Educators may perform and display their own educational multimedia projects created under Section 2 for curriculum-based instruction to students in the following situations:

1. Face-to-face instruction
2. Assigned to students for directed self-study
3. For remote instruction to students enrolled in curriculum-based courses and located at remote sites, provided over the educational institution's secure electronic network in real-time, or for after class review or directed self-study, provided there are technological limitations on access to the network and educational multimedia project (such as a password or PIN) and provided further that the technology prevents the making of copies of copyrighted material.

Motion Media

Up to 10% or 3 minutes, whichever is less, in the aggregate of a copyrighted motion media work may be reproduced.

Text Material

Up to 10% or 1000 words, whichever is less, in the aggregate of a copyrighted work consisting of text material may be reproduced or otherwise incorporated as part of a multimedia projects. A poem of less than 250 words may be used, but no more than three poems by one poet, or five poems by different poets from any anthology may be used. For poems of greater length, 250 words may be used but no more than three excerpts by a poet, or five excerpts by different poets from a single anthology may be used.

Music, Lyrics, and Music Video

Up to 10%, but in no event more than 30 seconds, of the music and lyrics from an individual musical work (or in the aggregate of extracts from an individual work), whether the musical work is embodied in copies, or audio or audiovisual works, may be reproduced or otherwise incorporated as a part of a multimedia project.

Illustrations and Photographs

The reproduction or incorporation of photographs and illustrations is more difficult to define with regard to fair use because fair use usually precludes the use of an entire work. Under these guidelines a photograph or illustration may be used in its entirety but no more than 5 images by an artist or photographer may be reproduced or otherwise incorporated as part of an educational multimedia project. When using photographs and illustrations from a published collective work, not more than 10% or 15 images, whichever is less, may be reproduced or otherwise incorporated as part of an educational multimedia project.

Numerical Data Sets

Up to 10% or 2500 fields or cell entries, whichever is less, from a copyrighted database or data table may be reproduced or otherwise incorporated as part of an educational multimedia project. A field entry is defined as a specific item of information. A cell entry is defined as the intersection where a row and a column meet on a spreadsheet.

Caution in Downloading Material from the Internet

Educators and students are advised to exercise caution in using digital material downloaded from the Internet in producing their own educational multimedia projects, because there is a mix of works protected by copyright and works in the public domain on the network. Access to works on the Internet does not automatically mean that these can be reproduced and reused without permission or royalty payment and, furthermore, some copyrighted works may have been posted to the Internet without authorization of the copyright holder.

NOTE: It is strongly suggested to research this topic further go to UT Texas website as it is the source for Copyright questions on the TExES Exam.

Crisis Management Plan (CMP)
Crisis Intervention Plan (CIP)

The dictionary describes crisis as:" An unstable or crucial time or state of affairs in which a decisive change is impending, especially one with the distinct possibility of a highly undesirable outcome." This means a crisis is a critical situation where a school campus could be faced with inadequate information, not enough time, and insufficient resources, but in which leaders must make one or more crucial decisions.

Crisis is a daily part of the day-to-day on the modern public school campus. They range in scope and intensity from incidents that directly impact the entire school and its community, to incidents that impact a single student.

All Texas school districts and campuses must have Crisis Management (CMP) or Crisis Intervention Plan (CIP). The overall plan may be created at the district and/or campus levels. **The plan must identify factors where the district and/or campus must handle a situation with internal resources.**

Crisis management is a continuous process in which all phases of a plan are being reviewed and revised by the team. **A good crisis plan is a living plan that alters and changes to its environment of need.**

Plans need to address many types of crisis whether they are made by people or nature:
- Natural disasters (earthquake, tornado, hurricane, flood)
- Severe weather
- Fires
- Chemical or hazardous material spills
- Bus crashes
- School shootings
- Bomb threats
- Medical emergencies
- Student or staff deaths (suicide, homicide, unintentional, or natural)
- Acts of terror or war
- Outbreaks of disease or infections

There are four phases of crisis management:
1. **Mitigation/Prevention -** Addresses what schools and districts can do to reduce or eliminate the risk to life and property.
2. **Preparedness** - The process of planning for the worst-case scenario.
3. **Response** - Developing the steps to take during a crisis.
4. **Recovery** - Developing the steps on how to restore the learning and teaching environment after a crisis.

Key principles for effective crisis planning

Effective leadership helps with:
- Policy agenda decisions
- Seeking and/or securing funds
- Effective team building
- School and Community communication

Reminder – Do not overlook these four key points as you complete your CMP or CIP. They are essential.
- **The plan is not developed in a vacuum (must have internal and external influences)**
- **The plan is a natural extension of the district, campus and community's efforts to create a safe learning environment.**
- **The plan should enhance all school functions.**
- **The plan should incorporate needs assessments and other school data.**

Open and clear communication between the district, campus, and community well in advance of a crisis. Integration of internal and external groups must be included.

- School maintenance
- School financial team
- School medical
- School police
- Public law enforcement
- Fire safety officials
- Emergency medical services
- State and local mental health professionals
- Both district, campus and local community leaders

Reminder – Do not overlook these three key points as you complete your CMP or CIP. They are essential.
- **The development of specific vocabulary that all internal and external groups understand.**
- **The plan should be tailored to the district and campus needs.**
- **The plan should not be one document. It should be a series of documents targeted for the various needs of the specific campuses.**

Ready access to the plan is critical. All internal and external support groups must have access to the plan. Training and Practice are essential for the implementation of the crisis plan.

NOTE: *This short article is not inclusive and the student (Principal Candidate) should review the state and national Crisis Management Plan (CIP) Manual as well as the SBDM Manual.*

Curriculum of the Instructional Program

Purpose:

Requirements for instructional programs are well defined and in most cases mandated by the state. However, the management and oversight role in implementing these programs and ensuring adherence to established standards is the responsibility of individual districts.

Policies/Procedures:

1. Procedures established for textbook inventory and replacement including:
   - Maintaining a comprehensive textbook inventory
   - Properly accounting for funds for replacement books
   - Providing for accurate reporting of all textbooks to administration by each campus

2. Procedures established for allocation for instructional supplies and materials (other than textbooks) including:
   - Providing opportunity for input from campuses regarding needs
   - Providing resources for supplemental instructional materials and supplies
   - Allowing maximum flexibility for use of instructional funds
   - A budget monitoring process to provide accountability of campus budgets
   - An inventory of instructional materials and supplies maintained by campus
   - Maintenance of cost data to ensure general per pupil, grade level and subject matter equity

3. **The principal's questions to determine usefulness of the present curriculum**
   - Is the curriculum consistent with the campus mission statement?
   - Is the curriculum consistently applied across the learning environment by the classroom teacher?
   - Does the curriculum have a set of intended learning outcomes that articulate the latest state standards?
   - Is the curriculum learning outcomes clearly and consistently reviewed through the evaluation instrument?

Important!
Remember the Curriculum and all changes must be an SBDM process. Communication (Domain I) to ALL constituents will be the responsibility of the building administrator. NEVER let curriculum change come as a surprise!

NOTE: Compiled from the TEA Management Manual 8.5.2.1

Cyberbullying and Student First Amendment Rights

The leading case on student speech is *Tinker V. Des Moines Ind. Community School District* (1969).

The main challenge for administrators? When should they discipline a student for off-campus cyberbullying when the student later claims that the discipline violated their First Amendment freedom of speech rights.

1. The First Amendment protects freedom of speech rights:
   - The right of expression,
   - The right from "compelled expression

Tinker v. Des Moines Ind. Community School District (1969)

2. Recent court cases have recognized that students "can't hide" behind the First Amendment to protect their right in regard to:
   - Abuse and intimidating other students at the school.
   - Disruption in the school.
   - Deprives fellow students of his/her access to educational opportunities.

Sypniewski v. Warren Hills Regional Bd. of Education (2002).

3. Since *Tinker*, the Supreme Court has identified several categories of speech that school officials may constitutionally regulate: * check your policy procedures ALWAYS consult with your superintendent.
   - On-Campus vulgar, lewd, obscene, and plainly offensive speech. - *Bethel School District v. Fraser (1986)*
   - School –sponsored speech, when reasonably related to legitimate pedagogical concerns. - *Hazelwood Sch. District v. Kuhmeier (1988)*
   - Speech is promoting illegal drug use. - *Morse v. Frederick (2007)*
   - True threat. - *Watts v. United States (1969)*

With regard to, on and off-campus speech the Supreme Court has not spoken. **BUT, lower courts decisions reveal two categories that can be subject to school discipline:**
   1. **Speech that constitutes a "true threat."**
   2. **Conduct that reaches the school and causes a "material and substantial disruption' or is reasonably likely to cause such a disruption under the Tinker standard.**

NOTE: Data extracted from West Law, School Policy, and Texas School Digest

CYBER SECURITY

In accordance with HB 3171, Section 38.023, the Texas Education Agency has developed and made available to school districts a list of resources related to Internet Safety.

By nature of the content, the site and its information are constantly evolving; therefore, emerging content and resource URLs will be continuously added to the site.

Knowledge + Application = Internet Safety

Information security means protecting information and information systems from unauthorized access, use, disclosure, disruption, modification or destruction. *Know this definition!!*

Compiled from other sites recommended by TEA for administrators:

Although the internet serves as a valuable learning tool, youth should be educated by both parents and teachers regarding safe internet practices. With over 90% of teenagers engaging in online use, the internet serves as a dominant medium of information gathering and sharing for the vast majority of youth (Lenhart, Purcell, Smith & Zickuhr, 2010). Social media sites, such as Facebook and Twitter, pervade the lives of youth. Additionally, with cell phone ownership at over 75% for teens, the manner in which youth communicate with peers has vastly changed in the last decade (Lenhart et al., 2010). The ease of internet accessibility for youth lends itself to a continuous online presence, thus potential for subsequent victimization by adults and other peers. Although research suggests incidents of online victimization targeting youth impact a small portion of the population, these dangers still exist and must be addressed at the onset of internet use (Mitchell, Finkelhor, Wolak, Ybarra, & Turner, 2011).

Over the past decade, technology has altered the way youth communicate and interact with their peers. Over 75% of teenagers own cell phones, and one-third send over 3,000 text messages a month (Lenhart, 2010). Consequently, new forms of electronic communication (e.g., Facebook, Twitter, texting) have created concern among parents, health care professionals, educators, and law enforcement regarding the harmful behaviors youth may engage in as these types of communication become more prevalent (Mitchell, & Finkelhor, 2011; Mitchell, Finkelhor, Jones, & Wolak, 2012; Wolak & Finkelhor, 2011). Some of these harmful behaviors include engaging in cyberbullying, publicly posting sexual images, and communicating with or being solicited by prospective sexual predators online. Although there is no consistent legal definition for the term "sexting", most state laws generally concentrate on images that are transmitted through cell phones.

Important Points for Computer Security:

- Use security software that updates automatically
- Treat your personal information like cash
- Check out companies to find out whom you're really dealing with
- Protect your passwords
- Back up your files

<u>Every administrator in a school</u> environment has an <u>obligation to be knowledgeable</u> about cyber security, including district-level administrators, such as superintendents, community directors and finance managers, as well as school-level administrators, **such as principals, guidance counselors and libraries**. Safeguarding computers in the schools is not just for technology professionals: it is every <u>administrator's responsibility</u>. While most school districts have security measures in place to ensure computer network protection, responsible administrators, must guarantee that these systems are as secure as possible so that:

1. Student and staff data remain private

2. School technology property is not damaged during attacks from email viruses, Inquisitive student "hackers" or malicious external infiltration
3. Student, teachers, and district staff have access to online information and network services through secure internet and network connections.

Network Security Knowledge for School Administrators

Every district should have:

- **Antiv-Virus Software on every computer and every server.**

- **Firewall Protection to make the school network "invisible" on the internet and blocks communication from unauthorized sources.**

- **Data Backup is a system to backup data "off site."**

Data:

- Guidelines must be established and understood by the administrator for electronic data storage and security.

- Guidelines must be established and understood by the administrator to secure data from external sources

- Guidelines and protocol must be established and understood by the administrator for access to network information, both on and off site.

- Guidelines must be established and understood by the administrator for electronic communication – email. The process of encryption before distribution for certain files should be understood, and the protocols in place for its usage.

Basic Rules for Administrators:

- Establish Bi-Yearly "network Security checks" to keep up with the latest advances in computer and data management security

- Educate the School Community about Cyber Security

- Set-up password maintenance and security rules

- Set-up email security communication protocol about receiving unknown emails

- Set-up on-line chat protocol, discuss inappropriate websites, too much personal information and, "unknown" visitors to public sites

- Set-up rules about instant messaging and concerns about "real-time" electronic communication and the spread of computer viruses.

Violation of Acceptable Use Policy for Computer Systems:

- **Copying and sharing images, music, movies, or other copyrighted material using the district and/or campus computers.**

- **Making unlicensed copies of CD or DVD for others.**

- **Posting or plagiarizing copyrighted material.**

- **Downloading any copyright-protected files which you have not already legally procured (e.g., licensed copies of software, MP3s, movies).**

Note: Data extracted from West Law, School Policy, and Texas School Digest. However, the University of Texas "Crash Course" in Copyright Law has the complete list of violation of Acceptable Use Policy for Computer Systems.

Data Driven School Improvement

"One of the primary responsibilities of a leader is to help people confront problems. The way you confront problems is you identify them, and the way you identify problems is by looking at data."

- Terry Grier, superintendent, Guilford (N.C.) County Schools

Under this new environment of state and federal accountability requirements, the use of data-driven decision-making has begun to move beyond the purposes and evolve as a process. It now aims to systematically measure student progress, set school improvement goals and to increase the quality of curriculum and instruction to focus on increasing student achievement (Ainsworth & Viegut, 2006; Bernhardt, 2004a, 2004b; Datnow, Park, & Wahlstetter, 2007; Mandinach, Honey, & Light., 2006; Massell, 2000; Rogers., May 2011; Supovitz & Klein, 2003).

Five Elements to implementation:

1. Conduct a needs assessment or inventory audit
   - What do we want to learn?
   - Standardize the data management
   - Correlation of data elements across the system (standardized).
2. Analyze the data

    a. Interpretation of data (accuracy) is vital:
      - Provide ongoing training for campus users
      - Consider a "long-term" approach to data gathering
      - Data mining is critical
      - Data sharing is critical
      - The administration must create a "culture" of data sharing

3. Continuous Improvement
   - There is no end to data analysis

4. Communication
   - Sharing data in easy to read and understand documents and charts is critical (no educational jargon).

Data-driven decision-making techniques not only analyze test scores and student achievement, but also to:
- Narrow achievement gaps between student subgroups
- Improve teacher quality
- Improve curriculum
- Share best practices among schools and districts
- Communicate education issues more effectively with key stakeholders
- Promote parental involvement in the education process

Data-driven decision making is about:
- Collecting appropriate data
- Analyzing that data in a meaningful fashion
- Getting the data into the hands of the people who need it
- Using the data to increase school efficiencies and improve student achievement
- Communicating data-driven decisions to key stakeholders

Death: Dealing with Crisis at School
Practical Suggestions for Educators

The following are recommendations from several professional groups. **Texas schools depend on their Crisis Management plan and it protocol.** I have attached several here for your review. I have also attached a lengthy article from the National Association of School Psychologist and recommendation from the Department of Education. **First and foremost, follow your CMP!**

If you notice, both the plans attached are generic. The reason? All emergencies will dictate their own specific response. **The MAJOR areas you must respond to are:**

1. **Call 911, if appropriate**
2. Implement your CMP!
3. Follow through with all emergency contacts!

Large I.S.D.—Campus Emergency Plan (Example):

Death at School-Natural, Homicide, Suicide, Accident

1. Call 911. Call school nurse to site.
2. Activate Crisis Management Team.
3. Isolate the area.
4. Isolate the witnesses.
5. Suspend all bell schedules (everyone stays where he or she are)
6. Notify Central Administration.
7. Secure student/staff roster/emergency cards.

Other actions suggested:

1. Decide the method to inform parents, classmates and community of death, plans, and expected child reactions.
2. Ensure the family of the deceased is notified through pre-established method (personal visit preferred).
3. Alert counselors and nurse at schools in which siblings are enrolled.
4. Inform staff and student body.
5. Assign separate areas for media, parents, counseling.
6. Prepare a fact sheet and media statement.
7. Provide counseling individually or in groups.
8. Make home visits to counselors or crisis team members.
9. Hold faculty meeting as soon as possible to process feelings.
10. Prepare to hold community meetings.
11. Plan long-term response and follow-up counseling.
12. Permit students to leave only with parental permission.
13. Relay information, as it becomes available.
14. Communicate with the staff, include a written statement. (Utilize team leaders and department leaders if necessary).
15. Crisis Management Team meets to debrief at the end of the day.

Rural I.S.D. Campus Emergency Plan (Example):

SUICIDE OR ATTEMPTED SUICIDE

1. Call Police or 911
2. Activate CCMT
3. Isolate the area
4. Isolate the witnesses
5. Suspend bell schedule (everyone stays where he or she are)
6. Notify nurse
7. Notify Superintendent (specify needs, if any)
8. Secure emergency/health card
9. Notify parents (in person if possible)
10. Assign separate areas for media, parents, counseling
11. Communicate with the staff
12. Document all students checking out
13. Announce the availability of counseling and location
14. Teachers identify students who need counseling
15. Document who receives counseling and needs follow-up
16. CCMT meets to debrief at the end of the day

Notification and Announcement Procedures

Get the facts! Verification is very important and administrators should contact the family of the deceased and/or authorities to get the facts before providing post-vention. Give everyone the facts as quickly as possible to dispel rumors. Please verify that the student or staff member is deceased and not being maintained on life support systems. Age-appropriate language should be used. Acceptable sources of verification are:

1. School personnel who witnessed the death notification from the family of the deceased.
2. Notification from law enforcement agency.

Get help! Contact the key district administrators for assistance, and do so as quickly as possible. The administrators will also be helpful in interacting with the media. If the death was a suicide, it is essential that central administrators have input into post intervention planning.

Establish a calling tree: A calling tree should be utilized to notify district level personnel as well as building staff in the location where the deceased attended or worked. The calling tree can be used to notify all school personnel that a faculty meeting will be held before school to outline post-vention plans. If the death occurs during non-school hours or during vacations, this process allows staff members to work through their own issues before they assist their students.

If a death occurs when school is in session:

1. **Hand deliver a memorandum to all teachers.** The most frequent recommendation is to give all teachers the facts about the tragedy and instructions to share the information with their students, as well as suggestions for assisting students. This memo can also invite all staff to a faculty meeting after school. The majority of students should stay in their classroom. **Only those closest to the victim or those with tragic life situations of their own should be sent to the school's support personnel.**

2. Use the public announcement system. The administrator is urged to plan carefully and rehearse what he will say. Choice of words, voice tone, and inflection are very important and set the tone for management of the tragedy.

Parent Notification

It is very important to inform the parents of students at the school affected by the death that a death has occurred. There is a balance between providing enough information to dispel rumors and protecting the privacy of the deceased. It is recommended that a fact sheet or letter be sent to parents, either by mail or sent home via students. This letter, in most cases, would not contain the name of the deceased, especially when the death involves a student. The name would be used in communications within the school to the faculty, and in most cases with the students. The letter sent home would contain a brief description of the cause of death when the facts are known, but would avoid unnecessary details.

School personnel, especially those who have direct contact with parents either by phone or in person, should be given specific directions about appropriate information to share regarding the death. The letter to parents should encourage them to focus on the needs of their child and not on specific information about the deceased. The letter should clarify what types of services are available at the school to help their child cope with the tragedy. This letter should be reviewed by the superintendent or his designee prior to distribution.

Determine the Degree of Trauma

The following questions will help the administrator anticipate the amount of emotional trauma:

- Who was the person and were they a long-time popular member of the school?

- What happened? Murder and suicide are unexpected and violent, and thus more difficult to deal with than, for example, a death from a serious illness.

- Where did the death occur? A death that occurs on school grounds more difficult to deal with. It is important to find out who witnessed the death and provided them with counseling. Students may also reflect concerns with personal safety.

- What other tragedies have impacted this particular school recently? The latest death will cause other unresolved issues to surface for both staff and students.

- Who was the perpetrator? If the person believed to be responsible for the death is also a member of your school community, it adds to the emotionality.

Roles for School Personnel

There are a number of roles that should be performed by key personnel. It is important to recognize that each person has his or her own unique history with regard to crisis and loss. It is not unusual for old issues to resurface. Each student should be given permission to feel a range of emotions. There is no right or wrong way to feel. Typically, individuals go through a sequence of emotional reactions following a crisis:

- High anxiety
- Denial
- Anger
- Remorse
- Grief
- Reconciliation

Principal's Role
- **Direct intervention efforts**
- **Be visible, available, supportive, and empower staff**
- **Provide direction to teachers about how much to set aside the curriculum. Tests should be postponed in some classes.**
- **Communicate with central administration and other affected schools**
- **Contact family of the deceased**
- **Inform staff and students about funeral arrangements**
- **Ensure that memorials are appropriate**

What if the Death was a Suicide?

If the death was a suicide, postvention procedures outlined by the American Association of Sociology (AAS) should be followed, in addition to the recommendations above. The tasks of postvention are twofold:

1. To reduce the chances of anyone else committing suicide by avoiding glamorization of the deceased.
2. To assist staff and students with the grieving process. Postvention activities provide an opportunity to teach students the warning signs of suicide so that further suicides can be prevented. It is also important that school personnel receive training to recognize symptoms of depression and warnings of suicide ideation among students well before a crisis occurs. The main recommendations of the AAS include the following:

   - Don't dismiss school or encourage funeral attendance during school hours
   - Don't dedicate a memorial to the deceased
   - Don't have a large school assembly
   - Do give the facts to the students
   - Do emphasize prevention and everyone's role
   - Do provide individual and group counseling
   - Do emphasize that no one is to blame for the suicide
   - Do emphasize that help is available and that there are alternatives to suicide
   - Do contact the family of the deceased

NOTE: From National Association of School Psychologist, National Crisis Management Plans-DOE General Plan from a local I.S.D.

Disciplinary Alternative Education Program (DAEP) Placement

In deciding whether to place a student in a DAEP, regardless of whether the action is mandatory or discretionary, **the principal/campus behavior coordinator or appropriate administrator must review all proper procedures.**

Process

Removals to a DAEP shall be made by the principal/campus behavior coordinator or other appropriate administrator. In the event of a special needs student the ARD must be consulted.

1. **Conference** - When a student is removed from class for a DAEP offense, the principal/campus behavior coordinator or appropriate administrator shall schedule a conference within three school days with the student's parent, the student, and the teacher, in the case of a teacher removal. At the conference, the principal/campus behavior coordinator or appropriate administrator shall inform the student, orally or in writing, of the reasons for the removal and shall give the student an explanation of the basis for the removal and an opportunity to respond to the reasons for the removal. Following valid attempts to require attendance, the District may hold the conference and make a placement decision regardless of whether the student or the student's parents attend the conference. Until the conference is held, the principal may place a student in another appropriate classroom, in- school suspension or out-of-school suspension.

2. **Consideration of Mitigating Factors** - In deciding whether to place a student in a DAEP, regardless of whether the action is mandatory or discretionary, the principal/campus behavior coordinator or appropriate administrator shall take into consideration all ARD requirements, and recommendations.

3. **Placement Order** - After the conference, if the student is placed in the DAEP, the principal/campus behavior coordinator or appropriate administrator shall write a placement order. A copy of the DAEP placement order shall be sent to the student and the student's parent.

4. **Length of Placement** - The duration of a student's placement in a DAEP shall be determined by the principal/campus behavior coordinator, other appropriate administrator and the ARD.

5. **Appeals** - Questions from parents regarding disciplinary measures should be addressed to the campus administration. All appeal processes in the ARD must be addressed by the administration.

6. **Placement Review** - A student placed in a DAEP shall be provided a review of his or her status, including academic status, by the principal/campus behavior coordinator and the ARD at intervals pursuant to the determination of the ARD.

Discipline a Student with Disabilities

It is wise the first-year administrator should review not only this policy but also the ARD manual (pages 14-22). Between the two sources a much clearer picture of action will be available. **I would also visit with an ARD specialist and/or coordinator.** But as always, view the state documentation that is what the TExES is seeking.

A district shall conduct an evaluation in accordance with 34 C.F.R. 104.35(b) before taking any action with respect <u>to any significant change in placement of a student with a disability</u> who needs or is believed to need special education and related services. *34 C.F.R. 104.35(a)*

<u>All disciplinary actions regarding students with disabilities must be determined in accordance with 34 C.F.R. 300.101(a) and 300.530–300.536</u>; Education Code Chapter 37, Subchapter A; and 19 Administrative Code 89.1053 (relating to Procedures for Use of Restraint and Time-Out). *19 TAC 89.1050(j)*

Except as set forth below, <u>the placement of a student with a disability who receives special education services may be made only by a duly constituted admission, review, and dismissal (ARD) committee</u>. Any disciplinary action regarding the student shall be determined in accordance with federal law and regulations. *Education Code 37.004*

The methods adopted in the Student Code of Conduct [see FO] for discipline management and for preventing and intervening in student discipline problems must <u>provide that a student who is enrolled in the special education program may not be disciplined for bullying, harassment, or making hit lists until an ARD committee meeting has been held to review the conduct</u>. *Education Code 37.001(b-1)*

A student with a disability <u>who receives special education services may not be placed in a disciplinary alternative education program (DAEP) solely for educational purposes</u>. A teacher in a DAEP who has a special education assignment must hold an appropriate certificate or permit for that assignment. *Education Code 37.004(c)–(d)*

School personnel may remove a student with a disability who violates a student code of conduct from his or her current placement to an appropriate interim alternative educational setting, another setting, or suspension, for not more than <u>ten consecutive school days</u>, to the extent those alternatives are applied to children without disabilities. *20 U.S.C. 1415(k)(1)(B); 34 C.F.R. 300.530(b)(1)*

A district is required to provide services during the period of removal if the district provides services to a child without disabilities who is similarly removed. *34 C.F.R. 300.530(d)*

School personnel may remove the student, for not more than ten consecutive school days in that same school year <u>for separate incidents of misconduct, as long as those removals do not constitute a change in placement (see below)</u>. *34 C.F.R. 300.530(b)(1)*

After a student has been removed from his or her current placement for ten school days in the same school year, during any subsequent removal of ten consecutive school days or less, school personnel, in consultation with at least one of the student's teachers, shall determine the extent to which services are needed so as to enable the student to continue to participate in the general education curriculum, although in another setting, and to progress toward meeting the goals set out in the student's IEP. *20 U.S.C. 1415(k)(1)(D); 34 C.F.R. 300.530(d)(4)*

Not later than the date on which the decision to take the disciplinary action is made, a district shall notify the student's parents of the decision and of all procedural safeguards [see EHBAE]. *20 U.S.C. 1415(k)(1)(H)*

Any disciplinary action that would constitute a change in placement may be taken only after the student's <u>ARD committee conducts a manifestation determination review [see MANIFESTATION DETERMINATION, below]</u>. *Education Code 37.004*

For purposes of disciplinary removal of a student with a disability, a change in placement occurs if a student is:
   a. Removed from the student's current educational placement for more than ten consecutive school days; or
   b. Subjected to a series of removals that constitute a pattern because:
   c. The series of removals total more than ten school days in a school year;
   d. The student's behavior is substantially similar to the student's behavior in the previous incidents that resulted in the series of removals; and
   e. Additional factors exist, such as the length of each removal, the total amount of time the student is removed, and the proximity of the removals to one another.

The district determines, on a case-by-case basis, whether a pattern of removals constitutes a change in placement. The district's determination is subject to review through due process and judicial proceedings. *34 C.F.R. 300.536*

School personnel may consider any unique circumstances on a case-by-case basis when determining whether to order a change in placement for a student who violates a code of student conduct. *20 U.S.C. 1415(k)(1)(A)*

Within ten school days of any decision to change the placement of a student because of a violation of a code of student conduct, a district, parents, and relevant members of the ARD committee (as determined by the parent and the district) shall review all relevant information in the student's file, including the student's IEP, any teacher observations, and any relevant information provided by the parents to determine whether the conduct in question was:

   a. Caused by, or had a direct and substantial relationship to, the student's disability; or
   b. The direct result of the district's failure to implement the IEP.

If the district, the parent, and relevant members of the ARD committee determine that either of the above is applicable, the conduct shall be determined to be a manifestation of the student's disability. *20 U.S.C. 1415(k)(1)(E); 34 C.F.R. 300.530(e)*

If the determination is that the student's behavior was not a manifestation of the student's disability, school personnel may apply the relevant disciplinary procedures to the student in the same manner and for the same duration as for students without disabilities. The ARD committee shall determine the interim alternative educational setting. *20 U.S.C. 1415(k)(1)(C), (k)(2); 34 C.F.R. 300.530(c)*

The student must:
   a. Continue to receive educational services so as to enable the student to continue to participate in the general education curriculum, although in another setting, and to progress toward meeting the goals in the student's IEP.
   b. Receive, as appropriate, a functional behavioral assessment, and behavioral intervention services and modifications, that are designed to address the behavior violation so that it does not re-occur.

These services may be provided in an interim alternative educational setting. *34 C.F.R. 300.530(d)(1)–(2)*

If the district, the parents, and relevant members of the ARD committee determine that the conduct was <u>a **manifestation of the student's** disability</u>, **the ARD committee shall**:

   a. Conduct a functional behavioral assessment (FBA), unless the district had conducted an FBA before the behavior that resulted in the change in placement occurred, and implement a behavioral intervention plan (BIP) for the student; or
   b. If a BIP has already been developed, review the BIP and modify it, as necessary, to address the behavior.

c. Except as provided at SPECIAL CIRCUMSTANCES, below, the ARD committee shall return the student to the placement from which the student was removed, unless the parent and the district agree to a change in placement as part of the modification of the BIP.

20 U.S.C. 1415(k)(1)(F); 34 C.F.R. 300.530(f)

School personnel may remove a student to an interim alternative educational setting for not more than 45 school days without regard to whether the behavior is determined to be a manifestation of the student's disability, if the student:

a. Has inflicted serious bodily injury upon another person while at school, on school premises, or at a school function under the jurisdiction of TEA or the district. *20 U.S.C. 1415(k)(1)(G); 34 C.F.R. 300.530(g)*

b. **The ARD committee shall** determine the interim alternative education setting. *20 U.S.C. 1415(k)(2)*

The student must:

a. Continue to receive educational services so as to enable the student to continue to participate in the general education curriculum, although in another setting, and to progress toward meeting the goals in the student's IEP.

b. Receive, as appropriate, a functional behavioral assessment, and behavioral intervention services and modifications, that are designed to address the behavior violation so that it does not recur.

NOTE: From *District Policy FOF 2015*

Documentation
Texas Documentation Handbook

It is recommended by both Dr. Vance and Sandy Cortez-Rucker, that documentation begin at *the second* occurrence of a reoccurring incident. Example would be teacher and/ or staff tardiness—the bane of the modern principal.

While it is always important to maintain a good working relationship, you can't rely on oral directives when a consistent infraction becomes apparent. Documentation must begin to protect yourself, your district and give the legal department the justification to move on whatever recommendation you seek.

When to Document:
- **District Policy requires it!**
- **A pattern has occurred**
- **A serious incident has occurred!**

Types of Documentation:

1. <u>Notes to a file</u>
   a. All files kept by you are reviewable by the employee through the Texas Public Information Act.
   b. Do NOT write comments on the side of notes.
   c. Do NOT send a copy to the teacher/staff.
   d. Teacher/staff must be notified that a note to file has been done.
   e. Teacher/staff may request a copy. *this is the documentation they received it!*

2. **Performance Appraisal**
   Follow all documentation format, policy, and procedures.

3. <u>**Final Memo**</u>

   View all the above but conclude the above was accomplished, and the incidents continued. <u>**Do not fail to indicate danger of impact to the contract.**</u>

NOTE: Texas Documentation Handbook from Texas Legal Digest – You will find this is a clear, concise, and a must to have for the first-time administrators.

Documentation: WHY?

Texas Legal Digest – Principal's Handbook

1. **Three considerations to document:**
    - **Legal** – Fifth Circuit disregards testimony not verified with documentation.
    - **Ethical** – unfair decisions may be determined if not verifiable with documentation
    - **Political** – fairness in the decision reduces political fallout if documented.

2. Concerns about a lack of documentation:
    - Testimony that is not verifiable through documentation will be considered as hearsay!
    - The absence of carefully prepared documentation WILL jeopardize a district's case before the state commissioner or a state court.
    - The absence of careful documentation can impact an administrator's credibility during a harassment and/or bullying challenge.
    - The absence of careful documentation may indicate to a state commissioner and/or state court a perception of "indifference" on the part of the school district or administration.

> "Obstacles don't have to stop you. If you run into a wall, don't turn around and give up. Figure out how to climb it, go through it, or work around it."
>
> - Michael Jordan

Effective Texas Classroom Environment

What should I see as the building principal? The State of Texas has a very clear definition of what should be happening, in the modern classroom. The PDAS and other literature make it very clear and again, this would be very beneficial for the young principal to know and understand.

When the modern principal is evaluating either formative or as a walk-through there are many aspects that must be on his/her mind. As you read through the lists below, remember the **Quantity/Quality Rubric: Did I see it? Did it happen? Did it often happen? How many students impacted**?

Quality Classroom Lesson will have:
- **Effective delivery and presentation.**
- **Effective motivation and an indicators that students have a desire to learn.**
- **Effective variety is viewed, and indicators are present indicating impact on all students.**
- **Effective alignment is indicated through the communication of the teacher in identifying state and national standards.**

Lesson will be:
- Effective high cognitive level thinking is indicated through a variety of teaching models.
- Effective depth and complexity to the lesson produces curiosity and a desire to learn.
- Effective content is significant.
- Effective connection across disciplines and work or life applications.

Impact of the Lesson will be:
- Promotes student success.
- Effective use of assessment by the teacher to create the lesson.
- Data-driven decision-making.
- Indicates a level of responsibility for the student.
- Indicates a level of reflection for the student.
- Indicates a level of challenge for the student.

The Lesson will be:
- **Varied**
- **Differentiated**
- **Supportive with strategies and serves all students.**
- **Aligned to all curriculum and assessments.**

Formal collaborative planning:

The educational professional should work *in a collaborative planning team*. **This allows the teacher to:**
- Understand student needs,
- Understand the application of standards and their assessment on state instruments,
- Understand the application of standards to the campus and/or district scope and sequence.

Choice of teaching strategies **allows the teacher (in a collaborative team) to:**
- Identify effective research-based strategies and their appropriate resources,
- Identify and select appropriate assessment techniques.

Formal Collaborative Planning *develops a common core of lessons:*
- Develops a common plan with agreed lesson objectives,
- Develops agreed materials and classroom procedures,
- Develops agreed on time frames, activities and student assessment targets.

Formal Collaborative Planning develops *a clear process of implementation*.
- Delivers the agreed lessons within the accepted time frame.
- Delivers the assessment results and creates a dialogue for professional discussion about task and difficulty.

Formal Collaborative Planning allows for disaggregation of assessment and classroom data.
- Compares the assessment data to standards for identification of student success,
- Compares student work to standards for identification of student success.
- Compares student strengths, weaknesses and implications of teaching models of instruction.

Formal Collaborative Planning allows for the corrective communication process to flourish.
- Reflection on common teaching methods during the teaching cycle.
- Reflection on strengths, weaknesses, and alternate teaching models.
- Reflect on refining the process.

ELL and the Modern Principal

Every student who has a home language other than English and who is identified as an English language learner(ELL) shall be provided a full opportunity to participate in a bilingual education or English as a second language (ESL) program. Each school district with an enrollment of 20 or more limited English proficient students in the same grade level shall offer a bilingual education program as described in Texas Administrative Code *Chapter 89.1205.*

The goal of the Language Proficiency Assessment Committee(LPAC) is to identify and educate all English Language Learners (ELL).

- The **campus principal** will establish a Language Proficiency Assessment Committee (LPAC) for the campus and designate who shall serve on the LPAC.
- The **campus principal** will assure each member of the LPAC is adequately oriented and trained at least annually and prior to the first LPAC meeting on the campus.
- Within 20 school days of the student's enrollment on the campus, the campus principal will assure the LPAC meets to review the placement and program of the ELL student.
- At least annually, the campus principal will assure the LPAC meets on every ELL student on the campus to monitor the student's academic performance and progress toward language acquisition

Six Things Principals can do to support their English Language Learners:

1. Set a vision of high expectations - Principals can communicate to teachers their belief that ELLs, with appropriate instruction and supports, can succeed in learning challenging content.
2. Make the families of ELLs feel welcome - Principals can ensure outgoing communication—such as notices sent home to parents—are translated into home languages and provide interpreters at school events.
3. Ensure that ELLs receive English Language development - Principals can facilitate specifically designated time for English language development (ELD), a time when they learn sentence structure, additional vocabulary, and how English is used in academic settings.
4. Provide Ell-focused professional development to all teachers - Principals can facilitate the professional development that will build a shared understanding of Ells' needs and a common commitment to the instructional practices that support them.
5. Protect time for general-education or content teachers to collaborate with ESL specialist - Principals can avoid the disconnect and reduce the isolation by building collaboration time into the schedule. Specialists can join teachers for grade-level meetings or have overlapping planning periods.
6. Monitor Ells' achievement in the content areas and their development of English - Principals review data, when teachers meet in grade-level teams to examine data, or when teachers look at formative assessments within their own classrooms, they need data showing the progress of ELLs and comparisons to non-ELLs.

The campus principal will assure the LPAC:

1. Gives prior notice to the parent
    - Although parent attendance is not required, parents must be given every opportunity to participate in the decision-making process.
    - Document all decisions including placement, test scores, TELPAS performance, STAAR performance, grades, accommodations, and testing decisions in the LPAC documents.

2. Obtains signatures of LPAC members
   - Parent signature must be obtained if services are denied.
   - Parent signatures must be obtained when student is initially placed in the ESL or DLE program.
3. Maintains records in the LPAC folder on the campus - Assures the records are maintained appropriately and the confidentiality of the information is protected.
4. Reviews the progress of each ELL at least annually - The campus principal shall determine if the LPAC needs to meet on a student more than one time per year. The determination should be based on special academic circumstances of the student.

Policy References: Board Policy EHBE; EHBAB: EHBE; EKB; EIE: 19 Texas Administrative Code (TAC), Chapter 89. Adaptations for Special Populations: Subchapter BB: Commissioners Rules Concerning State Plan for Educating English Language Learners: Texas Education Code (TEC), Subchapter B. Bilingual Education and Special Language Programs (Chapter 29.051-29.066)

"Believe me, the reward is not great without the struggle."
— Wilma Rudolph

ELL Strategies

A major concern that many teachers consistently discuss with their peers is that English-language learner (ELL) students lack the basic literacy skills needed to grasp grade-level content. **The top three challenges facing secondary teachers regarding English-language learners:**

- **Communicating with English-language learners about academic, social, and personal issues**
- **Encouraging and motivating English-language learners**
- **Addressing the individual and diverse needs of English-language learners in both academic skills and English-language acquisition**

In response to these challenges, University of Texas has shared Six Key Strategies for Teachers of English Learners. **The six strategies** are based on multiple research studies from the past decade that identify effective methods for developing English-language learners' content knowledge, use of the academic language associated with math, literature, history, and science, and basic interpersonal communication skills in English.

The first of the six key strategies is vocabulary and language development, through which teachers introduce new concepts by discussing vocabulary words key to that concept. Exploring specific academic terms like algorithm starts a sequence of lessons on larger math concepts and builds the student's background knowledge.

The second strategy is guided interaction. With this method, teachers structure lessons, so students work together to understand what they read—by listening, speaking, reading, and writing collaboratively about the academic concepts in the text.

The third strategy is metacognition and authentic assessment. Rather than having students simply memorize information, teachers model and explicitly teach thinking skills (metacognition) crucial to learning new concepts. Research shows that metacognition is a critical skill for learning a second language and a skill used by highly proficient readers of any language. With authentic assessments, teachers use a variety of activities to check students' understanding, acknowledging that students learning a second language need a variety of ways to demonstrate their understanding of concepts that are not wholly reliant on advanced language skills.

The fourth strategy is explicit instruction, or direct teaching of concepts, academic language and reading comprehension strategies needed to complete classroom tasks.

The fifth strategy is the use of meaning-based context and universal themes, referring to taking something meaningful from the students' everyday lives and using it as a springboard to interest them in academic concepts. Research shows that when students are interested in something and can connect it to their lives or cultural backgrounds they are more highly motivated and learn at a better rate.

The final strategy is the use of modeling, graphic organizers, and visuals. The use of a variety of visual aids, including pictures, diagrams, and charts, helps all students—and especially ELL students—easily recognize essential information and its relationship to supporting ideas. Visuals make both the language and the content more accessible to students.

NOTE: Information compiled from: UT Texas, California Dept. of Education, and the Colorado Department of Education

Emergency Management

Schools, both K-12 and post-secondary institutions, continually face emergencies that vary in severity, duration, and expenditure. Therefore, emergency management is at the forefront of school safety and security related issues. The Federal Emergency Management Agency (FEMA) defines emergency management as "the protection of the civilian population and property from the destructive forces of natural and man-made disasters through a comprehensive program of mitigation, preparedness, response, and recovery" (FEMA, 2010). Thus, schools must take preemptive action to successfully fulfill their primary mission, which is educating students. These preventative measures include planning, drilling and training for a variety of emergencies. Furthermore, these measures should be assessed to ensure they are current and effective.

Preparedness and Drills in Schools

Drills are a first and important step in keeping schools safe and secure. They are filled with teachable moments and they are as important to schools as reading, writing and arithmetic. The purpose of drills is to save lives and property. An Emergency Operations Plan (EOP) is only as good as the ability of students, faculty and staff to execute it. Following the established plan requires a quick but careful assessment of the situation and practiced decisions as to the best course of action.

When everyone at the campus regularly practices the plan, school personnel are more confident in making decisions to effectively and efficiently manage an emergency or major event. With good training and practice, everyone involved will be better able to react appropriately to emergency events.

Safety

Always review safety precautions before starting a drill. It is important that all staff take part in the drill as they would for a realistic event. Key staff, however, should be assigned a "safety officer" role, similar to the assignment they would receive in an actual event. The following safety considerations should be in place for any drill:

- Make sure that **all** staff members are vigilant about actual emergencies or accidents that occur during a drill. If a student or staff member is injured, or becomes ill, provide aid and contact first responders if necessary. In such a situation, it **may** be necessary to end the drill.

- At the start of each drill and during subsequent announcements, ensure that the communication includes clear language to everyone that "This is a Drill". This includes clearly communicating when the drill is concluded.

- Set up a command post for a drill and make sure that staff members know its location. From here the drill is managed, accountability assured and real emergencies reported.

- Since fire drills should be the first drill of each school year, it is recommended that the school announce the first fire drill of each semester so that staff, students and parents are ready and have a chance to review expectations. It may not be necessary to publicize all subsequent drills. The decision to do so is based upon district policy.

- Drills are not conducted if an actual threat exists that could confuse or alarm participants and the community. For example, do not conduct a severe weather drill on a stormy day.

- It is the responsibility of all persons associated with the drill to stop the drill if, in their opinion, a real safety problem exists.

- Never endanger students for the sake of a drill. If protocol is to move students off site, consider simulating this by moving them to a far corner of campus and then discuss with them what would happen next.

- When drills are conducted, **all** staff and visitors should be expected to participate. Staff members should not get in the habit of thinking a drill doesn't apply to them; this includes faculty members who have an off/conference period and all non-instructional staff, and may require posting signs in the office to indicate that a drill is in process, temporarily disrupting normal activities.

- Volunteers, non-campus based support staff and other visitors who are on campus should be part of the drill as well. If parents are present to check-out their students from school or to drop off items, they should be asked to wait until the drill is over as vehicles moving through the parking lot can be a hazard to students who are being evacuated.

- Considerations should be made for people with disabilities. Although people with disabilities are not excluded from drills, the routines they practice may not mirror those of all students. This may require that buses, additional staff assistance and other relocation areas need to be identified in advance.

- Consider inviting first responders to drills when possible, and at least once a year. Not only does this help them understand the nuances of school emergencies, but it also provides campus staff an opportunity to see how students react to emergency vehicles and become aware of how first responders are likely to position their vehicles in an emergency. This helps reduce the risk of students moving into the path of responders.

- Special arrangements may be needed to help classes under the care of substitute teachers. During drills, assign buddy teachers or staff who can help guide the substitute teacher through the process.

Safety Comes FIRST!

DRILL TYPE	FREQUENCY (AT LEAST)	GUIDANCE
Fire / Evacuation	One fire drill each month that has 10 or more school days (including summer school), including one drill within 10 das of the beginning of classes. *TEC §61.1036 Section 3, F*	• One annoued drill (during first two weeks of new school year. • One obstructed drill each semester • One drill with special circumstances (scheduled during lunch, class change time, accountability / reunification issues, functional needs, etc) • Test evacuation procedures not usually addressed during fire drills. (Check with your local fire department about receiving fire drill credit for this drill.)
RECOMMENDED PRACTICES		
Lockdown	One drill **each semester** and each summer school session	• Allow time after the drill for teachers and students to talk about options and safety considerations • Provide ways for staff to share their own concerns, and those of their students with administrators
Reverse Evacuation	One drill **each semester** and each summer school session	Note: Consider conducting this dress in combination with other drills.
Severe Weather / Tornado	One drill **each semester** and each summer school session	
Shelter-in-Place (Hazmat)	One drill **each semester** and each summer school session	

NOTE: Retrieved from:
https://txssc.txstate.edu/tools/emergency-management-toolkit/role-of-districts/training-drills-exercises/drilling

Emergency Planning

Sample Drill & Exercise Guidance

Since drill are more than moving students and staff from one location to another, the following guidance is designed for schools to tailor to the threats and needs of their communities. The guidance provides recommendations to consider as part of the drill processes.

Fire/ Evacuation

Intent: Action schools will take to quickly move students and staff to safer locations outside of the building when a fire or other event requires that they leave the building. The primary objective of an evacuation is to quickly ensure all school staff, students, and visitors can quickly move away from the threat.

- In each classroom, evacuation maps should be posted on the inside of the door or adjacent to the door frame.
- Students should know the primary and secondary directions to exit their classroom.
- Students should know to use the nearest exit if they are not in their classroom and to report to the first teacher or administrator they encounter.
- Fire drills at the start of each semester should be announced to all students and staff; subsequent drills should be unannounced and be conducted at varying times of the day.
- Fire alarm pull stations should be used so students know what the alarm sounds like.
  - Drills using the alarms must be coordinated with the fire department and district administration to avoid triggering an actual response.
  - Fire drill schedules should vary and not only occur during regular class time. Some drills should be held during lunch, passing period or at the start or end of the school day.
- At least once each semester the campus should conduct an obstructed fire drill by blocking at least one primary exit. This may be accomplished by standing in a hallway with a sign or other obstruction to force students and staff to seek alternate exits.
- Other Evacuation drills should test a component not central to a fire drill, such as preparing students to be moved to a loading area as though to board buses or practicing an extended evacuation that would move them off campus toward a secondary safe location.

Document all of the above! (If it is not on paper, it is vapor.)

Lockdown

Intent: Action schools will take to secure school buildings and grounds during incidents that pose an immediate threat of violence in or around the school. The primary objective of a lockdown is to quickly ensure all school staff, students, and visitors are secured away from immediate danger.

- Areas of campus that cannot be secured should be evaluated for additional actions that allow vulnerable areas to be evacuated quickly and efficiently.
- Conduct at least one lockdown drill in areas other than classrooms, such as outside or in the cafeteria, to encourage fast and effective decision making.
- Place a sign on the main entry notifying parents and other visitors that the drill is in progress and that their access is restricted until the drill is over. Have a staff member standing by to field questions and concerns.

- Do not use role players or explosive sounds to enhance or simulate an attack.
- Designate time after the drill for teachers to talk with students about options and safety.
- At least annually, campus and district administrators should conduct a review of options and safety considerations in collaboration with local first responders.

Document all of the above!

Tornado/Severe Weather

Intent: Action schools will take to quickly move students and staff to remain indoors, perhaps for an extended period of time, because it is safer inside the building or a room than outside. Depending on the threat level (watch vs. warning), students and staff may be required to move to rooms without windows or to a weather shelter.

- Do not conduct weather drills on days when severe weather is expected or threatens.
- Identify good locations to protect from severe weather. Generally, the most dangerous locations are large rooms with expansive roofs such as cafeterias, gymnasiums, libraries and auditoriums. Rooms with large windows that may shatter can be extremely dangerous.
- Safer areas include: small interior rooms (with short roof spans), bathrooms, and interior hallways away from exterior doors and that have interior load-bearing walls. If the building has multiple levels, evacuate the upper levels. The lowest level is the safest.
- Consider placing small signs on the doors of safer areas.
- Use a floor plan to indicate the areas where people are to seek protection from severe weather. During drills have students practice moving to those places.
- Have students sit and face the walls. Instruct them to crouch and cover the back of their head and neck, linking their fingers. Demonstrate the protective posture and have them practice it. Do not expect them to hold the posture for long periods unless threat is eminent.
- Designated staff members should demonstrate knowledge of the location of the main shut off for gas and electricity so that in an actual occurrence they will be able to direct first responders to that location or complete the shut off themselves. However, during a drill they should not shut down the system.

Document all of the above!

Shelter-in-place

Intent: Action schools will take when students and staff are required to remain indoors, perhaps for an extended period of time, because it is safer inside the building or a room than outside. Depending on the threat or hazard, students and staff may be required to move to rooms that can be sealed (such as in the event of a chemical or biological hazard).

- Shelter-in-lace is designed to quickly protect students in areas that can be sealed from outside contaminates.
- Students and staff should be moved from large common areas such as cafeterias and gymnasiums into classrooms and other areas that can be sealed.
- Close doors and windows; turn off fans and other ventilation for the classroom.
- Designated staff members should demonstrate knowledge of the location of the main shut off valves for HVAC or the number to call to have the system turned off remotely. However, during a drill they should not shut down the system.
- Staff members should demonstrate knowledge of the location of barrier materials such as duct tape and plastic sheeting that can be used to seal the gaps around windows and doors, in the designated shelter area. **However, during a drill**

actual placement of barrier materials may not be required. Demonstration of barrier placement may be considered as a separate training during staff in-service.

- Complete a Shelter-in-Place drill with an evacuation, which would be the next step in the sheltering process (this also will allow credit for a fire/evacuation drill).

Document all of the Above!

Reverse Evacuation

Intent: Action schools will take to quickly move students and staff who are outdoors at school when an incident – natural or human caused – poses a potential threat. The primary objective of a reverse evacuation is to quickly ensure all school staff, students, and visitors are moved indoors and away from immediate danger.

- Reverse Evacuation is designed to move people who are outside to safety inside, away from potential threats. Incidents such as: lightning, vicious animals or bats in the vicinity or a car accident near the school may only require that students be brought inside rapidly. Events where a crime or threat is involved should include ensuring that the doors are locked and that staff monitor all doors. All staff should be prepared for further protective measures.

- Reverse Evacuation often is the first step to protective measures for various external threats; consequently, consider combining Shelter-in-Place, Severe Weather or Lockdown with Reverse Evacuation.

Document all of the Above!

IMPORTANT NOTE:

This is another group of manuals and documents you need in a file folder, or notebook. The emergency planning and subsequent exercise are an essential strategy of the modern campus and the responsibility of the building administrator. Do NOT take these responsibilities lightly.

Final Thoughts, remember DOCUMENT, DOCUMENT, DOCUMENT…all practices! Not just dates of the practice event but DETAILS. Document what happened, time taken for the event to be successful, good things, bad things, things to change. Be very proactive in your documentation. Remember the event is a practice in case of an emergency. PROVE through documentation that you have a campus which is prepared!

"It is the responsibility of administrators to ensure staff is trained and the district is adequately prepared to respond to and recover from these incidents." **(TSSC)**

"When disasters strike, it is sometimes difficult for people to think clearly and react in the appropriate manner. This is why it is important to practice drills: having safety practices internalized will ensure that staff and students remember how to behave in moments of crises." **(TSSC)**

NOTE: Additional information is available from Texas State, School Safety Center – Crisis Planning National Guide: https:// txssc.txstate.edu/

Emotional and Behavioral Assessment
TEA Guide to Effective Teaching

Assessing behavioral and emotional problems is important for developing successful interventions. Various standardized assessments can provide useful information, the following steps should also be undertaken **to identify a child's challenges and to understand his/her need:**

- Review the records and all related information
- Interview various people, including parents and teachers.
- Systematically observe the child across multiple settings (educational and social)

The various testing process includes but not limited to:
- **Behavior Rating Profile – evaluates problem behaviors of children 6-18. At home and school.**
- Child Behavior Checklist (CBCL) – widely used for clinical and research purposes.
- Conner's' Rating Scales – used to diagnose ADHD and comorbid disorders
- Pervasive Developmental Disorder Behavior Inventory – age norm instrument that assess pervasive developmental disorder (AU, AS, PDD-NOSS).

You must be able to answer questions such as the one below:
- What test would be given to determine problem behaviors in a special education student?

Equity in the Interview

A list of Strategies

<u>* ALWAYS follow your district's policy procedures during an interview! NEVER stray!! Deviation, could result in litigation and if you have not followed policies, procedures, and law, it falls back on you.</u>

Establish a Pool of Candidates to Interview:

- Select the Candidates and prepare a written justification for each interview and reasons for rejecting each applicant (pre-interview).
- The AAO must review all applicants and reason for rejection.
- Document all decisions

Pre-Interview and Committee Responsibility:

- Design interview questions that relate to the position, based on job descriptions. Ensure that the interview protocol is not biased (possibly reviewed by the AAO).
- Design an interview rating sheet with balanced weight for each question (reviewed by the AAO).
- Make sure the interview process and campus visits are in no way biased toward any candidate (review by the AAO).
- Review the interview committee for possible bias and/or equity concern. (AAO review).
- Document all decisions

Interview:

- Follow the interview questions, established and approved by the pre-interview committee.
- Use an interview rating sheet
- Document and tabulate all decisions.

" Unless you try to do something beyond what you have already mastered you will never grow."

\- Ronald E. Osborn

Evaluation and the Modern Principal PDAS Manual

* Soon To Move To The T-TESS

The goal of all evaluation instruments that review teaching methodology **is to improve student growth**. The results of these actions should be professional development and growth.

1. The PDAS has fifty-one evaluation criteria organized in eight domains. The domains are:
   - Domain I: Active, Successful Student Participation in the Learning Process
   - Domain II: Learner-Centered Instruction
   - Domain III: Evaluation and Feedback on Student Progress
   - Domain IV: Management of Student Discipline, Instructional Strategies, Time and Materials
   - Domain V: Professional Communication
   - Domain VI: Professional Development
   - Domain VII: Compliance with Policies, Operating Procedures and Requirements
   - Domain VIII: Improvement of Academic Performance of all Students on the Campus

2. Scoring of the domains are done primarily though classroom observational data, teacher input from their self-report (TSR) and other observances.

3. Each domain shall be scored independently.
   - Data will be gathered through the appraisal process by:
     - TSR (Teacher Self Report, and other documented sources.)
     - Contributions, by the teacher, in increasing student performance and achievement, school safety, an orderly climate and a stimulating learning environment must be clearly identified and described.
     - It is strongly advised that the new administrator read and understand the PDAS manual.

4. Domains I-VIII uses the following evaluation categories:
   - Exceeds expectations
   - Proficient
   - Below expectations
   - Unsatisfactory

5. Domains I-IV is directly related to students and the classroom:
   - Student participation in the learning process.
   - Learner-centered instruction
   - Teacher evaluation and feedback on student progress
   - Student discipline, instructional strategies, time on task and materials.

6. Domains V-VII is directly related to the professionalism of the teacher:
   - Professional communication
   - Professional development
   - Professional compliance with policies, procedures and other requirements
   - Domain VIII is directly related to the student academic performance, attendance, identification and assistance to at-risk and campus performance ratings.

7. Classroom Observation:
   - Formal observations will take place according to your district policy and procedures.
   - Walkthroughs can take place any time. <u>Walkthroughts are a holistic way to acquire a "snap shot".</u>

NOTE: This short article is not inclusive and the student must review the PDAS manual.

> *"If you learn from a defeat, you haven't really lost."*
> - Zig Ziglar

FERPA and the Modern Principal

The *family educational rights and privacy act* is a federal privacy law that gives parents certain protections with regard to their children's education records. These records include report cards, transcripts, disciplinary records, contact information, family information, and class schedules.

These rights transfer to the student when he or she reaches the age of 18 or attends a school beyond the high school level.

Parents or eligible students have the right to inspect and review the student's **education records** maintained by the school. Schools are not required to provide copies of records unless, for reasons such as great distance, it is impossible for parents or eligible students to review the records. Schools may charge a fee for copies.

Parents or eligible students have the right to request that a school **correct records** which they believe to be inaccurate or misleading. If the school decides not to amend the record, the parent or eligible student then has the right to a formal hearing. After the hearing, if the school still decides not to amend the record, the parent or eligible student has the right to place a statement with the record setting forth his or her view about the contested information.

Generally, **schools must have written permission from the parent or eligible student** in order to release any information from a student's education record. However, FERPA allows schools to disclose those records, without the consent, to the following parties or under the following conditions (34 CFR § 99.31):

- School officials with legitimate educational interest;
- Other schools to which a student is transferring;
- Specified officials for audit or evaluation purposes;
- Appropriate parties in connection with financial aid to a student;
- Organizations conducting certain studies for or on behalf of the school;
- Accrediting organizations;
- To comply with a judicial order or lawfully issued subpoena;
- Appropriate officials in cases of health and safety emergencies; and
- State and local authorities, within a juvenile justice system, pursuant to specific State law.

Schools may disclose, **without the consent, "directory" information** such as a student's name, address, telephone number, date and place of birth, honors, and awards, and dates of attendance. **However, schools must tell parents and eligible students about directory information and allow parents and eligible students a reasonable amount of time to request that the school not disclose directory information about them.** Schools must notify parents and eligible students annually of their rights under FERPA. The actual means of notification (special letter, inclusion in a PTA bulletin, student handbook, or newspaper article) is left to the discretion of each school.

Can a list of students' health issues be distributed to teachers or other staff?

A school-wide health concerns distribution list **violates FERPA and is not best practice**. If individual staff or faculty members need to be informed of a student's condition, that student requires an ECP (**emergency care plan**) listing symptoms to be alert for and the required response to those symptoms. It is recommended that parents, as a part of the IHP (individual health plan), participate in deciding who on staff and faculty requires identifiable health information for the child's safety. Staff and faculty who are trusted with personally identifiable health information should receive training regarding their responsibility to safeguard that information.

When can schools share health information with other agencies within their state?

Abuse or neglect: School employees are required to report suspected abuse or neglect. FERPA does not override that responsibility.

Certain reportable diseases: Some communicable diseases require emergent reporting while other diseases represent a less imminent public health threat. For example, the NH Department of Health and Human Services divides reportable disease into two categories: those that require reporting within 24 hours and those that must be reported within 72 hours. If reporting must occur within 24 hours, the Family Policy Compliance Office of the U.S. Department of Education has determined that indicates "imminent danger." As such, those illnesses may be reported without obtaining consent. The diseases on the 72-hour list do not pose imminent danger so school officials must obtain consent before disclosing this information.

Concern that a student may hurt self or others: if someone is in imminent danger, no consent is required.

De-identified data: It is permissible to share health related data that does not contain information that makes the student's identity readily traceable.

What if I am concerned that a student might hurt themselves or someone else, but I have no evidence?

If the school evaluates the information available at the time and feels that there is an "articulable and significant threat to the health or safety of a student or other individuals, it may disclose information from education records to any person whose knowledge of the information is necessary to protect the health or safety of the student or other individuals."

It is not necessary to first collect evidence before contacting those that can intervene to protect the student or others.

What about HIPAA? How does that affect school health services?

The Health Insurance Portability and Accountability Act is another federal law that dictates how health records are to be handled. A school is subject to HIPAA *only if it provides medical care and electronically transmits health information as part of a "covered transaction" (e.g., billing). See 45 CFR §160.103.*

NOTE: For most schools, HIPAA will only be an issue when you communicate with a student's medical provider.

Does FERPA apply to school health records?

Yes. Student health records maintained by school employees are considered part of the education record with only these two exceptions.

- The "treatment records" of an "eligible student" are not considered part of the education record.
- "Eligible student" is one who is at least 18 years old or attending a postsecondary institution (34 C.F.R §99.3).

Food Service Module: 8.5.1.9

Purpose:
The food service operation is an essential support service for all districts. In order to enhance participation and meet the needs of a more health-conscious clientele, many districts provide options such as a la carte menu items and salad bars.

A well-managed program can:

- Provide safe and nutritious meals for students and staff
- Provide surplus revenues which can finance future improvements of the operation
- Provide training and educational programs on nutrition and employee wellness.
- Provide nutrition education to students and staff that promote food choices for a healthful diet
- Promote healthy food choices by offering healthy foods and marketing healthy eating practices
- Create or support a healthy school nutrition environment

The food service operation should provide support of the educational program by providing:

- Nutrition education materials or resources to teachers
- Nutrition education activities for students
- Nutrition education activities involving the school and community to create or support a healthy school nutrition environment
- Nutrition information displayed in cafeteria or available for students or parents\
- Student advisory council's involvement in the nutrition program

Elementary school campuses
May not serve or provide access for students to (FMNV) or foods of minimal nutritional value. This refers to the four categories of foods and beverages (soda water, water ices, chewing gum, and certain candies) that are restricted by USDA under the child nutrition programs.

Middle school and junior high school campuses
May not serve or provide access for students to have (FMNV) or foods of minimal nutritional value. This refers to the four categories of foods and beverages (soda water, water ices, chewing gum, and certain candies) that are restricted by USDA under the child nutrition programs.

High school campuses
May not serve or provide access for students to have (FMNV) or foods of minimal nutritional value. This refers to the four categories of foods and beverages (soda water, water ices, chewing gum, and certain candies) that are restricted by USDA under the child nutrition programs.

Such foods and beverages may not be sold or given away to students on school premises by school administrators or staff (principals, coaches, teachers, etc.), students or student groups, parents or guest speakers or any other person, company or organizations.

EXCEPTIONS:

- **The above policies do NOT apply to <u>school nurses</u>** using FMNV's during the course of providing health care to individual students.

- **Special needs students whose <u>Individualized Education Program (IEP)</u> plan** indicates the use of any FMNV or candy for behavior modification (or other suitable need) may be given FMNV or candy items.

- Students **may** be given FMNV, candy items or other restricted food during the school day for up **<u>to three different events each school year to be determined by the campus</u>**. The exempted events must **<u>be approved by the school official</u>**. During these events, FMNV may not be given during meal times in the areas where school meals are being served or consumed, and regular meal service (breakfast and lunch) must continue to be available to all students in accordance with federal regulations.

- Schools and parents may provide one additional nutritious snack per day for **<u>students taking state exams</u>**. The snack must comply with the fat and sugar limits of the Public School Nutrition Policy and may not contain any FMNV or consist of candy, chips or dessert type items. Packaged snacks must be in single size servings.

- Teachers may use foods as long as the food items are not considered FMNV or candy. Students may consume food prepared in class for instructional purposes. These foods must be on an "occasional" basis and may not be provided or sold to other students or classes.

- School – **<u>approved field trips are exempt from (TPSNP)</u>** Texas Public School Nutrition Policy. A school official must approve the dates and purposes of the field trips in advance.

- The **<u>TPSNP does not apply to students who leave campus</u>** to travel to athletic, UIL, band or other competitions.

- **<u>The TPSNP does not apply to students after the "official" school day has ended</u>**. School activities, athletic functions, etc. that occur after the normal school day are not covered by the policy.

> *"Without courage, all other virtues lose their meaning."*
> - Winston Churchill

Grading Policy and Acceleration of Grades

SB 2033, passed by the 81st Texas Legislature, requires each school district to adopt a grading policy, including provisions for the assignment of grades on class assignments and examinations, before each school year. A district grading policy:

- Must require a classroom teacher to assign a grade that reflects the student's relative mastery of an assignment.

- May not require a classroom teacher to assign a minimum grade for an assignment without regard to the student's quality of work.

- May allow a student a reasonable opportunity to make up or redo a class assignment or examination for which the student received a failing grade.

TEA understands this legislation to also require honest grades for each grading period including six weeks, nine weeks, or semester grades for two reasons. First, if actual grades on assignments are not used in determining a six weeks' grade, the purpose of the legislation has been defeated. Second, since 1995, Texas Education Code, §28.021, has required decisions on promotion or course credit to be based on "academic achievement or demonstrated proficiency." If the six weeks' grades do not reflect the actual assignment grades, they would not reflect academic achievement or demonstrated proficiency.

A parent is entitled to:
(1) Petition the board of trustees designating the school in the district that the parent's child will attend, as provided by Section 25.033;
(2) reasonable access to the school principal, or to a designated **administrator with the authority to reassign** a student, to request a change in the class or teacher to which the parent's child has been assigned, if the reassignment or change would not affect the assignment or reassignment of another student;
(3) request, with the expectation that the request will not be unreasonably denied:
   (A) **the addition of a specific academic class in the course of study** of the parent's child in keeping with the required curriculum if sufficient interest is shown in the addition of the class to make it economically practical to offer the class;
   (B) **that the parent's child be permitted to attend a class for credit above the child's grade level**, whether in the child's school or another school, unless the board or its designated representative expects that the child cannot perform satisfactorily in the class; or
   (C) **that the parent's child be permitted to graduate from high school earlier than the child would normally graduate,** if the child completes each course required for graduation; and
(4) have a child who graduates early as provided by Subdivision (3)(C) participate in graduation ceremonies at the time the child graduates. (TEC. Title 2: Subtitle E. Chapter 26, 2016).

Assessment for acceleration in kindergarten through Grade 5.

(1) A school district must develop procedures for kindergarten acceleration that are approved by the school district board of trustees.
(2) A student in any of Grades 1-5 must be accelerated one grade if he or she meets the following requirements:
   (A) the student scores 80% on a criterion-referenced test for the grade level he or she wants to skip in each of the following areas: language arts, mathematics, science, and social studies;
   (B) a school district representative recommends that the student be accelerated; and
   (C) the student's parent or guardian gives written approval for the acceleration.(TAC. Chapter 74, Subchapter C. 74.24, 2016).

Grievances and the Modern Principal

What is a grievance?

The Texas Association of School Boards refer to the definition of a grievance as, "Virtually any topic can be the subject of a grievance. The terms complaint and grievance have the same meaning.

Examples of grievances are listed here but are not the only areas where a person or employee will seek redress.
- Evaluations, salary disputes, grading policies, sick leave, wages, work hours. condition of work, dismissal or termination
- Sexual harassment, bullying, instructional material
- Any other concern which may be deemed appropriate for communication from employee to employer

Must a school board hear a grievance?

Yes, state and federal law require school districts to have a grievance process and "apply" it.

Who may file a grievance?
The Texas Constitution grants citizens the right to redress grievances. Those being:
- Parents
- Students
- Employees
- General Community

Must a grievance from an employee be presented to the school board?
Yes, state education code (TEC 11.1513 (i) clearly permits each employee to present a grievance to the local school board.

Is there local board policy on Grievances?
All districts that follow the guidance of the TASB have in their policy manual:
- DGBA (local) for employee grievances;
- FNG (local) for student and parent grievances; and
- GF (local) for grievances by all others.

When the grievance process discusses and uses the term "day" what does that mean?

The term "day" shall mean district business days, unless otherwise noted in calculating time lines. The day a document is filed is day zero.

*TASB offers an excellent flip chart for principals! - To purchase Resolving Grievances in the Public Schools, visit http://store.tasb.org/products/Resolving/Grievances

What is the level one process for grievances?

At level one it is the desire of the district to resolve, as quickly as possible, the complaint by redress the issue and seeking a solution. The steps are:

- Schedule a conference with the employee at level one within ten days; or
- Refer the grievance within three days to an appropriate administrator below the level of associate/assistant superintendent, who will schedule a conference with the employee at level one within ten days of receipt of the referral.

Level One:

In most circumstances, employees on a school campus shall file level one complaints with the campus principal.

- The appropriate administrator shall investigate as necessary and a schedule a conference with the employee within ten days after receipt of the written complaint.
- The administrator shall provide the employee a written response within ten days following the conference.
- Level one record should contain but not limited to:
    - The original complaint form and all attachments.
    - All other documentation submitted by the employee
    - The written response issued at the level one and all attachments.
    - All other documentation used to determine the level one administrator's decision.

Level Two:

If the employee did not receive the relief requested from level one, the employee may request a conference with the appropriate associate/assistant superintendent or with a person designee to appeal the level one decision.

- The level one administrator must provide a written record of the proceedings and findings from level one for the level two administrator. Copies should be provided to all parties
- The level two administrator must provide a written response to the employee within ten days following the level two conference.
- The level two administrator response shall set forth the basis of the decision.

Level Three:

If the employee did not receive the relief requested from level two, the employee may request a conference with the Superintendent or designee.

- The level two administrator must prepare a written report for the level three administrator. The report should include but not limited to:
    - The level one report
    - The notice of appeal from level one to level two.
    - The written response issued at Level two and all attachments.

- The level three administrator shall schedule a conference within ten days.
- The conference shall be limited to the issues and documents considered at level one and level two. The employee may provide information concerning any documents or information relied upon by the administration for level two decision.

Level Four:

If the employee did not receive the relief requested from level three, the employee may request conference and appeal, within ten days, to the school board.

- The appeal must be placed on the board agenda.
- The superintendent or designee shall provide the board the following:
    o The level one, two and three records and all attachments.
    o All notices of appeal
    o All written responses
- The appeal shall be limited to the issues and documents considered at level three.
- The School Board shall determine whether the complaint will be present in open or closed meeting in accordance with the Texas Open Meeting Act.
- If the School Board shall consider the complaint. If the board does not make a decision regarding the complaint by the end of the next regularly scheduled meeting, the lack of response by the board upholds the administrative decision at level three.

May the employee record the proceedings?

As provided by law, an employee shall be permitted to make an audio recording of a conference or hearing under this school policy at which the substance of the employee's complaint is discussed. The employee shall notify all attendees present that an audio recording is taking place and the recording must be made available to all administrators and supervisors hearing the grievance. A copy of the recording shall be maintained with the level grievances.

Can all grievances go to the state education commissioner?

No, only a short list may actually move up to the commissioner of education. This includes:

- Breach of the employment contract coupled with economic harm
- A violation of a state law or regulation

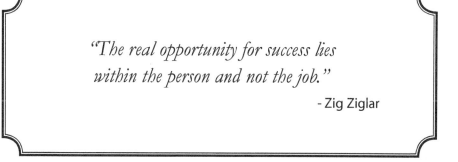

"The real opportunity for success lies within the person and not the job."
- Zig Ziglar

Homeless Students

A. Who is homeless?
   1. Individuals **who lack a fixed, regular, and adequate nighttime residence,** and
      a) children and youths who are sharing the housing due to hardships,
      b) housing may be identified as, but not limited to:
         - motels
         - hotels,
         - trailer parks,
         - camp grounds
         - emergency or transitional shelters,
         - abandoned building
         - awaiting foster care placement,
         - public or private place not normally used for sleeping
         - cars, parks, public spaces and building,
         - migratory children.
B. What is the District and Campus Responsibility?
   1. **Must provide educational stability for homeless students:**
      a) keep student in school of origin, unless against the parent's or guardian's wishes,
      b) permitted to continue attending **schools or origin** for duration of homeless experience and until the end of the academic year,
         - **School of Origin** – the school that the student attended when permanently housed; or
         - the school in which the child or youth was last enrolled.
         - *the school must remove barriers to the school enrollment and retention of children and youth in homeless situations.
   2. **Must provide immediate school access:**
      a) waive enrollment documentation
      b) obtain records from previous schools—while student is enrolled.
      c) obtain immunization and/or medical records—while student is enrolled.
C. District must have a local Homeless Education Liaison:
   1. Responsible for the identification, school enrollment, attendance and opportunities for academic success of the homeless student.
      a) public notices for educational rights,
      b) seek educational services for the homeless—Head start, Even start
      c) seek medical services for the homeless—dental, metal and medical
      d) seek shelter services for the homeless—family shelters, soup kitchens
      e) seek transportation services for the homeless—to and from school
D. Students experiencing homelessness are eligible for Title 1 services even when not attending a Title 1 campus
E. Teaching strategies for homeless students.
   1) Academic needs:
      a) stable learning environment with a structured routine,
      b) mini-lessons and units that can be completed in limited periods of time.
      c) a variety of levels in reading materials about the same content.
      d) assess students' interests to hook them in to learning.
      e) give credit to partially completed work.
   2) Technical needs:
      a) keep a supply of healthy snacks and extra school supplies,
      b) identify and connect with school support staff including:
         - guidance counselors,
         - homeless liaisons,
         - student support services

NOTE: Information Resource - McKinney-Vento

The complete text of the McKinney-Vento Homeless Assistance Act can be found at:
https://www2.ed.gov/policy/elsec/leg/esea02/pg116.html

http://tea.texas.gov/About_TEA/Laws_and_Rules/NCLB_and_ESEA/Title_X/Title_X,_Part_C__McKinney-Vento_Homeless_Assistance_Act/

For more information on collaboration between homeless education and Title I, Part A, including legislative excerpts, see NCHE's Title I brief at: http://www.serve.org/nche/downloads/briefs/titlei.pdf

> *"I don't think much of a man who is not wiser today than he was yesterday."*
> — Abraham Lincoln

Legal/Illegal Interview Questions

Note - First and foremost: <u>Follow your district's policy and procedures, in regards to the interview process. To waiver from the written "script" of the district interview questions places you personally liable.</u>

Question To Ask	Legal	Illegal
Address/Housing/Length of Residence	**CAN ASK:** • Place and length of current and previous address ("How long have you lived in [city]")? • For applicant's phone number or how s/he can be reached	• Specific inquiry into foreign addresses that would indicate national origin • Names or relationship of persons with whom applicant resides • Whether applicant rents or owns home
Age	**BEFORE HIRING ONLY:** • If a minor, require proof of age in the form of a work permit or a certificate of age • If age is a legal requirement, can ask "If hired, can you furnish proof of age?" or a statement that hire is subject to verification of age • Whether or not an applicant is younger than the employer's regular retirement age **AFTER HIRING <u>ONLY</u>:** • require proof of age by birth certificate	<u>**IT IS ILLEGAL TO ASK/REQUEST:**</u> • About the age or age group or date of birth of the applicant • Birth certificate or baptismal record before hiring • Questions that would tend to identify persons between 40 and 60 years of age.
Ancestry/ Birthplace/ National Origin	**CAN ASK:** • "After employment, can you submit a birth certificate or other proof of U.S. citizenship or other proof of the right to remain in or work in the U.S.?" • About foreign language skills (reading, speaking, and/or writing) if relevant to the job Be sensitive to cultural differences • Do not assume mispronunciation of English as a lack of education • Do not interpret silence as inability or unwillingness	<u>**IT IS ILLEGAL TO ASK/REQUEST**</u> • If an applicant is native-born or naturalized • The birthplace of applicant • Questions which identify customs or denomination • About birthplace of his/her parents, grandparents and/or spouse or other relatives • Require applicant submit a birth certificate or naturalization or baptismal record before employment • About any other inquiry into national origin (for applicant or his or her spouse or parents; maiden name of wife or mother) • First language • Date of arrival in U.S. • Port of entry
Citizenship	**CAN ASK:** • Whether a U.S. citizen • If no, whether intends to become one • If you are not a U.S. citizen, do you have the legal right to remain permanently in the U.S.? • If not a citizen, are you prevented from lawfully becoming employed because of visa or immigration status? • If spouse is a citizen • Statement that, if hired, applicant may be required to submit proof of citizenship. **AFTER HIRING <u>ONLY</u>:** • Require proof of citizenship	<u>**IT IS ILLEGAL TO ASK/REQUEST**</u> • "Of what country are you a citizen?" • If native born or naturalized (for applicant or his or her parents or spouse) • Proof of citizenship before hiring • Whether parents and/or spouse is native born or naturalized • Date of citizenship (for applicant or his or her parents or spouse)

Question To Ask	Legal	Illegal
Credit Rating	• NO questions may be asked regarding credit.	• You may not ask ANY questions regarding credit.
Criminal Record (Arrest and Convictions)	**CAN ASK:** • About actual convictions other than misdemeanors that relate reasonable to fitness to perform a particular job • About convictions or imprisonment if crimes relate to job duties and conviction or release from imprisonment occurred within the last ten years	**IT IS ILLEGAL TO ASK/REQUEST** • To inquire about arrests without convictions • Check into a person's arrest, court, or conviction record if not substantially related to functions and responsibilities of the particular job in question. • About any involvement in demonstrations
Disabilities	**Accommodations for the interview must be provided.** • Be careful how applicants with disabilities are evaluated. Do not make judgments based on communication skills of people with hearing and speech impairments. • To inquire for the purpose of determining applicant's capability to perform the job. (Burden of proof for non-discrimination lies with the employer.) **CAN ASK:** • Whether or not applicant is able to carry out all necessary job assignments/functions and perform them in a safe manner "How would you perform this particular task?" only if a disability has been identified by the candidate: • Applicant to indicate how and to what extent they are disabled. Employer must indicate to applicants that (1) compliance with the invitation is voluntary; (2) information is being sought only to remedy discrimination or provide opportunities for the disabled; (3) information will be kept confidential; and (4) refusing to provide information will not result in adverse treatment.	**AN EMPLOYER –** • The Rehabilitation Act of 1973 forbids employers from asking job applicants general questions about whether they are disabled or asking them about the nature and severity of their disabilities. • Don't ask the applicant about what kind of accommodation(s) he or she may need until after the interviewer has established that the applicant is qualified for the job and is considering that person for employment. • An employer must be prepared to prove that any physical and mental requirements for a job are due to "business" necessity" and the safe performance of the job. • Except in cases where undue hardship can be proven, employer must make "reasonable accommodations" for the physical and mental limitations of an employee or applicant. Includes alteration of duties, alteration of physical setting, and provision of aids. • To exclude disabled applicants as a class on the basis of their type of disability. (Each case must be determined on an individual basis by law.)
Gender/Sex	• Inquiry as to sex or restriction of employment to one's sex is permissible only where a bona fide occupational qualification exists. Burden of proof is on the employer to prove that the BFOQ does exist and that all members of the affected class are incapable of performing the job. **CAN INFORM:** • That the institution is an equal opportunity employer **AFTER HIRING ONLY:** • Can ask about gender for affirmative action plan statistics	**IT IS ILLEGAL TO ASK/REQUEST** • Sex of applicant • Anything which would indicate gender unless job related. (Only such jobs in education would be a full time locker room or restroom attendant.) • Sex is not a BFOQ because a job involves physical labor beyond the capacity of some women, nor can employment be restricted just because the job is traditionally labeled "men's work" or "women's work" • Sex cannot be used as a factor for determining whether an applicant will be satisfied in a particular job • Avoid questions concerning applicant's height or weight unless you can prove they are necessary requirements for the job to be performed.

Questions to ask	Legal	Illegal
Race/Color (also see Ancestry/ Birthplace/ National Origin)	• Can indicate that the institution is an equal opportunity employer **AFTER HIRING ONLY:** • Can ask race for affirmative action plan statistics	**IT IS ILLEGAL TO ASK/REQUEST** • Any inquiry that would indicate race and/or color • Color of applicant's skin, eyes, hair • Any other questions directly or indirectly relating race or color

> *"The mind is like a parachute - it doesn't work unless it's open."*
>
> \- Anonymous

LEADERSHIP

**Situational Leadership
And the Modern Principal**

LEADERSHIP

Transformation Leadership and the Modern Texas Principal

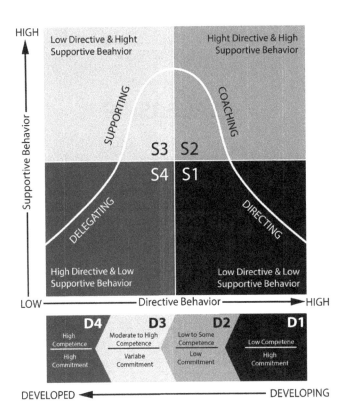

Explaining and Directing

There are four leadership behaviors needed from a leader under the situational leadership method. Examples of situational leadership can be based on these leadership behaviors. One is explaining and directing, wherein the leader defines the tasks of the team and closely supervises them. This is particularly true for inexperienced or first-time team members who need to be closely supervised by an experienced leader. This leadership style is particularly effective for team members who lack the competence but committed to achieving his or her roles. First-time team members in particular need to be told and directed by their team leaders for them to learn the rules of the trade.

Coaching

In this leadership behavior, a leader still defines and assigns roles and tasks but he or she is more receptive to getting ideas and suggestions from the team members. The leader still has the prerogative in making decisions, but in this scenario, the communication process is no longer one-sided. This type of leadership style is more suited for less experienced team members who still need guidance and supervision by their team leaders. This leadership style also helps in developing team members who may have the experience yet still lacking self-confidence in the performance of their work. Under this scenario, leaders may also follow closely the output of their team members and give them encouraging remarks in order for them to develop their self-confidence.

Supporting

The third in the list of examples of situational leadership is participating and supporting. Under this scenario, the team leader gives much control and minimal supervision on the team members. The team leader gives out day-to-day tasks and instructions on the processes required to achieve a certain task, but the team member has enough control or freedom on how to accomplish the said task. This scenario is best used when working with experienced team members who, for one reason or another, lack self-confidence and motivation. An example would be an experienced teacher who needs support and counsel after being assigned to a department chair position.

Delegating

The final example of a situation leadership method is delegation. In this scenario, the team leader still is involved in the decision-making process but the delegation of tasks and processes is fully given to the team members. This style is most suited to experienced team members who have the competence to set their own processes required in accomplishing certain goals. For instance, a 10-year veteran teacher can be depended upon to formulate his or her own lesson cycles based on the general directions or ideas formulated by his or her team leader. While the teacher can decide on how to go about with the lesson cycle he or she is still bounded by creative directions set by the team leader.

For further review go to:

http://www.brighthub.com/office/home/articles/83323.aspx
http://www.sayeconomy.com/situational-leadership-by-kenneth-blanchard-and-paul-hersey/
http://www.slideshare.net/ahmad1957/situational-leadership-revised2-presentation
http://www.americanchronicle.com/articles/view/26406
http://www.zundelsite.org/news_english/0028_patton.html

LEADERSHIP

Transformation Leadership and the Modern Texas Principal

School Transformation, is an initiative of the Texas Association of School Administrators and is aligned with the work of the Texas High Performance School consortiums (http://www.tasanet.org /Page/339, 2017).

This new material is based on, *Creating a New Vision for Public Education in Texas*, the work of the Public Education Visioning Institute.

Transformation of public school is based on the following principles:

- Digital Learning - Digital Learning: Meeting the Challenges and Embracing the Opportunities for Teachers, Manual

- High-Priority Learning standards - Review Principles and Goals on this site. http://www.tasanet.org//site/Default.aspx?PageID=544

- Multiple Assessments - Review Short-term and Long term solutions on this site. http://www.tasanet.org//site/Default.aspx?PageID=835

- College and Career Readiness - Review the great programs in your sister school districts based on "need assessments" for their individual communities. http://www.tasanet.org/site/Default.aspx?PageID=963

- Community-Based Accountability

    o Community-based accountability is not a way to escape standardized testing or a tool to pass judgment on individual students. It is a:

    - Locally developed system of evidence of student learning
    - Strategic and customized form of measuring student achievement
    - Rigorous descriptive reporting to parents and community members

    o The foundation of CBAS is a four-part system consisting of:

    - Student and classroom-centered evidence of learning
    - Strategic use of standardized testing
    - Performance reviews and validation of learning by highly trained visiting
    - Teams
    - Rigorous descriptive reporting to parents and communities

- Organizational Transformation

    o Review the material on this site: http://www.tasanet.org//site/Default.aspx?PageID=851

Management Overview
TEA Management Module #14

Management processes and practices have a direct link to overall accountability within a school district. The focus of management is the successful implementation of programs. Both the management structure and the execution of day-to-day management functions have an impact on student achievement as well as the quality of overall service delivery within the district.

Managing in the public school environment presents numerous challenges for school administrators. These include:

- **The governance structure** - Policy decisions are made by an elected Board of Trustees who often come from diverse backgrounds. Board members may also have divergent goals and objectives for the district. Although both of these factors are an integral part of the democratic process, school administrators are challenged to build the infrastructure for cohesive decision-making and provide support mechanisms to meet Board needs.

- **Public scrutiny** - There is an inherent skepticism about management of public school resources. Administrators face the demand for providing greater levels of service at decreased expenditure levels. This demand for providing "more for less" requires district management to be creative and seek alternatives to traditional service delivery methods. Additionally, parents and patrons of school districts have become increasingly involved in the decision-making process. Participation in site-based decision-making initiatives enables them to communicate with the board at scheduled meetings and workshops. School administrators are challenged to incorporate often diverse community demands for accountability at all levels of the district's organization.

- **Uncertainty of public school financing** - Financing the multi-billion dollar expenditures required to support public education in Texas has been a major issue for district administrators. Legislative action and subsequent court interpretations focusing on equalization make both short- and long-term financial planning and decision-making difficult.

- **External agency control** - Numerous external entities impact the operations of school districts. These include the legislature, Texas Education Agency, and other state and federal agencies. Responding to requirements, mandates, and requests add another level of complexity to an already complex management environment.

- **Operational diversity** - Public school districts, regardless of size, are complex and diverse organizations. **The school district is normally one of the largest employers in a community and <u>is required to provide services which include</u>**:

    - Instructional delivery

    - Food service

    - Transportation

    - Facility/Grounds maintenance

    - Custodial services

    - Financial services

    - Administration

Larger districts may provide other services including warehouse operations and security services.

The management structure, processes, and skills required to manage this enterprise significantly exceed that required for organizations with a singular focus or service output.

A challenge for school officials is the appropriate identification of the "problem(s)" to be addressed when developing a budget and making decisions about staffing and financial allocations. Herbert Simon, author of many books on public administration, like *Administrative Behavior: A Study of Decision-Making Processes* in Administrative Organizations explains that decision-making processes are facilitated when based upon a rigorous review of data and information, similar to activities involving engineering and scientific processes. **Decisions about personnel management issues and financial allocations should be based on data or evidence relating to the academic performance of students and the effectiveness of academic programs**, in addition to data explaining relative operating efficiencies of all instructional support and administrative functions. It is necessary to make comparisons between districts and campuses that have similar characteristics to obtain useful information about potential management issues. Software applications that benchmark academic and performance statistics are available from various sources. Decision-making processes in school districts are complex and administrative, and governance decisions are not effective, if the "problem(s)" is (are) not adequately identified before making decisions about resource allocations.

John Warfield, author of *A Science of Generic Design, Managing Complexity through Systems Design*, describes various processes for analyzing factors that contribute to or diminish an organization's efficiencies and effectiveness in accomplishing goals and objectives. Warfield also describes computer applications that provide functional capabilities to map complex multi-dimensional issues involving various aspects of the management of services and activities. These types of tools are also useful to management in obtaining an understanding of the "problem(s)."

Current Management and Organizational Trends

In the past, school districts have adopted several conventional management structures. These include:

- **Hierarchical organization structure** - The reporting relationship in most school districts is hierarchical adhering to an established chain of command. Cross-functional communication does exist. Clearly delineated functional responsibility and vertical reporting relationships dominate

- **Traditional business model -** The business model and business processes for school districts have been traditional and often historically based. Change has usually occurred slowly in response to mandates or to the demands of a special situation. The support tools for management of the district (such as technology) have lagged current trends.

- **Promotion from within** - Administrative positions have traditionally been filled from the ranks of existing employees either through promotion or transfer. Tenured employees most administrative positions (except superintendent) have been common.

Pressures generated by flat or declining revenue bases, demands increased quality of service, and the increasing cost of service delivery has created the need for school districts to analyze and implement more current management and organizational strategies. These include:

- **Rightsizing** - Rightsizing involves in-depth analysis of the organization structure and staffing levels to determine if personnel resources are adequate or excessive. It also focuses on organizational issues such as levels/layers of management, reporting relationships, and the ability of the organization to serve its "customers" or users. Rightsizing involves refocusing and realigning resources to perform functions that are "mission critical" for the district to be performing. It challenges historical staffing levels and the existing organization structure by focusing on key issues such as productivity, efficiency, effectiveness, and resource deployment. Rightsizing can benefit districts that face pressures to control administrative costs and to reallocate resources to the campus level to focus on instruction and student achievement.

- **Horizontal organization structure** - Also known as a matrix organization, a horizontal organization structure breaks down the traditional hierarchical organization structure and reporting relationships. A matrix organization allows for resources to be utilized in a cross-functional manner and provides for an administrator to utilize resources from other organizational units without going through "bureaucratic hoops". It allows more flexibility in matching the organization structure with its overall strategy and mission. Additionally, employees at various levels are empowered to participate indetermining realistically how they can best serve the organization. Lines of communication are also enhanced.

While most school districts adhere to a hierarchical structure, progress has been made through site-based management initiatives to allow for greater participation in management decisions and input regarding resource allocation. This initiative also appears to be a first step in providing a "bottom up" view of central administrative support requirements from both an organizational and staffing standpoint.

- **Reengineering** - Reengineering is a systematic approach to structuring and managing organizations. It differs dramatically from traditional management audits or organizational studies as it focuses on the fundamental rethinking of business processes. The results are normally a sharp departure from "legacy" processes of the past as the way work is performed fundamentally challenged and subsequently changed.

Improvement Opportunities are based on several basic premises:

An organization must constantly challenge itself and its methods of delivering services in order to meet the changing demands of today's society. A departure from the "we've always done it that way" service delivery philosophy is required.

An organization must be change oriented. This does not indicate that an organization must change for the sake of change, but rather that it is continually seeking improvement opportunities.

An organization must focus on results and seek to understand the "whys" of successes and failures. This means consistent evaluation and analysis of key operational components from instructional methods to transportation routing. Performance and productivity improvement are emphasized.

Improvement Challenges and Incentives

The premises are proactive in nature but should become basic tenets of a school district's management philosophy as challenges/obstacles to change and improvement will inherently occur. These may include:

- **Employee resistance** - Employees may be change-averse and feel threatened by new initiatives or implementation of new processes. This may be a result of fear of losing their jobs, insecurity relating to the ability to perform new duties, longevity within a position, or lack of understanding of the reason for a change. This resistance is normally overcome by providing for interactive participation in the change initiative, open communication, and the willingness to address (through corrective action) legitimate concerns.

- **Resource availability** - The availability of key resources such as time, personnel, or fiscal resources may inhibit change initiatives. However, this is a two-edged sword. The resources may not be available because of inefficient processes, improper resource allocation, or other reasons. All management improvement projects must include comprehensive planning to ensure that resource constraints do not block progressive actions.

- **Skill base** - The particular skill set involved in the change initiative may not be available within the district. The expertise to carry out the project and/or to implement project recommendations may not be available to district employees. It may be feasible to have an outside party (other district practitioners, professional organizations, or outside firms) to provide assistance. Employee skills can be enhanced by training prior to implementation of subsequent performance. Alternatively, staff changes may be required for the initiative to be successful.

    1. **Major incentives for improvements in district/campus management include: improved student performance**
    2. **Increased program effectiveness**
    3. **Cost savings**
    4. **Improved service delivery**
    5. **Problem resolution**
    6. **Improved board relations**
    7. **Enhanced community support**
    8. **Improved resource utilization**
    9. **Enhanced relations with governmental agencies**

No Pass, No Play

UIL - University Interscholastic League

Basics of No Pass, No Play

- **Must be passing all courses (except identified advanced classes).**

- Students lose eligibility for a three-week period, which is defined as 15 class days. Exception: one but only one of the three school weeks may consist of only three or four class days, provided the school has been dismissed for a scheduled holiday period. Two class days does not constitute a school week. Exception: Thanksgiving if schools are on holiday Wednesday, Thursday, and Friday.

- School week begins at 12:01 a.m. on the first instructional day of the calendar week and ends at the close of instruction on the last instructional day of the calendar week (excluding holidays).

- Ineligible students must wait seven (7) calendar days after a three-week evaluation period and the grading period to regain eligibility.

- **Students may regain eligibility an unlimited number of times throughout the school year. Passing means, a minimum grade of 70 on all courses (except identified advanced classes).**

- **Note: Spring break can't be part of the 3-week evaluation process.** All students are eligible during spring break.

Coach Gifts or Awards

Individuals who coach, direct or sponsor League activities in grades 9-12 may be suspended if:

- They accept more than $500 in money, product or service from any source (over and above the stipend paid by the school) in recognition of or appreciation for coaching, directing or sponsoring a UIL event. The $500 is cumulative for a calendar year and is not specific to any one particular gift.

- They accept money, products or services for entering a student in a UIL contest or activity.

- This section includes but is not limited to money, gifts, use of cars, insurance, club privileges, and any funds tendered by booster clubs for other services.

Exceptions:

- Scholarships
- Retirement
- UIL Sponsor Excellence Awards

An activity would be considered extracurricular if:

- **The activity is competitive;**
- **The activity is held in conjunction with another activity that is considered extracurricular;**
- **The general public is invited;**
- **An admission price is charged.**

Exception: If a student is enrolled in a state-approved course in which he or she must demonstrate mastery of the essential knowledge and skills in a public performance, then he or she may participate so long as the activity is not competitive, it is not held in conjunction with another activity that is competitive, and an admission price is not charged.

For example, a theater student may participate in a non-competitive, free presentation of a one-act play in which the public is invited to attend.

NOTE: UIL rules are extensive for athletics, high school sports, academics, music, theatre, speech, and debate.

The Novice Teacher and the Effective School Administrator

The creation and maintenance of a highly effective environment that assists novice teachers is critical to their success.

The discovery of "their place" in the campus community is essential. The present research seems to imply there are **four recurring themes in the creation of a successful relationship between a novice teacher and the school administrator**. These are:

1. **Positive relationships**
   - Principal support
   - School culture
   - Understanding the formal and informal school organization processes
2. **Positive expectations**
   - Positive role assistance for the novice teacher
3. **Positive perceptions of each other and others**
   - Positive assistance for the novice teacher teaching at the campus site
4. **Positive teacher development**
   - Positive mentoring by the building principal

Building a Successful Relationship Between the Building Administrator and the Novice Teacher

For the building process to be successful the building administrator must be able to MODEL:

- Personal Integrity
- Model a caring attitude and respect
- Be assessable
- Facilitate effective communication
- Use decentralized decision making
- Be supportive and model a teachers' value

Roles and Responsibilities of Principals (Texas Beginning Support System Standard #5)

Supported by district administration and specialized training, principals have unique responsibilities to ensure that newly hired beginning teachers are supported and retained by the school.

Quality Indicators of an Effective Mentoring Principal:

- Principals are knowledgeable about beginning teacher development and the role of the support system in retaining beginning teachers.
- Principals understand, inform the faculty of, and actively advocate the support system's rationale and goals.

- Principals secure assignments for beginning teachers that increase the likelihood for success early in their careers by:
- Reducing the number of difficult assignments,
- Giving beginning teachers their own classrooms,
- Assigning beginning teachers fewer students than veteran teachers,
- Assigning beginning teachers fewer students with special needs,
- Assigning beginning teachers single grade classrooms,
- Assigning beginning teachers classes only within their area of certification,
- Assigning beginning teachers, a limited number of class preparations, and
- Limiting extracurricular assignments.
- If beginning teachers must be assigned to work in difficult assignments, building principals provide them with additional assistance and resources. Principals facilitate the introduction of beginning teachers to the staff beginning teachers into the learning community by providing orientation and ongoing information on school resources, procedures, and policies.
- Principals understand the role of other support team members (e.g., mentors, educator preparation faculty members) and respect the confidentiality between team members and the beginning teacher.
- Principals differentiate between the Professional Development and Appraisal System (PDAS), an annual performance evaluation, and the formative collection of data for self- assessment.
- Principals schedule time and provide access to resources for mentors and beginning teachers to work together on a regular basis.
- Principals encourage the participation of beginning teachers in learning activities appropriate for their level of development (e.g., observing experienced teachers, participating in study groups, and attending workshops and conferences.)

> "The will to succeed is important, but what's even more important is the will to PREPARE."
> - Bobby Knight

Parental Rights and the Modern Principal

EDUCATION CODE
TITLE 2. PUBLIC EDUCATION
SUBTITLE E. STUDENTS AND PARENTS
CHAPTER 26. PARENTAL RIGHTS AND RESPONSIBILITIES:

PURPOSE.
- (a) **Parents are partners with educators, administrators and school district boards of trustees in their children's education.** Parents **shall be** encouraged to **participate actively in creating and implementing educational programs for their children.**

- (b) The rights listed in this chapter are not exclusive. This material does not limit a parent's rights under other law.

DEFINITION.
In this chapter, "parent" includes a person standing in parental relation. The term does not include a person as to whom the parent-child relationship has been terminated or a person not entitled to possession of or access to a child under a court order. Except as provided by federal law, all rights of a parent under Title 2 of this code and all educational rights under Section 151.003

RIGHTS CONCERNING ACADEMIC RECORDS.
- (a) **A parent is entitled to:**

1. **attendance records;**
2. **test scores;**
3. **grades;**
4. **disciplinary records;**
5. **counseling records;**
6. **psychological records;**
7. **applications for admission;**
8. **health and immunization information;**
9. **teacher and school counselor evaluations; and**
10. **reports of behavioral patterns.**

ACCESS TO STATE ASSESSMENTS.
- (a) Except as provided by Section 39.023(e), a parent is entitled to access to a copy of each state assessment instrument administered under Section 39.023 to the parent's child.***this is talking about counseling and not academic test instrument!**

ACCESS TO TEACHING MATERIALS.
- (a) A parent is entitled to:

- (1) review all teaching materials, instructional materials, and other teaching aids used in the classroom of the parent's child; and

- (2) review each test administered to the parent's child after the test is administered.

RIGHT TO FULL INFORMATION CONCERNING STUDENT.
- (a) A parent is entitled to full information regarding the school activities of a parent's child except as provided by Section 38.004.

38.004. CHILD ABUSE REPORTING AND PROGRAMS.
- (a) The agency shall develop a policy governing the child abuse reports required by Chapter 261, Family Code, of school districts and their employees. The policy must provide for cooperation with law enforcement child abuse investigations without the consent of the child's parents if necessary, including investigations by the Department of Protective and Regulatory Services. Each school district shall adopt the policy.
- (b) Each school district shall provide child abuse anti-victimization programs in elementary and secondary schools

A report of alleged or suspected abuse or neglect and the identity of the person making the report is confidential and not subject to release under Government Code Chapter 552 (Public Information Act). Such information may be disclosed only for purposes consistent with federal or state law or under rules adopted by an investigating agency. Family Code 261.201

Unless waived in writing by the person making the report, the identity of an individual making a report under this chapter is confidential and may be disclosed only to a law enforcement officer for the purposes of a criminal investigation of the report, or as ordered by a court under Family Code 261.201. Family Code 261.101(d)

> *"The people who get on in this world are the people who get up and look for the circumstances they want, and, if they can't find them, make them."*
> - George Benard Shaw

Professional Learning Communities and the Modern Principal (PLC)

Over the past several decades, both the public and education professionals have been vocal in their demands for new programs and practices in education. Simultaneously, these advocates have acknowledged that educators must come to an intimate understanding of the process of change for implementation to be successful and for the promises of new practices to be realized. (Hord, 2016).

Present research on Professional Learning Communities is varied and fraught with conflicting theory, approach and application. The following material is what was gleaned from multiple sources and applied from the building administrators point of view—as expressed by many RSC research articles.

Two vital issues to be resolved before implantation of the PLC process:
- How will you provide feedback and support to the teams?
- How will you evaluate the teams progress and effectiveness? (Hord, 1997)

Three vital issues to be reviewed before implementing the PLC process:
- Identifying materials and sources,
- Learning and developing new teaching strategies, and
- Application in the classroom.

What strategies must be implemented for teachers to buy into PLC's?
- The PLC must have relevance and value
- The PLC must show in its framework collegial support for the members
- The PLC must show a sense of urgency
- The PLC has implemented in its framework a strong mentoring strategy
- The PLC must show in its framework implementation for schoolwide initiatives

NOTE: It is strongly suggests that the student download the, "Professional Learning Teams: A facilitator's guide."

Records - Campus Based

Cumulative Folder and Other Record Challenges

1. What is a Cumulative Record?
   - Enrollment Forms,
   - Ethnicity Forms,
   - Birth Certificates,
   - Report Cards,
   - Language Survey,
   - LEP Forms,
   - Any documentation necessary for the student's well-being
   - Any information Principal may require,
   - Legal Documents
   - Other items needed by the campus and/or district.

2. Who may view records?
   - School Officials including teachers,
   - Parents and/or legal guardians,
   - Officials for audit or evaluation purposes,
   - Organizations conducting certain studies for or on behalf of the district and/or campus,
   - Accredited organizations,
   - Complying with a judicial order or lawfully issued subpoena,
   - Other legal issues.

NOTE: See parental rights and the Modern Principal

Response to Intervention: School Building Level

Response to Intervention (RtI) is the practice of providing high quality instruction and interventions matched to student need, monitoring progress frequently to make decisions about changes in instruction or goals and applying student response data to important educational decisions. RtI should be applied to decisions in general, remedial and special education, creating a well-integrated system of instruction/intervention guided by student outcome data.

Student outcome data are crucial to:

- Make accurate decisions about the effectiveness of general and remedial education instruction/interventions
- Undertake early identification/intervention with academic and behavioral problems
- Prevent unnecessary and excessive identification of students with disabilities
- Make decisions about eligibility for special programs, including special education
- Determine individual education programs and deliver and evaluate special education services

The campus is the unit of change in RTI. Implementation of RTI in practice typically proceeds through three stages.

- Consensus building – where RtI concepts are communicated broadly to implementers and the foundational "whys" are taught, discussed and embraced.
- Infrastructure building – where sites examine their implementations against the critical components of RtI, find aspects that are being implemented well and gaps that need to be addressed. Infrastructure building centers around closing these practice gaps.
- Implementation – where the structures and supports are put in place to support, stabilize and institutionalize RtI practices into a new "business as usual."

RtI is the practice of:

1. Providing high quality instruction/intervention matched to student needs
2. Using learning rate over time and level of performance
3. Make important educational decisions

These components of RtI are essential to the development of a successful RtI implementation strategy.

Organizing the School for Tiered Instruction:

The key to providing tiered instruction lies in the establishment of a workable schedule that maximizes school personnel resources and high degree of collaboration amount the teaching force.

Tier One: Foundation of the Program. Standards aligned instruction for ALL students.

Tier Two: Supplemental Intervention for Students at some risk (Strategic).

Tier Three: Supplemental Intervention for Students at high (Intensive). www.rtinetwork.org,2016

Building Principal's Role and Responsibilities

- **Sets a vision for the problem-solving process**
- **Supports development of expectations**
- **Responsible for allocation of resources**
- **Facilitates priority setting**
- **Ensures follow-up**
- **Supports program evaluation**
- **Monitors staff support/climate** (RTI Action Network, www.rtinetwork.org)

Note – It is strongly suggested the student download the entire manual for a referral resource. RTI is a major strategy in today's modern school and it will be wise that the administrator be acquainted with the concepts, strategies and processes.

Content compiled from the *Response to Intervention Blueprints: School Building Level Edition* (Texas Version, 2010)

> "There are no secrets to success. It is the result of preparation, hard work, and learning from our failure."
> - Colin L. Powell

Safe Routes to School Programs

Today, more than ever, there is a need to provide options that allow children to walk and bicycle to school safely. SRTS programs use a variety of education, engineering and enforcement strategies that help make routes safer for children to walk and bicycle to school and encouragement strategies to entice more children to walk and bicycle.

Campus Safe Routes Audit:

Student Drop-Off Areas:
- Are they designed so that students exiting or entering cars are protected from other vehicles?
- Do they have a continuous raised curb separating vehicles from pedestrians?
- Are there curb ramps for wheelchair access?
- Do the ramps have tactile warning strips or textured concrete?
- Are there posted vehicular signs?
- Are there posted pedestrian signs?
- Is the area lighted?
- Does traffic seem to move freely without congestion and backup?

Bus loading zones
- Are bus driveways physically separated from pedestrian and bicycle routes by raised curbs or bollards?
- Are bus driveways physically separated from parent pick-up and drop-off areas?
- If the buses are "double-stacked" in loading areas, are safety measures taken for students needing to cross in front of or behind a bus?
- Is traffic in the bus loading zone one-way?
- Does the bus zone meet the minimum width for drop-off/pull-out lanes?
- Is there a continuous curb and sidewalk adjacent to the drop-off/loading area into the school site?
- Is the bus loading/unloading zone lighted?

Sidewalks and Bicycle Routes
- Are current pedestrian and bicycle routes separated from motor vehicles by the use of sidewalks and separated paths?
- Are the bicycle routes designated by signage?
- Are marked bicycle lanes present?
- Are sidewalks and bicycle paths regularly maintained?
- Are there ramps for wheelchair access?
- Are the sidewalks continuous and without gaps?
- Do the ramps have tactile warning strips or textured concrete?

- Are the sidewalks lighted?
- Are the sidewalks used regularly?

Adjacent Intersections (intersections near school property)
- Are there high volumes of automobile traffic?
- Are there high volumes of pedestrian traffic?
- Are there painted crosswalks for all crossing intersections?
- Are there curb ramps located at all adjacent intersections?
- Is there appropriate vehicle signage?
- Is there traffic control, such as stoplights or stop signs?

Sight Distance (clear views between motorists and pedestrians)
- Are desirable sight distances (visibility free of obstructions) provided at all intersections within the walking zone?
- Do parked vehicles block the vision of other motorists, bicyclists or pedestrians?
- Has the placement of fences, walls, dumpsters and the location of parking areas been carefully considered in view of sight distance requirements?
- Are there pedestrian walk signals?

Traffic signs, speed control, signals and pavement markings.
- Are there school crossing signs, school speed limit signs, flashing beacons, and No Parking **and**
- No Standing signs?
- Is there an effective school traffic enforcement program?
- Is there a designated school zone?
- Are there any school pavement markings located on roadways adjacent to or in the vicinity of
- the school grounds?
- Are there currently traffic control measures used, such as different pavement surfaces, non-white paint, speed bumps and speed tables?

Scenario Strategy – Technical Reading

Below is a brief scenario. I have taken the storyline and indicated areas that impact the reading process of the students. Most are not trained in technical reading and will "read over" important details to the story line that impact the actual answer.

Scenario One:

Ms. McElroy has just been hired as the principal of Grover Middle School in a district with a large multinational population, including many bilingual and English-language learners. Within the first days of her arrival, teachers express an urgent concern about the inadequacy of the district's current approach to communicating with non-English-speaking parents. Teachers see limited involvement in parent-teacher conferences, parent-teacher organization (PTO) meetings, and special events. Additionally, because of the multinational character of the district, there is no single dominant language.

In response to the urgent request of the teachers, Ms. McElroy is making the improvement of communication with non-English-speaking parents a priority in her first year. Ms. McElroy has decided to implement a Parent Night for bilingual and English-language learners where parents meet the teachers, learn about how high school credits work and interact with other parents. The greatest benefit of Parent Night is that

As you read through the above scenario, you will see a large amount of information.

1. New principal
2. Large multinational population
3. Bilingual and English language learners
4. Teacher concerns
5. Present communication process
6. Principal possible strategy (explained)
7. Actual question --- "What is the benefit of a parent night?"
   - With ALL the information, the actual exam question could simply have been asked, "What are the benefits of parent night for your school?"
   - Both ways, the long scenario, and the short question ask the same question. The benefit?
   - So, the state is actually asking, **"Do you know the research that indicates the benefits of a Parent Night for your campus?"**

Scenario Two:

You are at home enjoying a great Saturday morning. Suddenly the doorbell rings, and a local TV news anchor is on your front stoop with camera and microphones. She asked about the death of one of your students on Friday night. She wants to know about the student and what your series of steps will be to handle the event. You answer the reporter to the best of your ability. The TV news anchor leaves you to return to your morning events.

Then a series of phone calls begin. The local teacher's groups are wanting to discuss a possible "prayer around the flagpole" for Monday morning. Just a few moments later the local pastor organization wishes to be present at school on Monday for any concerns students from their congregation. Later in the afternoon, your SHAC chairperson contacts you with a series of question and concerns about possible negative events on Monday morning.

By six that evening you receive a call from your Assistant Superintendent in Charge of District Administrators wanting you to prepare and then allow her to review a written statement to the press for Monday morning. Around 9:00 p.m. you get a call from your Superintendent upset over the amount of student information the local TV reporter has about the deceased student. The reporter quotes you in regard to the information. What process have you not followed correctly from the above scenario?

As you read through the above scenario, you will see a large amount of information.

1. The principal is at home
2. Local news reporter
   - These types of scenario's cause a lot of confusion for the student. Most to all districts require a principal to contact the district office the moment a news person shows up on the campus.
   - Also, many districts require that a principal NOT talks to news personnel. While this is good district policy, the state will NOT allow this within a scenario about such an event.
   - TEA/SBEC wants to know how a principal "would" respond and do they know "how" to respond.
3. Teacher groups and the flag pole has many "policy and procedure" question that are pulled up when the reader goes through this scenario.
4. Local pastor groups and "policy and procedure" question are mentally reviewed by the reader during these few seconds.
5. SHAC and SBDM responsibilities of the principal will be mentally reviewed by the reader.
6. Assistant superintendent request will cause the reader to begin the mental exercise toward creating a written response.
7. Superintendent call! HERE is the actual concern of the scenario. Student information shared with the news media---FERPA!

Scenario Three:

You have accepted the challenge of taking on the principal position of a large middle school at mid-year. Students and teachers will be arriving back from their winter holiday break in two weeks. As you review the student and teacher data, the concern is indicated. A first-year math teacher is struggling, and student assessment scores for that class are below the rest of the campus.

While there are many things, you are discovering about the campus and its needs this concern is at the forefront and requires action. The teacher mid-year formative evaluation files have the following data:

- First evaluation domain scores are low and below expectations.
- Interventions plan with objectives are in place with timelines for completion.
- Walkthroughs are clearly documented by the certified evaluation administration.
- Historical scores for the students are clearly documented. Before and in the present class.

When the students and teachers return from the holidays, you ask to see the first-year teacher. It is then you learn the teacher has no documentation showing the teacher was communicated with during the above data. The evaluation was given to the teacher to sign but without discussion. While the teacher is actively seeking to accomplish all the goals and objectives of the intervention plan. The teacher had no input into its creation. There have been no active discussions of support (no documentation) between the teacher and the former administrator—creator of the documentation.

It is now the middle of March, and you will have contract recommendations due by the end of March. As you review the data what question is the most important for you to consider?

As you read through the above scenario, you will see a large amount of information.

1. New principal mid-year
2. Weak teacher – first year
3. Weak scores
4. Evaluation process and evaluation folder information
5. Historical data
6. New teacher response to the present evaluation cycle (good or bad?)
7. As the student reads the possible answers, many will be considering that the teacher is NEW thus the evaluation process and needs do not apply! That is wrong. Local school boards WANT all employees to have the best possible remedial process use and documented. While this is NOT policy or actual law, <u>it is the best political action</u> for principals to take. Also, the TEA commissioners court will seek any and all documentation to make a determination of a non-renewal is challenge—NO MATTER ABOUT THE CONTRACT-because the decision is fraught with political overtones.
8. TIME CHANGE! Went from mid-term to March. Students reading all of the information of the scenario will miss the date (time change). THIS is what impacts the actual answers that are given.

> *"He who never fell never climbed."*
> - Anonymous

Sexual Harassment Investigations

The following "tips" are for your consideration. Always follow the school district's policy and procedures.

1. Promptly report the accusation to the school's HR/Superintendent.
2. Promptly initiate the investigation.
3. Be VERY familiar with Policy and Procedures.
4. Develop adequate documentation.
5. Interview all potential witnesses.
6. Take interim remedial measures, as suggested by HR/Legal.
7. Take steps to avoid retaliation by either party.
8. Most difficult—Confidentiality still counts!
9. Be consistent.
10. Be fair.

Conducting an investigation: Simple Steps

The process below is simple to follow. **Remember to contact the HR/Superintendent for advice.** If district legal decides to step in and investigate, breathe a sigh of relief then watch and learn. If not, follow policy and procedures…as closely as you can!

Do NOT delay the beginning an investigation:

A. Once an allegation has been presented, you must decide whether an investigation is warranted. If the violation of board policy is proven, then proceed.

B. In allegations of employee sexual harassment or abuse of students, you alert your Title IX coordinator and depending on circumstances campus security.

C. If the allegation involves a student, under TEX 26.004 and 26.008, the parents must be considered "full partners" in the matter. Parents as "partners" are highly desirable for the student, you, and your district. They may be in on all interviews and may bring legal counsel.

D. All interviews must be done separately. If your district has a witness statement form use it. Make sure you are following policy and procedures. You cannot promise confidentiality.

   1. While the allegations may not be protected, the student's personally identifiable information about the student or families is protected (FERPA).

Note -- Legal Reminder: Document, Document, Document! If it is NOT on paper, it is vapor!

Technology and the Principal's Role

A. **The most effective way school administrators can promote technology use?**
  1. **be knowledgeable of the use of technology on the campus and in the classroom**
  2. **be effective in the use of the technology on the campus and in the classroom**

B. Model the application of Technology by:
  1. support and encourage teachers to attend technology themed conferences and staff development.
  2. use technology in the day-to-day routine of the campus by:
     - use of e-mail notices to staff and faculty
     - use of electronic agendas instead of paper
     - have all lesson plans submitted electronically
     - seek support from parents by requesting and using their personnel e-mail addresses for all records and correspondence
     - have classes develop web sites
     - be a proactive administrator by attending technology conferences and staff development programs at other campuses
     - sharing with administrative colleagues about the use and implementation of technology
     - use technology to create, record and save all campus committee meetings
     - focus sufficient budgetary funds in the support of technology and its implementation
     - promote technology integration by providing time for planning, collaboration, and implementation of technology based activities

Section 3 will gather school administrator proficiencies and will be completed by the campus principal. Only campus principals are required to complete the school administrator self-assessment.

Section 3 – School Administrator Proficiencies

Data Required: Unduplicated number of school personnel achieving acceptable performance on standards. Data Required: Unduplicated number of school personnel achieving acceptable performance on standards-based performance profiles of technology user skills as defined by the state (Title II, Part D of ESEA as required by the Results Act) by staff categories, including teachers, librarian/library media specialists and campus administrators.

Key points

- The teacher and librarian/library media specialist data will be aggregated from the Teaching & Learning and Educator Preparation & Development sections of the Teacher STaR Chart.

- The campus administrator data will be collected through the NCLB Technology Reporting System and will be based upon the overarching standards from the ISTE Technology Standards for School Administrators.

- <u>**Only campus principals are required to complete Section 3**</u>.

Overarching standards from the ISTE Technology Standards for School Administrators:

1. **Visionary Leadership:** Educational Administrators inspire and lead development and implementation of a shared vision for comprehensive integration of technology to promote excellence and support transformation throughout the organization.
2. **Digital Age Learning Culture:** Educational Administrators create, promote, and sustain a dynamic, digital age learning culture that provides a rigorous, relevant, and engaging education for all students.
3. **Excellence in Professional Practice:** Educational Administrators promote an environment of professional learning and innovation that empowers educators to enhance student learning through the infusion of contemporary technologies and digital resources.

4. **Systemic Improvement:** Educational Administrators provide digital-age leadership and management to continuously improve the organization through the effective use of information and technology resources.
5. **Digital Citizenship:** Educational Administrators model and facilitate understanding of social, ethical and legal issues and responsibilities related to an evolving digital culture.
   - It is strongly suggested that the, "STaR Chart for Technology" be downloaded from TEA and placed in the administrators' state and federal manual folder on his/her desktop for reference. This is an ongoing report that will change as the needs of the public school changes.
   - It is strongly suggested that the, "2014 Progress Report on the Long-Range Plan for Technology, 2006-2020" be downloaded from TEA and placed in the administrators' state and federal manual folder on his/her desktop for reference.

"The great thing in this world is not so much where we are but in what direction we are moving."
- Oliver Wendell Holmes

Transportation -- Module: 8.5.1.10

Purpose:

Transportation is a vital support service that demands sound management due to the large capital investment in bus fleets and annual expenditures required for maintenance and operation. Although numerous state regulations govern transportation services, districts have the flexibility of establishing procedures which can enhance operations.

The main goal of the School Bus Transportation Programs are to properly develop and maintain the knowledge, attitudes, and skills required **to provide a safe, reliable, and efficient student transportation system**.

Safety recommendation:
A review of emergency bus evacuation procedures, including a demonstration of the school bus emergency exits and the safe manner to exit, immediately **before each field trip involving transportation by school bus**.

Students riding a school bus should always:

- Arrive at the bus stop five minutes early.
- Stand at least 5 giant steps (10 feet) away from the edge of the road.
- Wait until the bus stops, the door opens, and the driver says its okay before stepping onto the bus.
- Be careful that clothing with drawstrings and book bags with straps or dangling objects do not get caught in the handrail or door when exiting the bus.
- Check both ways for cars before stepping off the bus.

Principal's Responsibilities:

- **Inform parents and students of school bus rules and consequences of violations.**
- **Investigate all complaints and referrals**
- **Confer with students, parent and bus driver when appropriate.**
- **Be present or appoint a designated representative to be at the campus loading zone during arrival and departure times.**
- **Meet with the drivers at the beginning of each school year and as needed throughout the year to discuss loading procedures, safety concerns, discipline procedures, etc.**

Transportation of Students

As field trips are off school grounds, transportation is normally needed. This can be provided using a variety of forms. Listed below are transportation options and issues related to each.

On the field trip Itinerary, be sure to specify:
- the means of transportation,
- the Parent/Guardian Field Trip Permission,
- Emergency Information, and
- Informed Consent Form.

Other district vehicles

Your district may use a passenger van to transport 14 or fewer students to and from school-related activities or events, such as field trips and activities or events for clubs, sports, and band.26 Transportation to these activities and events is the only type of student transportation for which a passenger van may be used.

If a passenger van is used for this purpose:
- The number of passengers in the vehicle must not exceed the manufacturer-designed seating capacity of the vehicle
- Each passenger must be properly secured by a safety belt or an appropriate child safety seat restraint

A passenger van is a motor vehicle, other than a motorcycle or passenger car, designed to transport 15 or fewer passengers, including the driver. A passenger van does not include a minivan or a sport-utility vehicle with a capacity of 10 or fewer.

The driver of a passenger vehicle (such as a van) transporting students must hold a valid driver's license but is NOT required to meet the other requirements that school bus drivers must meet (School Transportation Allotment Handbook, Pg. 39).

Purchase of Insurance when Leasing/Renting a Vehicle (ALWAYS Verify the statement below-all Texas School District are different but this is the norm). Dr. CR

Insurance for non-owned or lease/rental **vehicles is included** in the district's liability insurance coverage. If a vehicle is leased/rented **by an employee** for the purpose of district business, that person is covered under the district's policy for liability. If additional insurance is taken during the leasing/rental process for any vehicle being used for district business, the person who has signed that lease/rental agreement will be responsible for the cost of the additional coverage. The district will not reimburse additional insurance coverage for any lease/rental vehicle being used by an employee for district business.

Language Proficiency Assessment Committee (LPAC)

Language Proficiency Assessment Committee
LPAC and the Assessment Committee
LPAC Manual

As an advocate for the LEP student, the LPAC becomes the voice that:

1. Initiates
2. Articulates
3. Deliberates
4. Determines the best instructional program for the student

The LPAC functions **as a link between the home and the school** in making appropriate decisions regarding:

1. Placement
2. Instructional practices
3. Assessment
4. Special programs that impact the student

The LPAC process is related to NCLB and Title III.

Chapter 89. Adaptations for Special Populations Subchapter BB.
Commissioner's Rules Concerning State Plan for Educating
Limited English Proficient Students

Statutory Authority: The provisions of this Subchapter BB issued under the Texas Education Code, §§29.051, 29.054, 29.056, 29.0561, and 29.060 unless otherwise noted.

§89.1201. Policy.
(a) It is the policy of the state that every student in the state who has a home language other than English and who is identified as limited English proficient shall be provided a full opportunity to participate in a bilingual education or English as a second language program, as required by the Texas Education Code, Chapter 29, Subchapter B. To ensure equal educational opportunity, as required by the Texas Education Code, §1.002(a), each school district shall:

(1) identify limited English proficient students based on criteria established by the state;

(2) provide bilingual education and English as second language programs as integral parts of the regular program as described in the Texas Education Code, §4.002;

(3) seek certified teaching personnel to ensure that limited English proficient students are afforded full opportunity to master the essential skills and knowledge required by the state; and

(4) assess the achievement of essential skills and knowledge in accordance with the Texas Education Code, Chapter 39, to ensure accountability for limited English proficient students and the schools that serve them.

(a) <u>The goal of bilingual education programs shall be to enable limited English proficient students to become competent in the comprehension, speaking, reading, and composition of the English language through the development of literacy and academic skills in the primary language and English.</u> Such programs shall emphasize the mastery of English language skills, as well as mathematics, science and social studies, as integral parts of the academic goals for all students to enable limited English proficient students to participate equitably in school.

   (b) <u>The goal of English as a second language programs shall be to enable limited English proficient students to become competent in the comprehension, speaking, reading, and composition of the English language through the integrated use of second language methods.</u> The English as a second language program shall emphasize the mastery of English language skills, as well as mathematics, science and social studies, as integral parts of the academic goals for all students to enable limited English proficient students to participate equitably in school.

NOTE: This is a major area of legal entanglement for the modern principal. Learn this! Details can be found in the LPAC manual.

> *"Man must cease attributing his problems to his environment and learn again to exercise his will - his personal responsibiity."*
>
> - Albert Schweitzen

LPAC and Placement

What is the requirement to have a bilingual education program or a special language program in Texas?

- Each district with an **enrollment of 20 or more students of limited English proficiency** in any language classification in the same grade level shall offer a bilingual education or special language program. TEC §29.053(c)

- For Bilingual Education: **Each district that is required to offer bilingual education and special language programs** shall offer: **Bilingual education in kindergarten through the elementary grades**

- **Bilingual education, instruction** in English as a second language, or other transitional language instruction approved by the agency in **post-elementary grades through Grade 8**

- Instruction in English as a second language in Grades 9 through 12. **Districts may join with other districts** to provide **bilingual education or English as a Second language programs**.

What if my district does not meet the 20 or more student threshold?
All limited English proficient students for whom a district is not required to offer a bilingual education program shall be provided an English as a second language program, regardless of the students' grade levels and home languages, and regardless of the number of such students.

What is the definition of a Limited English Proficient (LEP) student?
"Students of limited English proficiency" means a student whose primary language is other than English and whose English language skills are such that the student has difficulty performing ordinary classwork in English. TEC §29.052(1)

(The terms LEP and English Language Learners (ELLs) are used interchangeably.)

Which tests are administered to each student who has a language other than English as identified on the home language survey?
Grades 2-12 = a TEA approved oral language proficiency test (OLPT) (listening and speaking) in English (and primary language for bilingual programs) and the reading and language arts sections of an English norm-referenced standardized achievement test approved by the state (unless the English ability is so low that it would invalidate the test)

When does a district officially classify a student as "LEP"?
The date that the parent approval form is signed is the date the student's official Public Education Information Management System (PEIMS) status becomes LEP. From that date the student is identified as LEP, regardless of permission or denial.

When should a student be identified as limited English proficient in the academic school year?
Within the first four weeks (20 school days) of the student's enrollment in the district, the LPAC shall identify the student as limited English proficient and enrolled into the required bilingual education or English as a second language program. TEC §29.053(b)

What criterion is needed for a student to exit from a bilingual education or English as a second language program?
To exit from a bilingual education or English as a second language program, a student may be classified as English proficient at the end of the school year in which a student would be able to participate equally in a regular, all-English, instructional program.

What is the exit criteria for removing the student from the bilingual or ESL programs?

- TEA-approved tests that measure the extent to which the student has developed oral and written language proficiency and specific language skills in English; Satisfactory performance on the reading assessment instrument under the Texas Education Code, §39.023(a), or

- TEA-approved English language arts assessment instrument administered in English, or a score at or above the 40th percentile on both the English reading and the English language arts section of a TEA-approved norm-referenced assessment instrument for a student who is enrolled in Grade 1 or 2; and

- TEA-approved criterion-referenced written tests when available and the results of a subjective teacher evaluation.

Does the LPAC evaluate the student's progress after exiting the bilingual education or a special language program?

The language proficiency assessment committee **shall reevaluate a student** who is **transferred out** of a bilingual education or special language program during the **first two years after a student is exited IF** the **student earns a failing grade in a subject in the foundation curriculum during any grading period** and **determine whether the student should be reenrolled** in a bilingual education or special language program. TEC§29.0561(g)

> *"There is no use whatever trying to help people who do not help themselves. You cannot push anyone up a ladder unless he is willing to climb himself."*
> - Andrew Carnegie

LPAC Meeting

MEMBERSHIP

---

§89. 1220. Language Proficiency Assessment Committee.
   (a) Districts shall by local board policy establish and operate a language proficiency assessment committee. The district shall have on file policy and procedures for the selection, appointment and training of members of the language proficiency assessment committee(s).

   (b) In districts required to provide a bilingual education program, the language proficiency assessment committee shall be composed of the membership described in the Texas Education Code, §29.063. If the district does not have an individual in one or more of the school job classifications required, the district shall designate another professional staff member to serve on the language proficiency assessment committee. The district may add other members to the committee in any of the required categories.

   (c) In districts and grade levels not required to provide a bilingual education program, the language proficiency assessment committee shall be composed of one or more professional personnel and a parent of a limited English proficient student participating in the program designated by the district.

   (d) No parent serving on the language proficiency assessment committee shall be an employee of the school district.

   (e) A district shall establish and operate a sufficient number of language proficiency assessment committees to enable them to discharge their duties within four weeks of the enrollment of limited English proficient students.

   (f) All members of the language proficiency assessment committee, including parents, shall be acting for the school district and shall observe all laws and rules governing confidentiality of information concerning individual students. The district shall be responsible for the orientation and training of all members, including the parents, of the language proficiency assessment committee.

Each school district that is required to offer bilingual education and special language programs shall establish a language proficiency assessment committee.

Each committee shall include:
1. Professional bilingual educator
2. Professional transitional language educator
3. Parent of a limited English proficiency student
4. Campus administrator

Responsibilities

§89.1220. Language Proficiency Assessment Committee.

(g) Upon their initial enrollment and at the end of each school year, the language proficiency assessment committee shall review all pertinent information on all limited English proficient students identified in accordance with §89.1225(f) of this title (relating to Testing and Classification of Students) and shall:

(1) designate the language proficiency level of each limited English proficient student in accordance with the guidelines issued pursuant to §89.1210(b) and (d) of this title (relating to Program Content and Design);

(2) designate the level of academic achievement of each limited English proficient student;

(3) designate, subject to parental approval, the initial instructional placement of each limited English proficient student in the required program;

(4) facilitate the participation of limited English proficient students in other special programs for which they are eligible provided by the district with either state or federal funds; and

(5) classify students as English proficient in accordance with the criteria described in §89.1225(h) of this title (relating to Testing and Classification of Students), and recommend their exit from the bilingual education or English as a second language program.

The language proficiency assessment committee shall:

1. Review all pertinent information on limited English proficiency students, including the home language survey
2. The language proficiency tests in English and the primary language
3. Each student's achievement in content areas
4. Each student's emotional and social attainment

The LPAC shall make recommendations concerning:

1. The most appropriate placement for the educational advancement of the limited English proficiency student after the elementary grades
2. Review each limited English proficiency student's progress at the end of the school year in order to determine future appropriate placement
3. Monitor the progress of students formerly classified as limited English proficiency who have transferred out of the bilingual education or special language program
4. Based on the information, designate the most appropriate placement for such students
5. Determine the appropriateness of a program that extends beyond the regular school year based on the needs of each limited English proficiency student

Exiting the Program
§29.063(c)(4).

(h) For exit from a bilingual education or English as a second language program, a student may be classified as English profiient at the end of the school year in which a student would be able to participate equally in a regular, all-English, instructional program. This determination shall be based upon all of the following:

(1) TEA-approved tests that measure the extent to which the student has developed oral and written language proficiency and specific language skills in English;

(2) satisfactory performance on the reading assessment instrument under the Texas Education Code, §39.023(a), or a TEA-approved English language arts assessment instrument administered in English, or a score at or above the 40th percentile on both the English reading and the English language arts sections of a TEA-approved norm- referenced assessment instrument for a student who is enrolled in Grade 1 or 2; and

(3) TEA-approved criterion-referenced written tests when available and the results of a subjective teacher evaluation.

(i) **<u>A student may not be exited from the bilingual education or English as a second language program in prekindergarten or kindergarten</u>**. A district must ensure that limited English proficient students are prepared to meet academic standards required by TEC, §28.0211.

(j) For determining whether a student who has been exited from a bilingual education or English as a second language program **is academically successful**, the following criteria shall be used at the end of the school year:

(1) **the student meets state performance standards in English of the criterion-referenced assessment instrument required in the Texas Education Code, §39.023, for the grade level as applicable; and**
(2) **the student has passing grades in all subjects and courses taken.**

(k) The ARD **committee in conjunction with the language proficiency assessment committee shall determine an appropriate assessment instrument and performance standard requirement for exit under subsection** (h) of this section for students for whom those tests would be inappropriate as part of the IEP. The decision to exit a student who receives both special education and special language services from the bilingual education or English as a second language program is determined by the ARD committee in conjunction with the language proficiency assessment committee in accordance with applicable provisions of subsection (h) of this section.

"You measure the size of the accomplishment by the obstacles you had to overcome to reach your goals."
- Booker T. Washington

Site Based Decision Making (SBDM)

Site Based Decision Making

Overview of SBDM Manual

An Overview

The basic premise of site-based decision-making is that the most effective decisions are made by those who will actually implement the decisions. The belief is that people involved at the campus level have a greater opportunity to identify problems, develop problem resolution and change strategy than people located off-campus. Site-based decision making concepts also recognize that people at the campus level are more likely to internalize change and to support its implementation if they are involved in the decision making than if they are not.

The objective of site-based decision-making is to improve student performance and to enhance accountability. Each campus should have the freedom to set its own educational objectives, consistent with the school district's goals.

Site-based Decision Making Initiative

Site-based decision-making implementation has been mandated for all Texas school districts since 1992. TEA defines site-based decision making as follows:

Site-based decision making is a process of decentralizing decisions to improve the educational outcomes at every school campus through a collaborative effort by which principals, teachers, campus staff, district staff, parents, and community representatives assess educational outcomes of all students, determine goals and strategies, and ensure that strategies are implemented and adjusted to improve student achievement.

The atmosphere in the United States has become more demanding of public school systems' central administration. Often the public asks that centralized decision-making units be broken into smaller, more workable groups that will provide them opportunities to have input into local education decisions. To empower the local public school system, a balance between freedom and accountability must be achieved. The schools must have freedom to take ownership of the education process.

The expected outcome of site-based decision making is improved student performance as a result of:
- Effective campus and school district planning for the purpose of improved student performance
- Improved community involvement in the school improvement process
- Clearly established accountability parameters for student performance
- Increased staff productivity and satisfaction
- Improved communication and information flow
- Consensus-based, decision-making
- Pervasive and long-range commitment to implementation
- Increased flexibility at the campus level in the allocation and use of both human and fiscal resources
- Coordination of "regular" and special program or service components
- **Site-based decision-making strives to decentralize decisions to the campus level** and solicits the input of the following stakeholders in the decision-making process:

- Central administrative staff to provide support services to both the board members and schools in site-based decision-making initiatives
- **Principals to develop their respective school's site-based decision-making policies and procedures, as well as its campus improvement plan**
- Teachers, parents, students and community representatives to provide input on their respective school's site-based decision-making policies and procedures and campus improvement plan

Site-based decision-making <u>differs significantly</u> from traditional school organization practices in the following ways:

- Goals are determined on a campus level for a campus needs assessment and outcome data
- Activities are self-initiated and self-directed by the campus staff
- Budget development and allocation of resources are campus-controlled
- Staff selection criteria are guided by standards developed by a campus within the context of state and district guidelines
- Campus organization structure is arranged functionally to encourage and facilitate shared team decision-making and input
- The campus staff verifies that site-based decision-making is established and working
- The role of central administration in site-based decision-making is that of support. Central administration assists in site-based decision making through planning, providing alternative strategies, developing evaluation mechanisms and obtaining resources.

5.1.2 Roles and Responsibilities

Site-based decision-making advocates decision making by committee. In most cases, instructional related policies have been made by a limited number of high-level administrators.

Site-based decision-making (SBDM) now involves the input from many who are closely involved at the student level. Site-based decision-making policies and procedures without generally agreed upon objectives and **structure can create problems.** Thus, <u>**development of policies and procedures for site-based decision-making must place special emphasis on educating and training all individuals involved**</u>. The school district's mission must be clearly stated, and time should be invested to train all participants on the importance of a collaborative atmosphere for committee meetings and the process as a whole. Within the school district's policies and procedures for site-based decision-making, a clear delineation of each administrator's and committee member's role and their associated responsibilities is necessary.

Major Committees of the SBDM
- Budget
- Curricula
- Teacher In-service and training
- Site Health Action (SHAC)
- Homeless
- Safety and Emergency Preparedness
- others as designated

Site Based Decision Making (SBDM)
State Requirements

Each school district is required to adopt a policy and have administrative procedures to establish a district- and campus-level planning and decision-making process. This process must involve professional staff of the district, parents and community members in establishing and reviewing the district's and campuses' educational plans, goals, performance objectives and major classroom instructional programs

5.2.1 District- and Campus-level Committees

School districts are required to establish a district- and **campus-level planning and decision- making committees whose membership must include**:

- Professional staff
- Parents of students enrolled in the district
- Community members
- Business and industry representatives

The selection process for the district-level and campus-level committees must be conducted in a manner that provides for appropriate representation of the community's diversity. **These committees must hold at least one public meeting per year which must take place after the receipt of the annual district performance report from TEA.** These meetings are for the purpose of discussing the performance of the district and the district performance objectives.

Specifically, both the **campus and district-level planning and decision-making committees** roles address the areas of:

- Planning
- Budgeting
- Curriculum
- Staffing patterns
- Staff development
- School organization

In addition, the district-level committee must be actively involved in establishing the administrative procedure that defines the respective roles and responsibilities related to planning and decision-making at the district and campus levels.

Additional duties of the district- and campus-level committees include the following:

- For teacher appraisal, the school district may use an appraisal process and performance criteria developed by the district- and campus-level planning and decision-making committees. This process and related criteria must be adopted by the board of trustee.

- Each school district shall adopt a student code of conduct for the district with the advice of its district-level planning and decision-making committee and as appropriate, with the juvenile board of each county in which the district is located.

- Each school district shall adopt and implement a dating violence policy and provide the specifics of the policy (in the district plan), including the provision of dating violence safety planning, enforcement of protective orders and school-based alternative to protective orders, staff training and counseling for affected students, and awareness education for students and parents enacted by HB 121, 80th Legislature).

- A school campus or district seeking a waiver must submit a written application to the commissioner which must include: A written plan approved by the board of trustees that states the achievement objectives of the campus or district and the inhibition imposed on the accomplishment of those objectives by the existing requirement, restriction or prohibition

- Written comments from the campus or district-level committee.

- The campus-level committee shall determine the use of the funds awarded to a school under the Texas Successful School Awards System.

- Staff development must be predominantly campus-based, related to achieving campus performance objectives established by the principal with the assistance of the campus-level planning and decision-making committee. Staff development must be developed and approved by the campus-level committee.

5.2.3 Campus Improvement Plans

Each school year the principal of each school campus, with the assistance of the campus-level committee, must develop, review and revise the campus improvement plan. The purpose of this plan is to improve student performance on the state's student achievement indicators for all student populations, as well as improve performance on any other performance measures for special needs populations. The campus improvement plan must be supportive of the objectives of the district improvement plan and must, at a minimum, support the state goals and objectives for education.

The Texas Education Code, Section 11.251, also requires that the board of trustees ensures that the district and all campus plans be developed, reviewed and revised annually for the purpose of improving the performance of all students. Annual board approval must ensure that the district and campus plans are mutually supportive to accomplish the identified objectives and support the state goals and objectives listed in Chapter 4 of the Texas Education Code.

Each campus improvement plan must:

1. **Assess the academic achievement** for each student in the school using the student achievement indicator system as described in Section 39.053;
2. **Set the campus performance objectives** based on the student achievement indicator system, including objectives for special needs populations, including students in special education programs under Subchapter A, Chapter 29;
3. **Identify how the campus goals will be met** for each student;
4. **Determine the resources needed** to implement the plan;
5. **Identify the staff needed** to implement the plan;
6. **Set timelines for reaching the goals;**
7. **Measure progress** toward the performance objectives periodically to ensure that the plan is resulting in academic improvement;
8. **Include goals and methods for violence prevention and intervention** on campus;
9. **Provide for a program to encourage parental involvement** in the campus and
10. If the campus is an elementary, middle, or junior high school, **set goals and objectives for the coordinated health program** at the campus based on:
    a. student fitness assessment data, including any data from research-based assessments such as the school health index assessment and planning tool created by the federal Centers for Disease Control and Prevention;
    b. student academic performance data;
    c. student attendance rates;

d. the percentage of students who are educationally disadvantaged;
e. the use and success of any method to ensure that students participate in moderate to vigorous physical activity as required by Section 28.002(1); and
f. any other indicator recommended by the local school advisory council.

In addressing the needs of students at risk of dropping out of school, the state compensatory education program must be addressed in the comprehensive needs assessment, be described in the campus improvement plan if the program is implemented at the campus level, or be described in the district improvement plan if the program is implemented districtwide. The district and/or campus improvement plan, as appropriate, must also include the following:

- Comprehensive needs assessment - conducted to identify the strengths and weaknesses of existing programs, practices, procedures, and activities

- Total amount of state compensatory education funds allocated for resources and staff

- Identified strategies - aligned with the comprehensive needs assessment

- Supplemental financial resources for state compensatory education

- Supplemental FTEs for state compensatory education (This is not necessary if the schoolwide campus is at or above 40% and is combining SCE funds to support their Title I, Part A program.)

- Measurable performance objectives - stated in terms of what the student is expected to do and stated in terms of measurable and/or observable behavior to ensure that the plan is resulting in academic improvement

- Timelines for monitoring strategies and reaching goals – specific schedule for data collection during the school year

- Formative and summative evaluation criteria - Formative evaluation includes periodic measures that are utilized during the actual implementation of the interventions or strategies. The summative evaluation occurs at the end of the implementation period to provide the overall project and process evaluation.

Law requires the district/**campus improvement plan and is the primary record supporting expenditures attributed to the state compensatory education program.**

The district must design the state compensatory education program based on the identified needs of students at risk of dropping out of school. In determining the appropriate accelerated, intensive compensatory programs and/or services, districts must use student performance data from the TAKS and other appropriate assessment instruments and achievement tests administered under Subchapter B, Chapter 39 of the Texas Education Code.

Many districts utilize their regional education service centers to assist in the development of their campus and/or district improvement plans. ESCs provide technical assistance to school districts and can provide a wealth of information on best practices and model programs.

Evaluation of Site-based Decision Making

<u>At least every two years</u>, each district must evaluate the effectiveness of the district's decision-making and planning policies, procedures and staff development activities related to district- and campus-level decision-making and planning to ensure that they are structured effectively to positively impact student performance   (TEC 11.252 (d)).

<u>The statute gives no specified guidelines</u> for this bi-annual evaluation, other than that its scope must include all decision-making policies, procedures, and staff development.

5.3 Site-based Budgeting

A major management process which should be adopted by school districts is site-based budgeting. The concept of site-based budgeting **provides for input from community members, teachers, and other campus staff in the resource allocation decisions which affect their respective schools.** Although site-based decision-making allows for the involvement of these individuals in formulating campus goals, objectives and plans, site-based budgeting takes the process a step further by delegating more authority over financial resources to campus decision makers. Thus, **site-based budgeting is more flexible than traditional budgeting because it decentralizes budgetary decision making to those individuals who best understand the needs of individual schools**.

5.3.2 Site-based Budgeting Roles and Responsibilities

School districts that adopt site-based budgeting should select plans that segregate budgetary responsibilities between campus and district levels. This selection should be made as a district develops and approves its annual budget preparation process. A school district should develop a budget preparation process which is tailored to its own goals, objectives, and needs. A method by which a school district may assign budget preparation responsibilities is:

- State law mandates that the superintendent prepare, or cause to be prepared, the budget. Thus, the superintendent is responsible for preparing and presenting the preliminary budget to the board. Although the superintendent and other district administrators may be very involved in the preparation of the school district's budget, site-based budgeting delegates much of the authority to make resource allocations to the campus level. Campus decision makers, however, still require guidance and technical assistance from school district administrators to prepare campus budgets. School district administrators may provide such elements as enrollment projections, standard per pupil resource allocations, staffing guidelines, etc. The business office may also provide information to campuses about their budget status and expenditure reports. The business office often supplies valuable assistance in the areas of purchasing, the use of grant funds and amending the budget.

- In addition, **school district administrators may prepare budgets for support services which are critical to the needs of the individual schools.** For example, the director of personnel provides qualified personnel to each school. Directors of food services, transportation and plant maintenance (or their equivalents) control important services necessary to the operations of the campuses. Given the importance of such services to individual campuses, campus and district staffs should work closely during the budget preparation process to ensure that all campus/district expenditure items are included in the budget at the appropriate level.

- **The principal is responsible for developing and maintaining the campus budget**. Principals should work with campus resource planning groups (or their equivalents), department heads, and campus improvement teams to determine campus resource allocation and to develop non-allocated requests. **Principals may also act as the representative of the campus in school district budget meetings** as campus resource allocations, and non-allocated requests are reviewed and approved. Because the budget provides financial resources necessary for the achievement of the campus goals, the principal is responsible for directing these resources to their most effective use.

5.4 Site-based Accounting

Site-based accounting encompasses those administrative duties performed by campus-level personnel to provide accurate reporting of the school's activities. In this section, the following discussions will familiarize the campus-based personnel with basic terminology and key concepts related to campus-level accounting.

- Financial Accounting
- Overview of Accounting System
- Roles and Responsibilities

5.4.2 Roles and Responsibilities

Site-based decision-making has been implemented to give campus level personnel the opportunity to respond to the school's unique needs. Underlying this opportunity is the responsibility for site-based accounting procedures. These site-based accounting procedures will enable schools to monitor their own budgets and provide other users the financial information they need. Thus, the authority and responsibility for site-based accounting are placed at the campus-level.

School Principal or Designee

The school principal or other designated campus administrator is primarily responsible for site-based accounting procedures. The principal or campus administrator is often assisted by grade-level principals, assistant principals, secretaries, clerks or volunteers. All personnel performing site-based accounting procedures should be familiar with this manual and other local district guidance. Everyone should strive for the correct, consistent and concise application of site-based accounting procedures.

Campus-Based Personnel Financial Accounting Responsibilities

Financial accounting procedures performed at each campus by campus-level personnel are:
- Supplies and materials ordering
- Capital asset purchasing
- Cash receipting
- Petty cah accounting
- School and student activity fund accounting

Common among each of these broad accounting areas is the need to classify transactions for proper accounts (e.g., coding a purchase order and recording the proceeds received from candy sales).

SBDM Membership as Described by Texas Education Codes 11.251 and 11.252

It is wise that the administrator candidate reviews the Texas Education Code below as it pertains to the SBDM and membership. The student candidate will get very confused if they review their school districts SBDM policy and then compare to the TEC. Remember the Texas Principal Exam will seek to ascertain your knowledge of state code and policy. In regard to the difference to state and school district policy, there is an old adage, "you can add to state law you can't take away." Keep that in mind.

(b) Each district's policy and procedures shall establish campus-level planning and decision-making committees as provided for through the procedures **provided by Sections 11.251(b)-(e).**

Sections 11.251(b)-(e).
- (b) The board shall adopt a policy to establish a district- and campus-level planning and decision-making process that will involve the <u>professional staff of the district, parents, and community members in establishing and reviewing the district's and campuses' educational plans, goals, performance objectives, and major classroom instructional programs.</u> The board shall establish a procedure under which meetings are held regularly by district- and campus-level planning and decision-making committees that include representative professional staff, including, if practicable, at least one representative with the primary responsibility for educating students with disabilities, parents of students enrolled in the district, business representatives, and community members. The committees shall include a business representative without regard to whether the representative resides in the district or whether the business the person represents is located in the district. The board, or the board's designee, shall periodically meet with the district-level committee to review the district-level committee's deliberations.
- (c) For purposes of establishing the composition of committees under this section:
    - (1) a person who stands in parental relation to a student is considered a parent;
    - (2) a parent who is an employee of the school district is not considered a parent representative on the committee;
    - (3) a parent is not considered a representative of community members on the committee; and
    - (4) community members must reside in the district and must be at least 18 years of age.
- (d) The board shall also ensure that an administrative procedure is provided to clearly define the respective roles and responsibilities of the superintendent, central office staff, principals, teachers, district-level committee members, and campus-level committee members in the areas of planning, budgeting, curriculum, staffing patterns, staff development, and school organization. The board shall ensure that the district-level planning and decision-making committee will be actively involved in establishing the administrative procedure that defines the respective roles and responsibilities pertaining to planning and decision-making at the district and campus levels.
- (e) The board shall adopt a procedure, consistent with Section 21.407(a), for the professional staff in the district to nominate and elect the professional staff representatives who shall meet with the board or the board designee as required under this section.

TEC 21.407
- (a) A school district board of trustees or school district employee may not directly or indirectly require or coerce any teacher to join any group, club, committee, organization, or association.
- (b) A school district board of trustees or school district employee may not directly or indirectly coerce any teacher to refrain from participating in political affairs in the teacher's community, state, or nation.
http://codes.findlaw.com/tx/education-code/educ-sect-21-407.html#sthash.5xrp2uHi.dpuf

<u>At least two-thirds of the elected professional staff representatives must be classroom teachers.</u> The remaining staff representatives shall include both campus- and district-level professional staff members. If practicable, the committee membership shall include at least one professional staff representative with the primary responsibility for educating students with disabilities. Board policy must provide procedures for:
(1) the selection of parents to the district-level and campus-level committees; and
(2) the selection of community members and business representatives to serve on the district-level committee in a manner that provides for appropriate representation of the community's diversity.

(f) The district policy must provide that all pertinent federal planning requirements are addressed through the district- and campus-level planning process.
http://codes.findlaw.com/tx/education-code/educ-sect11251.html#sthash.DXnR5Mv7.dpuf

(c) Each school year, the principal of each school campus, with the assistance of the campus-level committee, shall develop, review, and revise the campus improvement plan for the purpose of improving student performance for all student populations, including students in special education programs under Subchapter A, Chapter 29, [FN1] with respect to the achievement indicators adopted under Sections 39.053(c)(1)-(4) and any other appropriate performance measures for special needs populations.

(d) Each campus improvement plan must:
  (1) assess the academic achievement for each student in the school using the achievement indicator system as described by Section 39.053;
  (2) set the campus performance objectives based on the achievement indicator system, including objectives for special needs populations, including students in special education programs under Subchapter A, Chapter 29;
  (3) identify how the campus goals will be met for each student;
  (4) determine the resources needed to implement the plan;
  (5) identify staff needed to implement the plan;
  (6) set timelines for reaching the goals;
  (7) measure progress toward the performance objectives periodically to ensure that the plan is resulting in academic improvement;
  (8) include goals and methods for violence prevention and intervention on campus;
  (9) provide for a program to encourage parental involvement at the campus; and
  (10) if the campus is an elementary, middle, or junior high school, set goals and objectives for the coordinated health program at the campus based on:
    (A) student fitness assessment data, including any data from research-based assessments such as the school health index assessment and planning tool created by the federal Centers for Disease Control and Prevention;
    (B) student academic performance data;
    (C) student attendance rates;
    (D) the percentage of students who are educationally disadvantaged;
    (E) the use and success of any method to ensure that students participate in moderate to vigorous physical activity as required by Section 28.002(l); and
    (F) any other indicator recommended by the local school health advisory council.

(e) In accordance with the administrative procedures established under Section 11.251(b), the campus-level committee shall be involved in decisions in the areas of planning, budgeting, curriculum, staffing patterns, staff development, and school organization. The campus-level committee must approve the portions of the campus plan addressing campus staff development needs.

(g) Each campus-level committee shall hold at least one public meeting per year. The required meeting shall be held after receipt of the annual campus rating from the agency to discuss the performance of the campus and the campus performance objectives. District policy and campus procedures must be established to ensure that systematic communications measures are in place to periodically obtain broad-based community, parent, and staff input, and to provide information to those persons regarding the recommendations of the campus-level committees.

(h) A principal shall regularly consult the campus-level committee in the planning, operation, supervision, and evaluation of the campus educational program.
http://codes.findlaw.com/tx/education-code/educ-sect-11-253.html#sthash.m2y9yL5v.dpuf

What Does All the Above Mean?

Membership:
The professional staff serving on decision-making committees must be nominated and elected by other professional staff members. At least two-thirds of the elected professional staff must be classroom teachers. **There is no state-designated ratio of professional staff versus non-staff members. Local policy defines how the other members (e.g., parents, community, and business representatives) are selected.** Statute does not prohibit boards from establishing policies for means of

receiving input from others, including students or paraprofessional staff, in planning and decision making at the district or campus level [TEC § 11.251 (g)(2)].

- Professional staff of the district,
- Parents,
- Community member
- If practicable, at least one representative with the primary responsibility for educating students with disabilities,
- A business representative without regard to whether the representative resides in the district or whether the business the person represents is in the district.
- Nominate and elect a professional staff representative
    - At least two-thirds of the elected professional staff representatives must be classroom teachers. The remaining staff representatives shall include both campus- and district-level professional staff members.

What is the SIZE of the SBDM committee?
The committees must be comprised of elected professional staff and other members, including parents, community, and business representatives. Two thirds of the elected professional staff must be classroom teachers. The professional staff must also include district-level staff. (This does not necessarily mean "central office" staff. District-level staff may be any professional staff member who is not assigned to one particular campus.) Although statute does not specify any certain ratio of professional staff to non-staff members, local districts may consider specifying such a ratio, if desired.

It is important to develop a system for election and selection of members that is both logical and streamlined. **The focus should be on creating a representation of members that allows for effective consideration of student performance needs. Other considerations (e.g., representing the community's diversity and providing linkage between campus and district committees) may tend to increase the size of the committee.**

Note -- <u>up front answer to the above. Size of SBDM committee is determined by your campus needs.</u>

How many meetings per year?
Each campus-level committee shall hold at least one public meeting per year. The required meeting shall be held after receipt of the annual campus rating from the agency to discuss the performance of the campus and the campus performance objectives.

What does this committee do?
- Planning,
- Budgeting,
- Curriculum,
- Staffing patterns,
- Staff development,
- And school organization.
- The campus-level committee **must approve** the portions of the campus plan addressing campus staff development needs.

School districts are required to establish **campus-level** planning and decision-making committees whose membership must include:

- Professional staff
- Parents of students enrolled in the district
- Community members
- Business and industry representatives

The selection process for the campus-level committees must be conducted in a manner that provides for appropriate representation of the community's diversity (TEC 11.251 (e)). These committees must hold **at least one public meeting per year** which must take place *after the receipt of the annual district performance report from TEA*. These meetings are for the purpose of discussing the performance of the district and the district performance objectives (TEC 11.252 (e), 11.253 (g)).

Specifically, campus-level planning and decision-making committees' roles address the areas of:

- Planning
- Budgeting
- Curriculum
- Staffing patterns
- Staff development
- School organization

Additional duties:

- Student Code of Conduct – TEC 37.001
- Health and Safety Issues -- TEC 37,.0831
- Campus Appraisal Process -- TEC 21.352
- Use of Texas Successful School Awards System – TEC 39.094

SBDM – Schoolwide Program Implementation

The <u>underlying purpose</u> of the schoolwide approach is to enable campuses with high numbers of students at risk of not meeting state standards to <u>combine the services that it funds from federal, state, and local resources.</u> A growing body of evidence shows that it is possible to create campuses in which all students achieve high standards, even when most are poor or disadvantaged. These campuses are most likely to be effective if they make significant changes to the way they deliver services. By making systemic changes to combine services into a comprehensive framework, campuses will have a better chance of increasing the academic success of all of their students.

The schoolwide program model also reflects the following fundamental principles of Title I, Part A, as amended by the No Child Left Behind Act of 2001 (NCLB):

> Accountability for results. In a schoolwide program, the campus shares accountability for results throughout the campus. The campus expects all students to meet the state's standards, and gives timely, effective, and additional assistance to students who experience difficulty mastering those standards. Teachers use information about student performance and share ways to improve instruction to meet a wide range of student needs. The campus keeps parents informed of individual student achievement and of the campus's progress toward meeting its goals.

Research-based practices. Schoolwide programs operate according to a campus improvement plan that contains proven, research-based strategies designed to facilitate schoolwide reform and improvement. The campus bases its professional development activities upon practices proven to be successful in helping teachers improve the quality of their instruction.

School and community engagement. Staff in schoolwide programs engage parents and the community in their work as planners, participants, and decision makers in the operation of the campus. The campus bases this collaboration upon a shared vision of the campus's values and overall mission. These partnerships strengthen the campus's ability to meet the needs of all students and improve the campus.

When it implements a schoolwide program, a campus may consolidate federal, state, and local funds to implement the campus's campus improvement plan to upgrade its entire educational program (Section 1114[a][1]). In consolidating state and local funds with funds from Title I, Part A and most other federal elementary and secondary programs administered by the U.S. Department of Education, a schoolwide program campus does not need to meet most of the statutory and regulatory requirements of the federal programs included in the consolidation as long as it meets the intents and purposes of each of those programs (Section 1114[a][3][A], [B]).

Moreover, the campus is not required to maintain separate fiscal accounting records by program that identify the specific activities supported by those particular funds to demonstrate that the activities are allowable under the program (Section [a][3][C]). Each campus, however, must identify the specific programs being consolidated, and the amount each program contributes to the consolidation (Section 1114[b][2][A][iii]). The campus must also maintain records that demonstrate that the schoolwide program addresses the intents and purposes of each of the federal programs whose funds are consolidated to support the schoolwide program (Section 1114[a][3][C]).

SBDM - Campus Improvement Plan - CIP

Each school year the principal of each school campus, with the assistance of the campus-level committee (SBDM), must develop, review and revise the campus improvement plan. **The purpose of this plan is to improve student performance** on the state's student achievement indicators for all student populations, as well as improve performance on any other performance measures for special needs populations. **The campus improvement plan must be supportive of the objectives of the district improvement plan and must, at a minimum, support the state goals and objectives for education.** TEC 11.251

The campus improvement plan must:

- Assess the academic achievement for each student in the school using the student achievement indicator system as described by Section 39.053;
- Set the campus performance objectives based on the student achievement indicator system, including objectives for special needs populations, including students in special education programs under Subchapter A, Chapter 29;
- Identify how the campus goals will be met for each student;
- Determine the resources needed to implement the plan;
- Identify staff needed to implement the plan;
- Set timelines for reaching the goals;
- Measure progress toward the performance objectives periodically to ensure that the plan is resulting in academic improvement;
- Include goals and methods for violence prevention and intervention on campus;
- Provide for a program to encourage parental involvement at the campus and
- If the campus is an elementary, middle, or junior high school, set goals and objectives for the coordinated health program at the campus based on:
    o Student fitness assessment data, including any data from research-based assessments such as the school health index assessment and planning tool created by the federal Centers for Disease Control and Prevention;
    o Student academic performance data;
    o Student attendance rates;
    o The percentage of students who are educationally disadvantaged;
    o The use and success of any method to ensure that students participate in moderate to vigorous physical activity as required by Section 28.002(l); and
    o Any other indicator recommended by the local school advisory council.

Additional responsibilities for the Plan include:

- Comprehensive needs assessment - conducted to identify the strengths and weaknesses of existing programs, practices, procedures, and activities
- Total amount of state compensatory education funds allocated for resources and staff
- Identified strategies - aligned with the comprehensive needs assessment
- Supplemental financial resources for state compensatory education

- Supplemental FTEs for state compensatory education (This is not necessary if the school wide campus is at or above 40% and is combining SCE funds to support their Title I, Part A program.)

- Measurable performance objectives - stated in terms of what the student is expected to do and stated in terms of measurable and/or observable behavior to ensure that the plan is resulting in academic improvement

- Timelines for monitoring strategies and reaching goals – specific schedule for data collection during the school year

- Formative and summative evaluation criteria - Formative evaluation includes periodic measures that are utilized during the actual implementation of the interventions or strategies. The summative evaluation occurs at the end of the implementation period to provide the overall project and process evaluation.

Texas Law requires the campus improvement plan is the primary record supporting Expenditures attributed to the state compensatory education program.

School Health Advisory Council (SHAC)

CHAPTER 28.004. LOCAL SCHOOL HEALTH ADVISORY COUNCIL AND HEALTH EDUCATION INSTRUCTION.

It is important for the "new" administrator to realize that **the Campus Improvement SHAC uses outline below and is responsible for accomplishing the outline (below) at the site level.**

It is further advantageous to understand that the building principal will work within his/her campus SBDM and the SHAC at the district level. The state has determined that this school health committee design be integrated into the SBDM and be an active participant in the decision making process for the campus and the district.

A. The board of trustees of each school district <u>shall</u> establish a local school health advisory council to assist the district in ensuring that local community values are reflected in the district's health education instruction.
B. A school district <u>must</u> consider the recommendations of the local school health advisory council before changing the district's health education curriculum or instruction.
A. The local school health advisory council's duties include recommending:
   (1) the number of hours of instruction to be provided in health education;
   (2) curriculum appropriate for specific grade levels designed to prevent obesity, cardiovascular disease, and Type 2 diabetes through coordination of:
       (A) **health education;**
       (B) **physical education and physical activity;**
       (C) **nutrition services;**
       (D) **parental involvement; and**
       (E) **instruction to prevent the use of tobacco;**
   (3) appropriate grade levels and methods of instruction for human sexuality instruction; and
   (4) strategies for integrating the curriculum components specified by Subdivision (2) with the following elements in a coordinated school health program for the district:
       (A) school health services;
       (B) counseling and guidance services;
       (C) a safe and healthy school environment; and
       (D) school employee wellness.

D. The board of trustees shall appoint members to the local school health advisory council.
   A majority of the members must be persons who are parents of students enrolled in the district and who are not employed by the district. The board of trustees also <u>may</u> appoint one or more persons from each of the following groups or a representative from a group other than a group specified under this subsection:
   (1) public school teachers;
   (2) public school administrators;
   (3) district students;
   (4) health care professionals;
   (5) the business community;
   (6) law enforcement;
   (7) senior citizens;
   (8) the clergy; and
   (9) nonprofit health organizations.

E. Any course materials and instruction relating to human sexuality, sexually transmitted diseases, or human immunodeficiency virus or acquired immune deficiency syndrome shall be selected by the board of trustees with the advice of the local school health advisory council and must:

   (1) present abstinence from sexual activity as the preferred choice of behavior in relationship to all sexual activity for unmarried persons of school age;
   (2) devote more attention to abstinence from sexual activity than to any other behavior;
   (3) emphasize that abstinence from sexual activity, if used consistently and correctly, is the only method that is 100 percent effective in preventing pregnancy, sexually transmitted diseases, infection with human immunodeficiency virus or acquired immune deficiency syndrome, and the emotional trauma associated with adolescent sexual activity;
   (4) direct adolescents to a standard of behavior in which abstinence from sexual activity before marriage is the most effective way to prevent pregnancy, sexually transmitted diseases, and infection with human immunodeficiency virus or acquired immune deficiency syndrome; and
   (5) teach contraception and condom use in terms of human use reality rates instead of theoretical laboratory rates, if instruction on contraception and condoms is included in curriculum content.

F. A school district may not distribute condoms in connection with instruction relating to human sexuality. A school

G. district that provides human sexuality instruction may separate students according to sex for instructional purposes.

H. The board of trustees shall determine the specific content of the district's instruction in human sexuality.

I. A school district shall notify a parent of each student enrolled in the district of:

   (1) the basic content of the district's human sexuality instruction to be provided to the student; and
   (2) the parent's right to remove the student from any part of the district's human sexuality instruction.

I. A school district shall make all curriculum materials used in the district's human sexuality instruction available for reasonable public inspection.

J. A school district shall publish in the student handbook and post on the district's Internet website, if the district has an Internet website:

   1) a statement of the policies adopted to ensure that elementary school, middle school, and junior high school students engage in at least 30 minutes per school day or 135 minutes per school week of physical activity; and
   2) a statement of:
      a. the number of times during the preceding year the district's school health advisory council has met;
      b. whether the district has adopted and enforces policies to ensure that district campuses comply with agency vending machine and food service guidelines for restricting student access to vending machines; and
      c. whether the district has adopted and enforces policies and procedures that prescribe penalties for the use of tobacco products by students and others on school campuses or at school-sponsored or school-related activities.

K. **SHAC membership selection:**

   1) **There are primarily three methods for selecting SHAC members.**
      a. **recruitment**
      a. **appointment**
      b. **volunteer**

L. **Sources of SHAC members:**

   1) **Parents (majority – required by law)**
   2) **Medical professionals/ hospitals/clinics**
   3) **Social service agencies/public health agencies**
   4) **Business/industry**

5) **Volunteer health agencies**
6) **Churches/synagogues**
7) **Civic and service organizations/ professional societies**
8) **Colleges/universities**
9) **Public media: print/electronic**
10) **Attorneys and law enforcement officials**
11) **Schools: administrators, nurses, classroom, health/P.E. teachers, nutrition services managers**
12) **Youth groups/students**
13) **City/County/State government officials**

M. **Principal responsibilities within the SHAC:**

1) The school administrator attends SHAC meetings, keeps the superintendent informed and assists in the development of reports to the school board.

Site Based Decision Making and the Modern Principal

Principal's SBDM Responsibilities

Why is the SBDM important on the TExES?

Legal Foundations---Texas Education Code (TEC
- TEC -11.251 Planning and Decision Making Process

Level Planning and Decision Making
- 11.253 Campus Planning and Site

Based Decision Making ---Financial Accountability System Resource Guide
- Section 9.2.3 District and Campus Improvement Plans
- Section 9.2.7 Evaluation of SCE programs
- Section 9.4 Risk Assessment

Public Law (P.L.) 107
- 110 [NCLB}
- 1114 (b) Components of a Title I School Wide Program (SWP)
- 1115 (c) Components of a Title I Targeted Assistance Program

1. The TExES exam focuses much of its energy on the SBDM and the modern principal.

2. The logistical life of the campus is enveloped in the application of the SBDM process. **The SBDM and its positive application is the state's guide to management and leadership on the campus.** This belief is reinforced through the number of questions located on the TExES for first year administrators.

Site Based Decision Making
Structure of the SBDM And It's impact on the Campus

Below are a series of events that most principals have embedded in their brains. It would be wise to review and learn.

Student Achievement Scores are out and dispensed from the district office!

1. **The principal shall:**
   - Review the results and compare to the Campus Improvement goals.
   - Share the results with the faculty and department heads (in view of the Campus Improvement goals)
   - Share the report with the SBDM

2. **The SBDM shall:**
   - Compare the student results with the Campus Improvement Plans goals.
   - Establish a list of recommendations in lieu of those results.
   - This list shall impact the decision process of the campus budget.

3. **The principal shall:**
   - Review the recommendations of the SBDM
   - Begin the process of budgetary oversight in view of the new recommendations
   - With the support of the SBDM build a new budget that reflects the recommendations.
   - Establish a new or revised series of goals in view of the new recommendations.

4. **The SBDM Recommendation shall impact:**
   - Campus planning,
   - Budget
   - Staff development
   - Staffing patterns
   - School organizational patterns
   - Curriculum

SBDM and the Mental Picture of the First-Year Administrator

Overview of Site-based Decision Making

The basic premise of site-based decision making is that the most effective decisions are made by those who will actually implement the decisions. The belief is that people involved at the campus level have a greater opportunity to identify problems, develop problem resolution and change strategy than people located off-campus. Site-based decision making concepts also recognize that people at the campus level are more likely to internalize change and to support its implementation if they are involved in the decision making than if they are not.

The objective of site-based decision making is to improve student performance and to enhance accountability. Each campus should have the freedom to set its own educational objectives, consistent with the school district's goals.

* **All of the above information is developed into possible test questions on the TExES**.

Site-based Decision Making Initiative

Site-based decision making implementation has been *mandated for all Texas school districts since 1992*. TEA defines site-based decision making as follows:

> **Site-based decision making is a process for decentralizing** decisions to improve the educational outcomes at every school campus through a collaborative effort **by which principals, teachers, campus staff, district staff, parents, and community representatives assess educational outcomes of all students, determine goals and strategies,** and ensure that strategies are implemented and adjusted to improve student achievement.

The expected outcome of site-based decision making is improved student performance as a result of:

- Effective campus and school district planning for the purpose of improved student performance
- Improved community involvement in the school improvement process
- Clearly established accountability parameters for student performance
- Increased staff productivity and satisfaction
- Improved communication and information flow
- Consensus-based, decision making
- Pervasive and long-range commitment to implementation
- Increased flexibility at the campus level in the allocation and use of both human and fiscal resources
- Coordination of "regular" and special program or service components

Site-based decision making differs significantly from traditional school organization practices in the following ways:

Possible question on the TExES "How is the SBDM different than traditional?"

- Goals are determined on a campus level from a campus needs assessment and **outcome data----**

Possible question on the TExES "What drives the needs assessment?"

- Activities are self-initiated and self-directed by the campus staff
- Budget development and allocation of resources are campus-controlled

Possible question on the TExES "What drives the budget development?"

- Staff selection criteria are guided by standards developed by a campus within the context of state and district guidelines
- Campus organization structure is arranged functionally to encourage and facilitate shared team decision making and input
- The campus staff verify that site-based decision making is established and working
- The role of central administration in site-based decision making is that of support

"You must have long-range goals to keep you from being frustrated by short-range failures."
- Anonymous

SBDM Planning Cycle ---IMPACT OF DATA

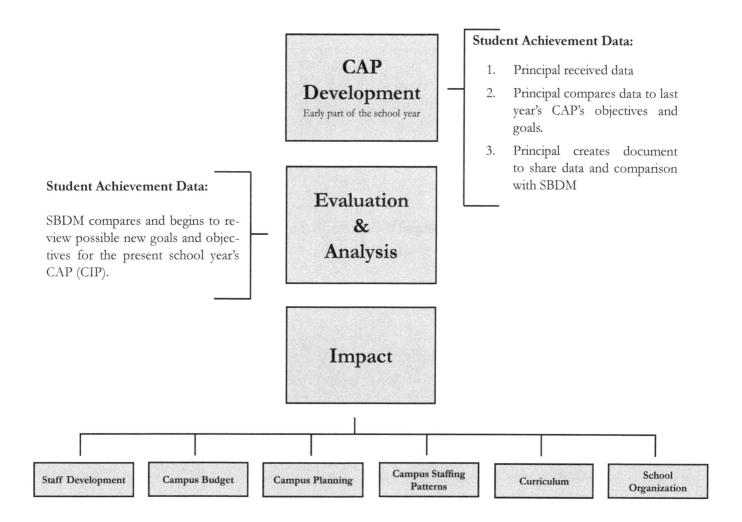

SBDM TAPR - Understanding Data Charts

Data visualization is a graphical representation of numerical data. The right data visualization tool can present a complex data set in a way that is simple to understand. A spreadsheet, which displays data in rows and columns (TAPR), is very useful for displaying small data sets. When the data set gets too large, however, it can be difficult for the viewer to grasp the relative significance of the data. The present TExES Principal exam is seeking to verify that the candidate for certification can understand and apply data from the TAPR data spreadsheet. This challenge comes in two forms. One is whether the candidate can ascertain which of the series of data pages will be used to clarify a scenario on the exam. Two is whether the candidate can read the spreadsheet and answer basic questions given in a scenario.

The TExES Student guide give great examples of the importance of knowing the "flow" of the data excel spreadsheets and their impact on the campus. The study guide gives four very valuable areas of importance that would be prudent to understand.

Basic questions that require a good understanding of the details in the data stream or spreadsheets:

1. If you are asked to identify the areas in the TAPR that are used to indicate equal opportunities for all students to succeed are evident. Where would that be?
   - The data set that indicates the differences between White students an other identified students subgroups. (grade sheets pages 1-3)

2. If you are asked to identify the areas in the TAPR that indicate the variables that affect and have the most influence on achievement for all students. Where would that be?
   - The data set that indicates and has the most influence on academic performance would be <u>socioeconomic status.</u>

3. If you were asked to determine which area of the TAPR should be used to determine teacher development. Where would that be?
   - The data sets indicating formative assessment that monitors student understanding.

4. If you were asked to indicate what personnel would likely be most helpful for achieving equal opportunities for all students. What should be the first answer?
   - Teaching staff and numbers that mirror the ethnic makeup of the student body.

Basic data understanding of the TAPR. You will also have basic questions about data.

1. Where would you locate ethnic distribution?
   - Student information sheet (pg. 7) middle of the page.

2. Where would you locate at-risk numbers?
   - Student information sheet (pg. 7) bottom of the page.

3. Differing grade group scores?
   - All grades page 1-3.

4. Economically disadvantaged comparison between state, district, and campus?
   - Student information sheet (pg. 7) bottom of the page.
   - Specifics are located on pages 1-2 and comparisons on pages 5-6.

5. Where would you locate class size comparison between state, district, and campus?
   - Student information page 8

Breakdown of the TAPR Charts * definitions provided below

STAAR Data – Pages 1-5

Attendance Data – Page 6

Student Information – Page 7
- Students by Grades
- Ethnic Distribution
- Economically Disadvantaged
- Non-Educationally Disadvantaged *
- ELL
- Student w/Disciple Placement *
- At-Risk *
- Mobility *

Student Information – Page 8
- Retention Rates
- Class Size

Staff Information – Page 9
- Professional Staff Breakdown
- Educational Aides
- Total Minority Staff
- Total Gender Breakdown
- Teachers by Years of Experience
- Number of students per teacher

Staff Information – Page 10
- Average Teacher Salaries
- Average Teacher Salaries by experience
- Instructional Staff
- Campus Admin

Program Information – Page 11
- Student enrollment by program
- Teachers by program

At-Risk: The count and percentage of students identified as being at risk of dropping out of school as defined by TEC §29.081(d) and (d-1).

For purposes of this section, "student at risk of dropping out of school" includes each student who is under 26 years of age and who:

(1) was not advanced from one grade level to the next for one or more school years;

(2) if the student is in grade 7, 8, 9, 10, 11, or 12, did not maintain an average equivalent to 70 on a scale of 100 in two or more subjects in the foundation curriculum during a semester in the preceding or current school year or is not maintaining such an average in two or more subjects in the foundation curriculum in the current semester;

(3) did not perform satisfactorily on an assessment instrument administered to the student under Subchapter B, Chapter 39, and who has not in the previous or current school year subsequently performed on that instrument or another appropriate instrument at a level equal to at least 110 percent of the level of satisfactory performance on that instrument;

(4) if the student is in prekindergarten, kindergarten, or grade 1, 2, or 3, did not perform satisfactorily on a readiness test or assessment instrument administered during the current school year;

(5) is pregnant or is a parent;

(6) has been placed in an alternative education program in accordance with Section 37.006 during the preceding or current school year;

(7) has been expelled in accordance with Section 37.007 during the preceding or current school year;

(8) is currently on parole, probation, deferred prosecution, or other conditional release;

(9) was previously reported through the Public Education Information Management System (PEIMS) to have dropped out of school;

(10) is a student of limited English proficiency, as defined by Section 29.052;

(11) is in the custody or care of the Department of Protective and Regulatory Services or has, during the current school year, been referred to the department by a school official, officer of the juvenile court, or law enforcement official;

(12) is homeless, as defined by 42 U.S.C. Section 11302, and its subsequent amendments; or placement facility in the district, including a detention facility, substance abuse treatment facility, emergency shelter, psychiatric hospital, halfway house, or foster group home.

(d-1) Notwithstanding Subsection (d)(1), a student is not considered a student at risk of dropping out of school if the student did not advance from prekindergarten or kindergarten to the next grade level only as the result of the request of the student's parent.

Mobility (*campus profile only*): The count and percentage of students who have been in membership at a school for less than 83% of the school year (i.e., missed six or more weeks). This rate is calculated at the campus level. The mobility rate shown in the "district" column is based on the count of mobile students identified at the campus level. The district mobility rate reflects school-to-school mobility within the same district or from outside the district.

Non-Educationally Disadvantaged: Those students not eligible to participate in free or reduced-price lunch or to receive any other public assistance. This is the complementary count and percentage to Economically Disadvantaged.

Students with Disciplinary Placements: The count and percentage of students placed in alternative education programs under Chapter 37 of the Texas Education Code (Discipline; Law and Order). Districts report the disciplinary actions taken toward students who are removed from the classroom for at least one day. Although students can have multiple removals throughout the year, this measure counts students only once and includes only those whose removal results in a placement in a disciplinary alternative education program or juvenile justice alternative education program

SBDM - Budgeting

SBDM - Budgeting

Budgeting is the process of allocating resources to the prioritized needs of a school district. Although budget formats and policies are by no means uniform in school districts, formal budgets play a far more important role in the planning, control and evaluation of school district operations than in those of privately owned organizations. In school districts, the adoption of a budget implies that a set of decisions has been made by school board members and school district administrators which culminate in matching a school district's resources with its needs. As such, the budget is a product of the planning process. The budget also provides an important tool for the control and evaluation of a school district's sources and uses of resources. With the assistance of the accounting system, administrators are able to execute and control the activities that have been authorized by the budget and evaluate performance based on comparisons between budgeted and actual operations.

A challenge for school officials are the appropriate identification of the "problem(s)" to be addressed when developing a budget and making decisions about staffing and financial allocations. Herbert Simon, author of many books on public administration, like *Administrative Behavior: A Study of Decision-Making Processes in Administrative Organizations*, explains that decision-making processes are facilitated when based upon a rigorous review of data and information, similar to activities involving engineering and scientific processes. **Decisions about personnel management issues and financial allocations <u>should be based on data or evidence relating to the academic performance of students and the effectiveness of academic programs</u>**, in addition to data explaining relative operating efficiencies of all instructional support and administrative functions. It is necessary to make comparisons between districts and campuses that have similar characteristics to obtain useful information about potential management issues. Software applications that benchmark academic and performance statistics are available from various sources. Decision-making processes in school districts are complex, and administrative, and governance decisions are not effective if the "problem(s)" is (are) not adequately identified before making decisions about resource allocations.

Importance is placed upon sound budget planning for the following reasons:

- The type, quantity, and quality of school district goods and services often are not subject to the market forces of supply and demand. The budget becomes the limiting force.

- These goods and services (e.g. instruction) are critical to the public interest.

- The scope and diversity of school district operations make comprehensive planning necessary for good decision-making.

- Planning is a process that is critical to the expression of citizen preferences and through which consensus is reached among citizens, school board members, and district/campus staff on the future direction of a district's operations.

The link between planning and budget preparation in school districts gives budgets a unique role in these organizations. Budgets in the public arena are often considered the ultimate policy document since they are the financial plan a school district uses to achieve its goals and objectives reflecting:

- Public choices about what goods and services the district will and will not produce.

- School districts' priorities among the wide range of activities in which they are involved.

- Relative weight is given to the influence of various participants and interest groups in the budget development process.

- How a school district has acquired and used its resources.

NOTE: The budget, itself, then becomes intrinsically a political document reflecting school district administrators' <u>accountability for fiduciary responsibility to citizens</u>.

In the educational context, budgeting is a valuable tool for both planning and evaluation processes. **Budgeting provides a vehicle for translating educational goals and programs into financial resource plans**. Thus, instruction planning (to attain student educational goals) should determine budgetary allocations. This link between instruction and financial planning is critical to effective budgeting. In addition, such a budgeting practice may enhance the evaluation of budgetary and educational performance since resource allocations are closely associated with instructional plans.

Objectives of Budgeting

Performance evaluation allows citizens and taxpayers to hold policymakers and administrators accountable for their actions. Because accountability to citizens often is stated explicitly in state laws and constitutions, it is considered a cornerstone of budgeting and financial reporting. The Governmental Accounting Standards Board (GASB) recognizes its importance with these objectives in its *GASB Concepts Statement No. 1*:

- Financial reporting should provide information to determine whether current-year revenues were sufficient to pay for current-year services.

- Financial reporting should demonstrate whether resources were obtained and used in accordance with the entity's legally adopted budget. It should also demonstrate compliance with other finance-related legal or contractual requirements.

- Financial reporting should provide information to assist users in assessing the service efforts, costs and accomplishments of the governmental entity.

Meeting these objectives requires budget preparation to include several concepts recognizing the accountability. Often these concepts have been mandated for state and local public sector budgets. They include requirements that budgets should:

- Be balanced so that current revenues are sufficient to pay for current services.

- Be prepared in accordance with all applicable federal, state, and local legal mandates and requirements.

- Provide a basis for the evaluation of a government's service efforts, costs, and accomplishments.

Budget Process Overview

The budgeting process is comprised of three major phases:
1. Planning,
2. Preparation
3. Evaluation

The budgetary process begins with sound planning. Planning defines the goals and objectives of campuses and the school district and develops programs to attain those goals and objectives. Once these programs and plans have been established, budgetary resource allocations are made to support them. Budgetary resource allocations are the preparation phase of budgeting. The allocations cannot be made, however until plans and programs have been established.

Finally, **the budget is evaluated** for its **effectiveness in attaining goals and objectives**. Evaluation typically involves an examination of how funds were expended, what outcomes resulted from the expenditure of funds, and to what degree these outcomes achieved the objectives stated during the planning phase. This evaluation phase is important in determining the following year's budgetary allocations. In summary, budget preparation is not a one-time exercise to determine how a school district will allocate funds. Rather, school district budget preparation is part of a continuous cycle of planning and evaluation to achieve district goals.

Budgetary Approaches

Over the past thirty years, a variety of budget types and formats have been utilized by school districts in the U.S. The development of more advanced budget philosophies reflects growth in both the scope and complexity of government operations and the need for systems which are capable of translating the variety of policy decisions into financial plans. Those **currently being used by school districts are:**

1. Line-item or "traditional" budgeting
2. Performance budgeting
3. Program and Planning, "programming" budgeting (PPB)
4. Zero base budgeting (ZBB)
5. **Site-based budgeting**

A single budgetary approach may be effective; however, many governments use a variety of hybridized versions of the four basic ones depending on their needs. Each of the five basic approaches has relative advantages and limitations.

For those students who wish to study the budgeting process, in detail, I recommend, "The Principal's Guide to School Budgeting," by Richard Sorenson and Lloyd Goldsmith.

Site-Based Budgeting

In recent years, educational leaders have sought to enhance the ability of principals to serve as effective instructional leaders. This effort has led to the development of a budgetary approach (which may be used in combination with any of the four discussed above) which emphasizes the decentralization of budgetary decision making, broadly referred to as site- based budgeting. **Site-based budgeting places the principal and other campus staff at the center of the budget preparation process. Principals act as budget managers for their individual schools, responsible for both the preparation and maintenance of the campus budget.**

Site-based budgeting, as its name implies, generally involves the granting of increased budgetary authority to the campus level. Campuses are normally allocated a certain level

of resources over which they have authority to allocate to educational and support services. These budgetary allocations are meant to cover those areas over which campus decision- makers have control. For example, campuses which have authority over staffing decisions would be allocated funds for staff costs. In contrast, campuses in a school district where staffing decisions are made centrally may not be granted funds for staff costs. These staff costs would be budgeted at the district level. As shown by this example, site-based budgeting takes many forms and may be implemented by school districts to varying degrees.

The main advantage of site-based budgeting is that it allows school personnel to make budgetary decisions on their own campuses. Thus, those whom best understand student needs at the campus level plan how funds are used to meet them. This decentralization of budgetary authority may also be a means of increasing school accountability. Another potential advantage of site-based budgeting is increasing the level of participation of both campus staff and parents in budget development. Many site-based budgeting systems create committees composed of campus staff, parents and other community members to determine campus budgetary allocations. These committees give parents and other community members a voice in school budgeting from its inception, rather than merely when the budget is presented for public review by the district board.

Legal requirements for school district budgets are formulated by the state, TEA, and the local district. In addition to these requirements, individual school districts also may have their own legal requirements for budget preparation. Additional legal requirements also may be imposed by state and federal grants; however, this section deals only with *state legal mandates, TEA legal requirements and local district requirements* for basic budget development and submission.

1. The summary of the budget should be presented in the following function areas: (A) Instruction – functions 11, 12, 13, 95
2. Instructional Support – functions 21, 23, 31, 32, 33, 36
3. Central Administration – function 41
4. District Operations – functions 51, 52, 53, 34, 35 (E) Debt Service – function 71
5. Other – functions 61, 81, 91, 92, 93, 97, 99

The "per student" will be based on student enrollment.

Annual Budget Responsibilities and Guidelines

The development of campus and district annual budgets should be part of ongoing planning processes at those levels. **The advent of site-based decision-making, mandated by the state, has increased integration of planning and budgeting at the campus level;** however, state guidance allows for considerable district autonomy in budget preparation. The organizational structure of a school district, the size and complexity of its administrative structure, the budgetary approach chosen, and the level of centralization in budget development all will affect the budget development process and the final budget document. Beyond the budgetary requirements for federal and state programs, a school district's budget preparation process and the related budget responsibilities largely will be determined by the school board and the district superintendent. The concept of site-based budgeting, endorsed by TEA, is the recommended approach outlined in this section.

Roles and Responsibilities

The budget preparation process and guidelines should be established through interaction between the school board and the superintendent. Thus, the delegation of budget responsibilities among district administrators (district-wide) and individual campuses (site- based) will reflect the consensus of the school board and the superintendent.

Exhibit 3 is an example of site-based budgeting roles and responsibilities used by a Texas school district. **This example includes the following individuals and groups which are involved in budget development:**

Campus Level:
1. **Campus staff**
2. **Resource Planning Groups (RPG) (or equivalents)**
3. **Campus resource planning groups composed of campus staff and/or special program administrators (nominated by school principals)**
4. **Campus Improvement Committees (CICs) - Campus resource planning groups composed of elected campus staff, community members, and parents**
5. **Principals (School Budget Managers)**

Development of Campus Budgets

The development of campus level budgets follows the budget preparation guidelines which are issued by the superintendent. While the revenue side of the district budget is prepared by district administrators, campus level budgets become the basis for the expenditure side of the district budget as that information filters up through the various levels of review. Additional budgeted expenditures for costs which are centrally budgeted such as debt service and interest costs normally are added when the district-wide preliminary budget is compiled.

Although a campus may receive an allocation of district resources based upon standard allocation formulas, the budgeting of these resources, exclusive of legal mandates, is at the discretion of the campus under the site-based decision making model. Consistent with the outcome focus, the development of campus budgets should evolve from the planning process. As such, campus budgeting should begin with the identification of a school's goals and objectives by the school's resource planning group (RPG) or equivalent (e.g. the campus improvement committee - CIC), as a first step in the campus budget development process. **These goals and objectives should be driven by the educational needs of the campus (i.e. instruction). In addition, the school's goals and objectives should be developed in accordance with long-term district educational goals and campus improvement plans.**

Budget Decentralization

Budget decentralization places the authority to make decisions related to the allocation of resources at the school level. This process gives each school the opportunity to identify and target the varied resources available to it and make decisions about how best to utilize these resources. Decisions about the use of resources involve more than financial resources. These decisions also include considerations relating to the use of people, time, information and technology. Simply stated, a decentralized system of budgeting allows schools to select the resources they need to meet the needs of their specific student population.

SBDM BUDGET CODE (Examples)

NOTE: You need to understand this material!

199-11-6399-00-001-X-11-0-00

Fund/Group	**199**
Function	**11**
Object	**6399**
Local Option Code 1 and 2	00
Organization	001
Fiscal Year	X
Program Intent Code	11
Local Option Code 3	0
Local Option Code 4 and 5	00

- Question: How is the expenditure financed?

- Answer: Fund/Group Code - **199** (e.g., general fund, special revenue funds, etc.; based on the definitions discussed in the Account Codes section).

- Question: Why was the expenditure made?

- Answer: Function Code - **11 or 12 or 13** - the fourth and fifth digits in the code structure. These are used exclusively for recording expenditures (e.g., instruction, Cocurricular/extracurricular activities, etc.).

- Question: What was purchased?

- Answer: Object Code - **6399** - these four-digit codes are the sixth through ninth digits in the code structure. These codes classify the item as a particular asset, liability, equity, revenue, expenditure, other resources or other uses.

Note: Must Remember:

A principal may **transfer** budgeted funds from Supplies and Materials (Object 6300) to Other Operating Costs (Object 6400) within Instruction (Function 11) without formal board approval. A request to **amend** funds from Supplies and Materials (Object 6300) in Function 11 to Supplies and Materials in Function 12 for a campus would require official board approval (SBDM Manual, 2017).

> *"Today's preparation determines tomorrow's achievement."*
> — Anonymous

Site Based Budgeting and the Principal

A major management process which should **be adopted is site-based budgeting**. The concept of site-based budgeting provides for input from community members, teachers, and other campus staff in the resource allocation decisions which affect their respective schools. Although site-based decision making allows for the involvement of these individuals in formulating campus goals, objectives and plans, site-based budgeting takes the process a step further by delegating more authority over financial resources to campus decision makers. Thus, site-based budgeting is more flexible than traditional budgeting because it decentralizes budgetary decision making to those individuals who best understand the needs of individual schools.

The principal is responsible for developing and maintaining the campus budget. Principals should work with campus planning groups (or their equivalents), department heads, and campus improvement teams to determine campus resource allocation and to develop non-allocated requests. Principals may also act as the representative of the campus in school district budget meetings as campus resource allocations and non-allocated requests are reviewed and approved. Because the budget provides financial resources necessary for the achievement of the campus goals, the principal is responsible for directing these resources to their most effective use.

The school principal or other designated campus administrator is primarily responsible for site-based budgetary accounting procedures. The principal or campus administrator is often assisted by grade-level principals, assistant principals, secretaries, clerks or volunteers. All personnel performing site-based accounting procedures should be familiar with the SBDM portion of the budget manual and other local-district guidance. Everyone should strive for the correct, consistent and concise application of site-based accounting procedures.

Financial accounting procedures performed at each campus by campus-level personnel are:
- Supplies and materials ordering
- Capital asset purchasing
- Cash receipting
- Petty cash accounting
- School and student activity fund accounting

Common among each of these broad accounting areas is the need to classify transactions for proper accounts (e.g., coding a purchase order and recording the proceeds received from candy sales).

* While specific question pertaining to the budget process have NOT been reported on the TExES the IMPLIED continued importance of everything <u>located IN the SBDM manual indicates</u> that this will change as test writers move to continue to improve the TExES exam.

<u>Major Committees of the SBDM</u>

- Budget
- Curricula
- Teacher In-service and training
- Site Health Action (SHAC)
- Homeless
- Safety and Emergency Preparedness
- others as designated

Campus Budget and the Modern Principal
TEA Budget Manual #14
SBDM Manual

The proper coding of the budget and classification of expenditures is critical for the accurate oversight of a school's budget. Time should be invested in training <u>the campus staff to ensure their understanding of the budgetary account structure and specific rules</u> associated with the use of special funds (e.g., federal grants). Because with site-based budgeting most budget activity is initiated at the campus, **campus budget managers must know what funds are available and how the available funds can be used**. Some school districts provide simple definitions of account code segments along with examples of classification of common expenses as part of their site-based budgeting documentation. Campus budget managers may be granted the authority (at the discretion of the school district board) to move budgeted funds from one expenditure object to another within a function. For example, a principal may transfer budgeted funds from Supplies and Materials (Object 6300) to Other Operating Costs (Object 6400) within Instruction (Function 11) without formal board approval. A request to amend funds from Supplies and Materials (Object 6300) in Function 11 to Supplies and Materials in Function 12 for a campus would require official board approval.

Fund code describes where the money is coming from. Often times, the fund is specific to a particular population as well and thus also represents a population that can be served. But this is not always the case. A mandatory 3-digit code (**box 1 in the Account Code Structure diagram**) is to be used for all financial transactions to identify the fund type:

The Code Structure

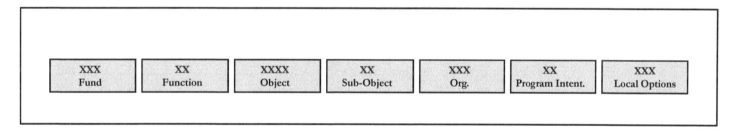

Function Codes are grouped according to related activities in the following major areas/classes:

The FUNCTION CODES are broken down further to identify the expenditure or expense **purpose**. Example the function code of 10. The code 10 indicates that funds within this code "range" can be used for Instruction and Instruction-Related Services. NOW while this indicates what general area these funds are identified it does not describe specifically. SO, the second digit "0" becomes the identifier for the budget manager. Example the function code of 10 indicates money for instruction BUT if the code is 11 then this clearly identifies the funds to pull (expenditure) are being removed from the overall function line of instruction but the identifier of "1" also now indicates the money is being spent for a specific AREA within instruction (see examples below).

10	Instruction and Instructional-Related Services (11,12 & 13)
20	Instructional and School Leadership (21 & 23)
30	Support Services – Student (Pupil) (31,32,33,34,35 & 36)
40	Administrative Support Services (41)
50	Support Services – Non-Student Based (51,52 & 53)
60	Ancillary Services (61)
70	Debt Service (71)
80	Capital Outlay (81)
90	Intergovernmental Charges (93,95 & 99)

Each of these major areas is further defined by detail function codes. **The code is required for PEIMS reporting purposes if such costs apply to the school district.**

Function 10 Instruction and Instruction-Related Services

Function 11 – Instruction

This function includes those activities dealing directly with the interaction between teachers and students. Teaching may be provided in a classroom or other learning situations. It is used for expenditures for direct classroom instruction and activities that deliver, enhance or direct the delivery of learning situations to students. **NOTE: Any teacher/instructional classroom aide substitutes, including substitutes used during staff development, will be coded to function 11.**

- Professional staff tutoring students (11)
- Auxiliary staff tutoring students (11)
- "Consultants" for student presentations (11)
- Access to online websites for instruction (11)
- Reading Materials for instructional use (11)
- Supplies for instructional use (11)
- Yellow school bus for instructional field trips (11)
- Student entrance fees for instructional field trips (11)

Function 12 – Instructional Media & Resources

This function is used for expenditures/expenses that are directly and exclusively used for resource centers, establishing and maintaining libraries and other major facilities dealing with educational resources and media.

Most position/departments using function 12:
- Librarian
- Library Aide
- Library
- Media Aide
- Media Center
- Campus Techs

Function 13 – Curriculum/Instructional Staff Development

This function includes those expenditures that are directly and exclusively used to aid instructional staff in planning, developing and evaluating the process of providing learning experiences for students. This includes in-service training and other staff development for instructional related personnel. Caution-do not include any teacher substitutes used during training.

This is coded to function 11. Most position/departments using function 13:
- Campus Instructional Specialist
- District Instructional Specialist
- Elementary Curriculum Department
- Secondary Curriculum Department

Function 20 -- Instructional and School Leadership

Function 21 – Instructional Leadership

This function is used for expenditures/expenses that are directly used for managing, directing, supervising and providing leadership for staff **who provide general and specific instructional services**.

Most positions/departments using function 21:
- Assistant Superintendent's Office
- Executive Director for Secondary Schools' Office
- Executive Directors for Elementary Schools' Office
- Administrative for Special Education Office

Function 23 – School Leadership

This function covers those expenditures/expenses, which have as their **purpose directing, managing, and supervising schools, i.e., campus principal's office and related costs**.

NOTE: Function 23 can only be used in a campus budget and not in a department budget.

Most positions/activities using function 23:
- Campus Principals
- Campus Assistant Principals
- Campus Secretaries
- Campus Improvement Plan
- Campus-wide Activities for staff

Function 30 -- Student Support Services

Function 31 – Guidance, Counseling & Evaluation Services

This function incorporates those activities, which have as their purpose assessing and testing pupils' abilities, aptitudes, and interests; counseling pupils with respect to career and educational opportunities, and helping them establish realistic goals. Includes costs of psychological services, identification of individual characteristics, testing, educational counseling, student evaluation and occupational counseling, and activities involved in maintaining information the course of study for each student.

Most positions/activities using function 31:
- Counselors
- Counseling Department/Office
- Assessment & Accountability
- Standardized Testing
- Diagnosticians

Function 32 – Social Work Services

This function encompasses those activities related to promoting and improving school attendance of students. Also, includes investigating and diagnosing student social needs arising out of the home, school or community; casework and group work services for the child, parent or both; interpreting the social needs of students for other staff members; and promoting modification of the circumstances surrounding the individual student which are related to his or her social needs.

Most positions/activities using function 32:
- Social Workers
- Attendance Officers/Department

Function 33 -- Health Services

This function is used to provide health services, which are not a part of direct instruction. Note this function is not used for speech, health, physical, or occupational therapy to assist special education students in the learning process. Those go to function 11.

Most positions/activities using function 33:
- Nurses, Clinic Aides, Campus Health Clinics
- Health Services Department

Function 34 -- Student (Pupil) Transportation – **Campuses will not use this**

This function covers the cost of providing management and operational services for regular school bus routes that transport students to and from school. Note this function is used only by the Transportation Department.

Function 35 -- Food Services – **Campuses will not use this**

This function encompasses activities, which have as their purpose the management of the food services program of the school or school system. Note this function is used only by the School Nutrition Department. Campuses will not use this.

Function 36 -- Extra-Curricular

This function is used for expenditures for school- sponsored activities outside of the school day. These activities are generally designed to provide students with experiences such as motivation and the enjoyment and improvement of skills in either a competitive or noncompetitive setting

Extracurricular activities include athletics and other activities that normally involve competition between schools (and frequently involve offsetting gate receipts or fees such as football, baseball, volleyball, track and tennis). Other kinds of related activities are included (such as drill team, pep squad and cheerleading, University Interscholastic League competition such as one-act plays, speech, debate, band, Future Farmers of America (FFA), National Honor Society, etc.).

Note: band instruments are charged to function 11 not to function 36.

Most positions/activities using function 36:

- Athletic department
- Athletic events/items
- Competitions
- Items for Resale

SBDM Budget - Redirection on the Campus

Because with site-based budgeting most budget activity is initiated at the campus, campus budget managers must know what funds are available and how the available funds can be used. Some school districts provide simple definitions of account code segments along with examples of classification of common expenses as part of their site-based budgeting documentation (SBDM Manual, 2017).

The school district's board adopted district budget projects available resources and how those resources are to be channeled to best meet student needs. <u>Unforeseen events or changes in priorities</u> which occur during the year often <u>require redirection of funds</u>. The budget is not intended to hinder these changes. **Rather, procedures** should be established which allow for necessary amendments to the school district budget (SBDM Manual, 2017).

As a result, budget amendments at the <u>campus level must be submitted for board approval when they affect fund or function totals at the district level</u>. Campus budget managers may be granted the authority (at the discretion of the school district board) to **move budgeted funds from one expenditure object to another within a function** (SBDM Manual, 2017).

For example, a principal may **transfer** budgeted funds from Supplies and Materials (Object 6300) to Other Operating Costs (Object 6400) within Instruction (Function 11) without formal board approval. A request to **amend** funds from Supplies and Materials (Object 6300) in Function 11 to Supplies and Materials in Function 12 for a campus would require official board approval (SBDM Manual, 2017).

Function 10 Instruction and Instruction-Related Services

Function 11 – Instruction – 6300 series of codes

This function includes those activities dealing directly with the interaction between teachers and students. Teaching may be provided in a classroom or other learning situations. It is used for expenditures for direct classroom instruction and activities that deliver, enhance or direct the delivery of learning situations to students. NOTE: Any teacher/instructional classroom aide substitutes, including substitutes used during staff development, will be coded to function 11.

- Professional staff tutoring students (11)
- Auxiliary staff tutoring students (11)
- "Consultants" for student presentations (11)
- Access to online websites for instruction (11)
- Reading Materials for instructional use (11)
- Supplies for instructional use (11)
- Yellow school bus for instructional field trips (11)
- Student entrance fees for instructional field trips (11)

Function 12 – Instructional Media & Resources -- 6300 series of codes

This function is used for expenditures/expenses that are directly and exclusively used for resource centers, establishing and maintaining libraries and other major facilities dealing with educational resources and media. Most position/departments using function 12:

- Librarian
- Library Aide

- Library
- Media Aide
- Media Center
- Campus Techs

Function 13 Curriculum/Instructional Staff Development – 6300 series of codes

This function includes those expenditures that are directly and exclusively used to aid instructional staff in planning, developing and evaluating the process of providing learning experiences for students. This includes in-service training and other staff development for instructional related personnel. Caution-do not include any teacher substitutes used during training. This is coded to function 11. Most position/department using function 13:

- Campus Instructional Specialist
- District Instructional Specialist
- Elementary Curriculum Department
- Secondary Curriculum Department

Looking at the above and understanding that the State wants you to be able to know the movement of funds on your campus. A basic question was asked by a student. "I am a little confused about the budget codes. I was reading and it's stated in our manual that funds can be transferred from Object 6300 to other functions within that object; without board approval. So, what codes are within 6300?"

What codes are within 6300? To answer that question, you must return to the SBDM Manual. It states for you! The codes are the list above. Easy! What you must remember is you can TRANSFER funds inside an existing budget code. You can never AMEND funds. Don't get those confused.

For example:
A principal may transfer budgeted funds from Supplies and Materials (Object 6300) to Other Operating Costs (Object 6400) within Instruction (Function 11) without formal board approval. A request to amend funds from Supplies and Materials (Object 6300) in Function 11 to Supplies and Materials in Function 12 for a campus would require official board approval (SBDM Manual, 2017).

SBDM Budget : Rural and Low-Income School Programs

The purpose of the **Rural and Low-Income School** (RLIS) or **Rural Education Achievement Program** (REAP) grant program is to provide rural districts with financial assistance for initiatives aimed at improving student achievement. The grant is non-competitive, and eligibility is determined by statute.

LEAs that receive RLIS grants may use the funds to carry out the following types of activities:

- Teacher recruitment and retention, including the use of signing bonuses and other financial incentives;

- Teacher professional development, including programs that train teachers to use technology to improve teaching and that train teacher of students with special needs;

- Parental involvement activities;

- Title I-A (Improving Basic Programs Operated by local education agencies)

    o Example: A school district develops an entrepreneurial education program to supplement its civics curriculum.

- Title II-A (Supporting Effective Instruction)

    o Example: A school district pays the stipend for a prospective teacher to work alongside an effective teacher, who is the teacher of record, for a full academic year.

- Title III (Language Instruction for English Learners and Immigrant Students)

    o Example: A school district offers an afterschool enrichment program for English learners.

- Title IV-A (Student Support and Academic Enrichment)

    o Example: A school district purchases bully prevention materials for all schools.

Note – Why is this material important? What if I ask," Your SBDM has asked you to locate funds for a new bully prevention program on the campus. Where would you locate the funds with the district finance officer?"

You may locate additional information at the following website: **https://www2.ed.gov/programs/reaprlisp/index.html**

Year Long Budget Process

Sept 16	Administration meets with the superintendent's Budget and Finance Advisory Committee to discuss the FY 20XX-20XX budget process.
Sept 21	Budget request templates are disseminated to all central department. • The board initiates the budget process with discussion on the approach for the FY 20XX-20XX budgeting process. Set initial budget parameters, and budget development calendar.
Sept 28	Budget hearing begin
Oct 19-23	Departments submit budget request for state mandated required increased expenditures. • Example: Mandatory increase (state request) spending on Special Service by 2% for the FY 20XX-20XX.
Oct - Feb	Discussion with Principals on budget priorities, student needs and options to address priorities. • What information would you use begin the discovery process early in August or September? TAPR and your Campus Improvement Plan
Oct	**Meeting with Principal to develop staffing formula recommendations for board action.**
Oct	Board reviews budget development and staffing formulas
Nov	Board approves budget development and staffing formulas
Nov – Jan	**Administration meets with Principal's to go over the budget development process, options on program reductions and balancing for FY 2016-117 budget.**
Nov - Jan	**Administrative staff conducts campus budget workshops**
Feb	Campuses submit budgets • By this time, you are also reviewing and discussing contracts for the next year!
Apr.	Superintendent present FY20XX-20XX <u>preliminary budget</u> to the board and public
May	Community meetings on the <u>preliminary budge</u>
May	Superintendent present FY20XX-XX <u>recommended budget</u> to the board
June	Board conducts community meetings on the <u>recommended budget</u>
June	Board adopts FY20XX-XX recommended budget with amendments
June	State reviews and accepts the recommended budget for the district (required).

SBDM Activity Funds and the Modern Principal

Activity funds are defined as funds consisting of resources received and held by the school as trustee to be expended or invested in accordance with conditions of the trust. Specifically, they are funds accumulated from various school-approved money-raising activities and the receipt of student dues or fees, commissions, investment interest and donations. These funds are to be used to promote the general welfare of the school and the educational development and morale of all students. All funds collected by school district personnel from students are defined as activity funds and must be handled through the activity funds accounts (SBDM, pg. 42).

The responsibility for activity funds involves principals, staff such as the school secretary or clerk, fund sponsors and auditors. The <u>responsibilities are</u> that of:

- **The school principal, or designate**, who is personally responsible for the proper collection, disbursement and control of all activity funds at the school. This responsibility includes providing for the safekeeping of funds at the school.

- Money on hand at the end of the school day ideally should be placed in a night depository at the school's bank. If this is not feasible, the principal should store the money in a locked, secured area.

- The principal is not responsible, however, for funds collected, disbursed and controlled by parents, patrons or alumni organizations, and these funds should not be accounted for in a school district's activity funds (i.e., Parent Teacher Organizations, athletic and band booster's clubs, etc.).

- The school secretary/clerk who is responsible for maintaining an adequate supply of various activity fund forms. This person should be responsible for issuing cash receipt books as needed to teachers and other persons authorized by the school principal. This clerk must keep a distribution record of all receipt books issued, which is part of the official activity fund records. The school secretary/clerk is commonly responsible for the depositing of activity funds into the bank, accounting and reporting for activity fund activities and cash management (if the school district uses a decentralized activity fund method).

- The individual activity fund sponsors who are responsible for managing their respective activity funds. This responsibility can include developing fund raising plans, monitoring the financial position of the activity fund, reviewing the activity fund financial statements, safekeeping activity fund money until it is deposited by the school district and other fiduciary responsibilities.

Campus-Based Personnel Financial Accounting Responsibilities

Financial accounting procedures performed at each campus by campus-level personnel are:

- Supplies and materials ordering
- Capital asset purchasing
- Cash receipting
- Petty cash accounting
- **School and student activity fund accounting**

Common among each of these broad accounting areas is the need to classify transactions for proper accounts (e.g., coding a purchase order and recording the proceeds received from candy sales).

Activity Fund Receipts

Cash receipts records are the means of accurately recording cash received and provide support to substantiate each bank deposit. Most school districts use pre-numbered cash receipts books or other similar forms to record all cash and/or checks received. In order to maintain effective cash control, if possible, at least two persons should be involved in the functions of collecting cash and receipting cash. The person who collects the cash should not be responsible for receipting cash receipts.

Activity Fund Receipts

Cash receipts records are the means of accurately recording cash received and provide support to substantiate each bank deposit. Most school districts use pre-numbered cash receipts books or other similar forms to record all cash and/or checks received. In order to maintain effective cash control, if possible, at least two persons should be involved in the functions of collecting cash and receipting cash. The person who collects the cash should not be responsible for receipting cash receipts.

The procedures that should be followed for activity fund receipting are:

- An official receipt should be prepared immediately for any cash and/or checks received. Receipts should be issued in pre-numbered sequence and should be prepared in ink. The school district should not accept postdated checks.

- A form that includes details about the payer and a description of the receipt should be **completed for cash receipts.**

- An actual cash count by the person signing the receipt should be made in the presence of the person turning in the money. The total of cash and checks should be **shown separately on the cash receipt.**

- The maker of a check must be indicated on the receipt if the maker is someone other than the person turning in the money. The account name should be placed on each check.

- A copy of the receipt should be given to the person paying the money.

- Originals of receipts must be retained in the activity fund **cash receipt book.**

- Under no circumstances should a receipt amount or the signature be altered. If either of these errors occurs in the preparation of a receipt, void the receipt and issue a new receipt.

- The original of the voided receipt must remain attached in the activity fund cash receipt book. The principal should approve the voiding of a receipt by signing the original receipt.

- Receipts are not to be pre-signed or predated.

- Deposit slips should include receipt numbers to allow for a proper audit trail for the disposition of all pre-numbered receipts.

Activity Fund Disbursement Vouchers

To limit irregularities, all expenditures **should be paid by pre-numbered check** from the activity fund checking account. In addition, checks made out to "cash" or to the paying school should never be issued. Many school districts require two signatures on the checks to further limit the possibility of irregularities.

Income received from a specific group should be expended for that group. No expenditure of funds should be approved by the principal unless sufficient funds are available in the appropriate activity account. Some school districts allow for transfers as loans between two or more activity funds. When transfers as loans occur, the school district should ensure that appropriate approvals have been received and that the loans are repaid by the end of the school year in which the loan was granted.

Petty Cash Funds

A petty cash fund may be established at the discretion of the principal for the purchase of small, miscellaneous items. Disbursements from petty cash funds should not exceed the school district's preset limit for petty cash purchases, and employee and other checks should not be cashed from petty cash funds.

All activity fund petty cash fund procedures should adhere to the school district's petty cash accounting policies. Original invoices or other suitable documentation must be obtained for all petty cash expenditures and should be defaced after payment.

Transfers of Funds between Activity Accounts

Some activity funds are revenue producing by their very nature (i.e. vending machine accounts, interest accumulation accounts) and many school districts routinely transfer these proceeds to other activity funds. **Any transfer of moneys between accounts should be approved by the school principal** as well as the involved activity fund sponsors.

> *"Whatever the cost of our libraries, the price is cheap compared to that of an ignorant nation."*
> - Walter Cronkite

Special Education and the Responsibilities of the Modern Principal

Special Education and the ARD Responsibilities of the Modern Principal

Procedural Safeguards

The *Procedural Safeguards* document addresses the specific rights and responsibilities of the parent in the special education process under the IDEA. The document, written in English and Spanish, defines common terms and explains specific rights related to activities and areas that impact a student's educational program and services

Parents will receive a copy of the Procedural Safeguards for the following activities:
1. Initial referral for evaluation
2. Each notification of an ARD meeting
3. Reevaluation of the student
4. Receipt of a request for due process hearing.

* make sure the parents get these copies—during conversations with the parents "bring it up" to make sure!!!

Basic Questions for the Principal

When is an ARD meeting necessary?
An ARD is needed for initial placement or any time the school staff or parents feel a change is needed in a student's special education program. The IEP must be reviewed at least once a year, but an ARD meeting may be held at other times. For example, an ARD will need to be held to review additional assessment.

When is written notice required for an ARD meeting?
Parents are entitled to receive their written notice at least five school days before the meeting is scheduled to take place.

When may the requirement for written notice be waived?
Sometimes it might be necessary to have an ARD meeting without waiting for the written notice but such situations should not happen very often. This usually happens if there is an emergency, but parents can refuse to waive the notice requirement.

Can an ARD meeting be held without the parent?
Parents are strongly encouraged to attend and be involved in their child's ARD meeting. Great efforts are made to schedule the ARDs during times that are convenient for both the parents and the school. In cases where the parents cannot attend, they usually have given permission for the school to proceed without them.

Participants of the ARD Meeting

At a minimum, the committee must include the following:
1. A representative from the local school district administration, someone designated and authorized to commit the

district's resources to implement the IEP. Often, the building principal, assistant principal or counselor serves in this role.

2. A teacher from general instruction
3. A teacher from special education
4. The student's parents, guardian, or designated representative
5. The student, when appropriate
6. A representative of the special education assessment team

Other specific types of professionals for students with specific disabilities (for example, a professional certified in education of the deaf, when a student with auditory impairment is being considered), or when other specialized needs (for example, vocational instruction or Limited English Proficiency) will be discussed.

NOTE: Participants should have some knowledge of the child to be discussed or some other involvement in the decisions being considered.

Discipline-related School Removals:

- Under IDEA, a free appropriate public education (FAPE) must be made available to all children with disabilities between the ages of 3 and 21, inclusive, including children who have been suspended or expelled from school, as provided in 34 CFR §300.530(d). See 20 USC §1412(a)(1) and 34 CFR §300.101(a).

- Therefore, students with disabilities removed from their current placements through suspension or expulsion must continue to receive educational services so as to enable them to continue to participate in the general education curriculum, although in another setting, and to progress toward meeting their Individualized Education Program (IEP) goals. See 34 CFR §300.530(d).

Short-term Removals for 10 Consecutive Days or Less

- Disciplinary removals for 10 consecutive school days or less do not trigger the requirement to hold an ARD committee meeting or conduct a manifestation determination.

- The school is only required to provide services to your child during a short-term removal if it provides services to a child without disabilities who is similarly removed.

NOTE: Do NOT allow beyond 10 days. Watch the discipline records!! If the student has more than "accumulated" 10 days, this will trigger a 'concern' through the PEIMS. So watch this.

Cumulative Removals Totaling 10 Days or More

- School officials may order additional short-term removals (not more than 10 consecutive school days) in the same school year for separate incidents of misconduct, provided that these removals do not constitute a change of placement.

- After the child, has been removed for 10 cumulative school days in the same school year, if the current removal is not for more than 10 consecutive school days and is not a change of placement, the school must provide services so as to enable the child to continue to participate in the general education curriculum, although in another setting, and to progress toward meeting the goals set out in the child's IEP.

- School personnel must consult with at least one of the child's teachers to decide which services are needed.

NOTE: Sometimes it is best to go ahead and get the ARD involved. You do NOT have to make these decisions by yourself!

SPECIAL EDUCATION
ARD Committee Decision-Making Process for the Texas Assessment Program

Purpose of the ARD

For students receiving special education services, assessment decisions are made by the admission, review, and dismissal (ARD) committee.

Who Needs to Be Trained on the Campus Level?
- Principal and other administrators
- Testing Coordinators and Test administrators
- Educational diagnosticians
- Licensed Specialist in school Psychology
- Counselors
- Teachers
- Special Education Personnel (Bilingual/ESL)
- Parents

Overview of Assessment Decisions

When making assessment decisions, the members of the ARD committee must weigh the benefits of rigorous and challenging expectations for the possibilities of success, given each student's individual strengths, needs, instruction, and accommodations. Keeping these high standards in mind, the <u>ARD committee determines the annual measurable goals</u> to be documented in each student's IEP and <u>chooses the assessment that best matches the educational needs of each student</u>. It is important to emphasize that the academic instructional decisions made by the ARD committee and documented in the IEP must always guide assessment decisions.

The Four Steps: Making Assessment Decisions

In order to make appropriate assessment decisions, the ARD committee should follow these steps:

1. Review the student's present level of academic achievement and functional performance (PLAAFP).
2. Review the student's instructional plan, including accommodations, modifications, or supports the student will need in order to access the grade-level TEKS.
3. Determine the appropriate assessment for the student: TAKS, TAKS (Accommodated), TAKS–M, or TAKS–Alt.
4. Document the appropriate assessment, including the accommodations or supports the student will need during the assessment.

Changing the Assessment Decision during the School Year

The ARD committee has the responsibility to make appropriate assessment decisions based on the needs of the student. As part of the ongoing process of monitoring the special education program for a student, the ARD committee may feel the assessment decision made at a previous meeting needs to be **revised because of a change in the student's instructional plan**. This change may be due to:

- A difference in how the student accesses the grade-level curriculum
- A revision of the student's instructional goals, or
- The addition or removal of certain accommodations. **Simply passing or failing a state assessment is not a sufficient reason to justify revising the assessment decision in the IEP.**

Any changes to assessment decisions must be considered carefully because the requirements of different assessments may impact a student (e.g., SSI requirements for multiple testing opportunities, requirements for graduating on the Recommended or Distinguished high school program).

The Student Success Initiative (SSI)

The Student Success Initiative (SSI) was enacted by the 76th Texas Legislature in 1999.

The SSI is composed of three initiatives that together support:
- Texas Reading Initiative,
- Texas Mathematics Initiative, and
- Grade advancement requirements in reading at grades 3, 5, and 8 and in mathematics at grades 5 and 8

The role of the ARD committee in making decisions about student's subject to SSI requirements is defined in the Texas Administrative Code (19 TAC §101.2003). For the students described in 19 TAC §101.2003, an ARD committee must make decisions regarding **appropriate:**

1. Assessment,
2. Accelerated instruction, and
3. Grade placement based on a student's specific disability-related needs.

The ARD committee decision regarding grade placement **does not have to be unanimous** but must follow the general rules governing ARD committee decision-making as set forth in **19 TAC, Chapter 89, Subchapter AA**.

Special Education and Change of Placement

If the school proposes a removal that will constitute a change of placement due to the student's violation of the code of student conduct, school officials must notify the parent of that decision and provide the parent with a copy of the Notice of Procedural Safeguards. This must be done on the date on which the decision is made to change the child's placement. Also, the school must arrange for a meeting of the ARD committee to determine whether the conduct was a manifestation of the child's disability.

Manifestation Determination Review (MDR)

Within 10 school days of any decision to change the placement of the student due to a violation of the code of student conduct, the ARD committee must meet and conduct an MDR.

When conducting an MDR, **the ARD committee must** review all relevant information in the student's file, including the IEP, any teacher observations, and any relevant information provided by the parent. The parent may present any relevant information at this time for the ARD committee to review when making the determination whether the student's conduct is a manifestation of his or her disability.

The ARD committee must then answer both of the following questions:

- Was the conduct in question caused by, or did it have a direct and substantial relationship to, the student's disability?
- Was the conduct in question the direct result of the school's failure to implement the IEP?

When Conduct is a Manifestation

If the ARD committee answers "yes" to either of the above questions, the conduct is a manifestation of the child's disability. In that event, the committee must either:

- Conduct a functional behavioral assessment (FBA), unless the school had conducted an FBA before the behavior that resulted in the change of placement occurred, and implement a behavior intervention plan (BIP), or
- If a BIP is already in place, review the BIP and modify it as necessary to address the behavior.

Also, if the committee concludes that the student's conduct was caused by the school's failure to implement the IEP, the school must take immediate steps to remedy the deficiencies.

If the ARD committee concludes that the student's behavior is a manifestation of his or her disability, the committee must return the student to the placement from which the student was removed unless: the parent and the school agree to a change of placement as part of the modification of the child's BIP, or the student's violation of the code of student conduct involves one of the "special circumstances" described below.

When Conduct is Not a Manifestation

If the ARD committee concludes that the student's conduct was not a manifestation of his or her disability, school personnel may discipline the student in the same manner as other children, except appropriate educational services must continue.

The child's ARD committee will determine the IAES in which the child will be served. In Texas, the IAES may be a disciplinary alternative education program (ARD Manual, pg. 14 and 15).

Special Education

I.E.P. Changes

SB (Senate Bill) 1259

Students with delayed skills or other disabilities will be eligible for special services that provide individualized education programs in public schools, free of charge to families.

The updated version of the Individuals with Disabilities Education Act (IDEA 2004) made parents of students with special needs even more crucial members of their child's education team.

Parents can now work with educators to develop a plan — the individualized education program (IEP) — to help students succeed in school. The IEP describes the goals the team sets for a child during the school year, as well as any special support needed to help achieve them.

There are four specific changes:

1. It requires that every district must have "a process" that can be used by any teacher who <u>instructs a student with a disability</u> to have "input in the development of the student's IEP."
2. It specifies that the "regular education teacher" who is a member of the ARD must "to the extent practicable, <u>be a teacher who is responsible for implementing</u> a portion of the child's IEP."
3. It specifies that the written documentation of the ARD meeting must include <u>the date</u> of <u>the meeting, the name, position,</u> and <u>signature of each member participation in the meeting</u> and "an indication of whether the child's parents, the adult student if applicable, and the administrator agreed or disagreed with the decisions of the committee."
4. Each member of the ARD committee who disagrees with the IEP development is entitled to include a statement of disagreement.

Key Point! Document, Document, Document – Remember, if it is not on paper, it is vapor!

> *"The quality of an individual is reflected in the standards they set for themselves."*
>
> *- Ray Kroc (founder of McDonalds)*

Special Education – Extended School Year (ESY)

Extended School Year Services—an individualized instructional program for eligible students with disabilities that are provided beyond the regular school year. The need for ESY services must be determined **on an individual basis** by the admission, review, and dismissal (ARD) committee.

Some students with disabilities have difficulty retaining skills during long school holidays and/or summer. (This is your definition for ESY—know it!) If a student requires a significant amount of time to recoup mastered skills, then the ARD committee should discuss whether the student needs extended educational and/or related services during school breaks.

The determination of whether a child will receive **ESY services will be made by the ARD committee**; and the individualized education program (IEP) developed for ESY must include goals and objectives.

Legal References Regarding ESY Services | Federal Regulations
Individuals with Disabilities Education Act (34 CFR Part 300)
300.309. **Extended school year services.**
§ (a) General.
  (1) Each public agency shall ensure that extended school year services are available as necessary to provide FAPE, consistent with paragraph (a)(2) of this section.

  (2) Extended school year services must be provided only if a child's IEP team determines, on an individual basis, in accordance with §§300.340-300.350, that the services are necessary for the provision of FAPE to the child.

  (3) In implementing the requirements of this section, a public agency may not—

   i. Limit extended school year services to particular categories of disability; or

   ii. **Unilaterally limit the type, amount, or duration of those services.**

(b) **Definition. As used in this section, the term extended school year services means special education and related services that—**

  (1) **Are provided to a child with a disability—**
   i. **Beyond the normal school year of the public agency;**

   ii. **In accordance with the child's IEP; and**

   iii. **At no cost to the parents of the child; and**

  1) **Meet the standards of the SEA.**

Related Services:
a) General. As used in this part, the term related services means transportation and such developmental, corrective, and other supportive services as are required to assist a child with a disability to benefit from special education, and includes speech-language pathology and audiology services, psychological services, physical and occupational therapy, recreation, including therapeutic recreation, early identification and assessment of disabilities in children, counseling services, including rehabilitation counseling, orientation and mobility services, and medical services for diagnostic or evaluation purposes. The term also includes school health services, social work services in schools, and parent counseling and training.

b) Individual terms defined. The terms used in this definition are defined as follows: (15) Transportation includes—

  (a) Travel to and from school and between schools;

  (b) Travel in and around school buildings; and

  (c) Specialized equipment (such as special or adapted buses, lifts, and ramps), if required to provide special transportation for a child with a disability.

Special Education Process -- Timeline

(15-45-30)

Initial Request for Referral made by Parent

Parent makes a **written request** to school for an evaluation to determine special education eligibility.

- Response - 15 school days of written request

Consent and Notice of Evaluation or Prior Written Notice given to Parent

Schools must provide a parent with an opportunity to provide written consent for the evaluation or if the school refuses to conduct the evaluation, the school must provide parent a notice of their procedural safeguards that explain their rights under the law.

- **Response – 45 school days of receipt of written signed consent.** School absence of 3 or more days will impact the response time. Must meet the 45-day response time.
    - **Full Initial Individual Evaluation (FIIE) Completed** - Assessing all areas of suspected disability
    - **Notice of ARD Meeting** - Provided to parent at least 5 days prior to ARD meeting
    - **ARD Meeting and Consent for Initial Placement** - To determine eligibility for special education, development of IEP and determine placement
- Response time – **within 30 calendar days see the differing time frame—CALENDAR Days**

Important notes:

- School days does not include any day a student is not in school including holidays, weekends, and staff development days.
- Review the entire process of parental rights at: Disability Rights Texas
- School days does not include any day a student is not in school including holidays, weekends, and staff development days.
- Review the entire process of parental rights at: Disability Rights Texas Web Site

Title Grants

Title Grants and the School Principal

TEA Data

Required for all independent school districts:

There are three major title grants that affect your campus; they are:
- Title I – Priority School Grants
- Title II – Teacher and Principal Training
- Title III – Language Instruction

The principal shall:

Principal - Has parent, teacher, student, counselor, and paraprofessional meetings, conferences, and walk-throughs. The Principal also communicates through corresponds through emails, newsletters, and flyers to have an up-to-date assessment of needs. In addition, the Principal reviews various data reports to desegregate the student and teacher gaps, barriers, and weaknesses.

The Principal will work with the district assigned personnel to assist with the day-to-day operations to ensure successful implementation and operation of the grant programs; provide guidance, support, training, and resources to campus personnel; assist in submitting financial and grant progress reports, and approve budget expenditures with the business office personnel.

The Principal will work closely with the teachers in reviewing and approving curriculum that is aligned with the state requirements and Title Programs. The campus administration will hold themselves accountable for meeting the Districts Annual Performance Goals and TEA's Performance Assessment and Evaluation targets. Benchmarks with target timelines will be set for each funding cycle.

Data collection will be developed to track the quarterly activities that show appropriate evidence of implementation, evaluation of the implementation, and evaluation of timelines. The following data will be tracked for each activity.

1. Academic Performance, including (but not limited to) Reading/ELA and Mathematics
   - Data-driven instruction
   - Curriculum Alignment (both horizontal and vertical)
   - On-going Monitoring of Instruction
2. Use of Quality Data to Drive Instruction
   - Data Disaggregation /Training
   - Data-driven Decisions
   - On-going Communication
3. Leadership Effectiveness
   - On-going Job Embedded Professional Development
   - Operational Flexibility
   - Resource/Data Utilization

4. Learning Time
    - Flexible Scheduling
    - Instructionally-focused Calendar
    - Staff Collaborative Planning
5. Parent/Community Involvement
    - Increased Opportunities for Input
    - Effective Communication
    - Accessible Community Services
6. School Climate
    - Increased Attendance
    - Decreased Discipline Referrals
    - Increased Involvement in Extra/Co-Curricular Activities
7. Teacher Quality
    - Locally Developed Appraisal Instruments
    - On-going Job Embedded Professional Development
    - Recruitment/Retention Strategies

Title I:
Funds provided will help schools with high concentrations of students from low income families provide a high-quality education that will enable all children to meet the state's student performance standards.

Title II:
Funds will be used to promote teacher and principal quality through strategies such as high quality professional development in core subject areas and development of mechanisms and initiatives to promote the retention and hiring of highly qualified teachers and principals, including class size reduction.

Title III:
Funds used English language instruction educational programs provided after school or on Saturday. Professional development for regular classroom teachers; teachers of LEP students, administrators, educational personnel, and personnel from community based education organizations on topics such as instructional strategies for LEP students, understanding assessment for LEP students, alignment of curricula and state standards, and subject matter knowledge for teachers. Parental involvement activities designed to assist parents of LEP students to them work with their children to their children's achievement.

Title I, Part A - Improving Basic Programs

The Improving Basic Programs Operated by Local Education Agencies effort in Title I, Part A of the Elementary and Secondary Education Act (ESEA), as amended by the No Child Left Behind Act (NCLB), provides supplemental funding to state and local education agencies. This funding pays for resources to assist schools with high concentrations of students from low-income families. These resources improve education quality and help ensure all children in low-income contexts meet the state's student performance standards. Title I, Part A provides support to schools in implementing either a school-wide program or a targeted assistance program. Title I, Part A programs use effective methods and instructional strategies that are grounded in scientific research (hhttp://tea.texas.gov, 2016).

Section 1114 of Title I of the ESEA allows a school in which 40 percent or more of its students are from low-income families to use its Title I funds, along with other Federal, State, and local funds, to operate a schoolwide program to upgrade the entire educational program in the school to improve the academic performance of all students, particularly the lowest-achieving students. [Section 1114(a)(1)] To operate a schoolwide program, a school must conduct a comprehensive needs assessment of the entire school and, using data from the needs assessment, develop a comprehensive plan that meets the requirements of the ESEA and §200.27 of the Title I regulations. [Section 1114(b); 34 CFR 200.27] A school operating a schoolwide program is not required to identify specific students as eligible to participate in the schoolwide program, or to demonstrate that the services provided with Title I funds are supplemental to services that would otherwise be provided. [Section 1114(a)(2)] This is in contrast to a targeted assistance program, in which Title I funds may be used only for supplementary educational services for children identified as being most at risk of not meeting State standards. [Section 1115(a)]

Using Title, I Schoolwide Programs to Support School Reform

A Title I schoolwide program is a comprehensive reform strategy designed to upgrade the entire educational program in a Title I school with a poverty percentage of 40 percent or more in order to improve the achievement of the lowest-achieving students (ESEA section 1114(a)(l)).

- **Any Title I school with 40 percent or more of its students living in poverty, regardless of the grades it serves, may operate a schoolwide program.**
- An SEA may request a waiver for certain schools to operate a schoolwide program without meeting the 40 percent poverty threshold through:
- The School Improvement Grants (SIG) program in a Tier I or Tier II school that receives SIG funds to implement one of the SIG intervention models; and
- ESEA flexibility in a priority school or focus school that implements interventions designed to enhance the entire educational program of the school.

Implementing a Schoolwide Program

There are three basic components of a schoolwide program that are essential to effective implementation:

- Conducting a comprehensive needs assessment of the entire school, using academic achievement data and perception data from school staff, parents, and others in the community. Using a systematic method, such as root-cause analysis, this comprehensive needs assessment should identify the major problem areas that the school needs to address.

- Preparing a comprehensive schoolwide plan that describes how the school will improve academic achievement throughout the school, but particularly for the lowest-achieving students, by addressing the major problem areas identified in the comprehensive needs assessment This plan may be integrated into an existing improvement plan.

- Annually reviewing the schoolwide plan, using data from the State's assessments, other indicators of academic achievement, and perception data to determine if the school wide program has been effective in addressing the major problem areas and, in turn, increasing student achievement, particularly for the lowest-achieving students. Schools need to annually revise the plan, as necessary, to ensure continuous improvement.

Title I School May use the program for:

- Title I funds may be used in a school wide reading and math instruction. program to support academic areas that the school's needs assessment identifies as needing improvement.

- The purpose of a schoolwide program is to remedial instruction. upgrade the entire educational program in the school in order to raise the achievement of the lowest-achieving students.

- At times, this may be best achieved by preparing low-achieving students to take advanced courses for example, providing an intensive summer school course designed to accelerate their knowledge and skills, offering an elective course to prepare them to take advanced courses, or providing after-school tutoring while they are taking advanced courses.

- Title I funds may be used to upgrade the achieving students. entire educational program in a school and, in doing so, all students may benefit from the use of Title I funds. However, consistent with the purpose of Title I, the reason to upgrade the entire educational program in a school is to improve the achievement of the lowest achieving students.

- Title I funds may be used to upgrade the entire educational program in a school and serve all students.

- Title I funds may be used for activities and strategies designed to raise the achievement of low-achieving students identified by a school's needs assessment and articulated in the school's comprehensive schoolwide plan. Title I children below kindergarten or the age of funds to operate, in whole or in part, a compulsory education. preschool program to improve cognitive, health, and social-emotional outcomes for children below the grade at which the LEA provides a free public elementary education.

McKinney-Vento Homeless Assistance Act

The McKinney-Vento program addresses the problems that homeless children and youth have faced in enrolling, attending, and succeeding in school. Under this program, State educational agencies (SEAs) must ensure that each homeless child and youth has equal access to the same free, appropriate public education—including a public preschool education—as other children and youth. LEAs must ensure homeless students have access to the services they are entitled to so they are empowered to achieve the same state academic standards required of all students. Homeless children and youth should be integrated into the student body at large and may not be separated from the mainstream school environment. States and districts are required to review and undertake steps to revise laws, regulations, practices, or policies that may act as a barrier to the enrollment, attendance, or success in school of homeless children and youth.

Title II and Teacher Professional Development

The purpose of Title II, Part A is to help Texas school districts ensure that all students have effective teachers; that is, teachers with the subject-matter knowledge and teaching skills necessary to help all children achieve high academic standards, regardless of individual learning styles or needs. In this regard, the program provides funding to help LEAs recruit, train, reward, and retain effective teachers. Title II, Part A and Title I, Part A also place particular emphasis on the need for LEAs to ensure that teachers of a core academic subject meet certain minimum requirements they need to become effective educators. The requirements to be considered "highly qualified" are that teachers hold at least a bachelor's degree, be fully certified in Texas, and demonstrate competency in the core academic subject area they are teaching.

Section 1119(a)(1) and (3)]. (TEA Policy Guidance-Improving Teacher Quality, 2016).

What is meant by "high-quality professional development"?

The term "high-quality professional development" means professional development that meets the criteria contained in the definition of professional development in Title IX, Section 9101(34) of NCLB. Professional development includes, but is not limited to, activities that:

- Improve and increase teachers' knowledge of academic subjects and enable teachers to become highly qualified;
- Are an integral part of broad schoolwide and districtwide educational improvement plans;
- Give teachers and principals the knowledge and skills to help students meet challenging State academic standards;
- Improve classroom management skills;
- Are sustained, intensive, and classroom-focused and are not one-day or short-term workshops;
- Advance teacher understanding of effective instruction strategies that are based on scientifically based research; and
- Are developed with extensive participation of teachers, principals, parents, and administrators.

What are some options by which LEAs can implement professional growth activities?

Too often, the best career advancement option currently available for teachers is to become school principals or LEA administrators. This leaves fewer excellent, experienced teachers working directly with children in the classroom. Teacher advancement initiatives that offer multiple career paths can provide professional opportunities without having teachers leave the classroom. For example, an LEA could establish a system whereby teachers could opt to pursue various career paths, such as:

- Becoming a career teacher, staying in the classroom with traditional instructional duties;
- Becoming a mentor teacher, staying in the classroom but taking on additional duties such as mentoring first-year teachers and receiving additional pay for these duties; or
- Becoming an exemplary teacher, based on a distinguished record of increasing student academic achievement, and training other teachers to do the same while receiving additional pay for these duties.

Does the law contain any restrictions on the amount of Title II, Part A funds that an LEA may spend on professional development?

No. However, in considering how to spend its funds, the LEA should focus on its need to ensure that all teachers who teach in core academic subjects meet the requirements for a highly-qualified teacher.

How can rural districts address teacher professional growth needs?

One possible way that rural districts can provide teachers with professional development activities is by offering distance-learning opportunities. Many colleges and universities may currently offer distance learning. Through distance learning a teacher in a rural area can take professional development courses that meet his/her specific needs.

What types of professional development can assist existing teachers to develop and demonstrate subject-matter competency?

- Participation in institutes, workshops, seminars, conferences, in-service or staff development activities given by an approved provider or sponsor, which are related to or enhance the professional knowledge and skills of the educator;

- Participation in interactive distance learning, video conferencing, or on-line activities or conferences;

- Independent study, not to exceed 20 percent of the required points, which may include self-study or relevant professional materials (books, journals, periodicals, video and audio tapes, computer software, and on-line information), or authoring a published work;

- Development of curriculum or CPE training materials;

- Teaching or presenting a CPE activity, not to exceed 10 percent of the required points;

- Providing professional guidance as a mentor educator, not to exceed 30 percent of the required points; and

- Serving as an assessor under TAC §241.35 (relating to the Principal Certificate), not to exceed 10 percent of the required points.

> *"Even when I went to the playground, I never picked the best players. I picked guys with less talent, but who were willing to work hard, who had the desire to be great."*
> - Earvin "Magic" Johnson

Title III, Part A

Title III, Part A of the Elementary and Secondary Education Act (ESEA), as reauthorized under the No Child Left Behind Act of 2001 (NCLB), aims to ensure that English language learners (ELL) and immigrant students attain English language proficiency and meet the state's challenging academic achievement standards.

Is it allowable to use Title III funds to pay for administrative costs?

Yes, it is allowable to use Title III funds to pay for administrative costs to implement the Title III program. However, the amount of Title III funds which may be used to pay administrative costs to implement the program must not exceed 2% of the program's entitlement amount (carryover is not included when calculating the 2% max.). In calculating total administrative costs subject to the 2% limit, all appropriate indirect and direct costs, such as administrative salaries, must be included. If the local education agency (LEA) contracts with an outside vendor to provide Title III services, the LEA must require that the contractor break out administrative costs, which are included within the 2% limit, as well.

Can Title III funds be used to pay 100% for a Bilingual/ESL Coordinator position that will assist with the monitoring and coordinating of all district and campus bilingual and ESL programs? The coordinator will also manage all student assessment data to ensure that effective interventions are occurring. The coordinator will also assist the campuses with all the district, state, and federal compliance issues. Coordination between campus administrators, classroom teachers, and the bilingual coordinator will occur to support the ongoing monitoring of student achievement. The position is supplemental to the daily practices that are occurring at each campus.

This is not allowable. The position duties as described are required by policy guidance under the Bilingual Education Allotment (BEA) and/or are federally/state mandated. It may possibly be allowable if split funded with local funds, however any duties performed that would be funded under T3A must be supplemental to local and state requirements as well as be supplemental to the Title I, Part A program.

Can Title III funds be used for extra duty pay for staff to carryout Title III-specific activities?

As long as the activity is Title III-specific and supplemental (and meets all other supporting conditions, such as necessary and reasonable, etc.), it is allowable.

NOTE: Use of the term, "extra-duty pay," typically refers to payment to staff already paid through the same program in question.

Can Title III funds be used to support sending staff to ELL-specific professional development (e.g., ELPS, LPAC, TELPAS, etc.) by paying for substitute teachers or extra-pay if the training is held outside the staff's work hours (e.g., after school, Saturday, etc.)?

One factor in determining if this is an allowable use of funds is that it must be supplemental.

If the training helps to fulfill a local, state, or other federal requirement, then it is not supplemental and, thus, would not be an allowable use of Title III funds. Examples to consider include:

- English Language Proficiency Standards (ELPS) – LEAs are required by the State to implement the ELPS, just as they are required to implement the TEKS (the State's curriculum standards); thus, training that is part of how the LEA meets this requirement is not supplemental. If, however, the training is provided above and beyond the LEA's plan for ensuring implementation of the ELPS, then it may be supplemental.

- Language Proficiency Assessment Committee (LPAC) – LEAs are required by the State to implement the LPAC process; thus, training that is a part of how the LEA meets this requirement is not supplemental.

- Texas English Language Proficiency Assessment System (TELPAS) – LEAs are required by the State to implement the TELPAS; thus, training that is part of how the LEA meets this requirement is not supplemental. If, however, the training is provided for a purpose above and beyond the processes required by the State, then it may be supplemental. For example, training that is solely on how to use student TELPAS data to inform or improve instruction of LEP students may be supplemental.

If the training is supplemental; it would be an allowable use of Title III funds if it reflects the remaining factors:

- Addressed in the application

- Extra duty (and substitutes pay, if for substitutes) is checked for Title III in budget schedule; and

- The professional development is specified in PS3106; if staff is attending a conference, the conference name is included under OTHER or Additional Information.

- Benefits LEP students – The participants serve LEP students.

- Costs are necessary and reasonable

Can an LEA use Title III funds for a Language Translator or Interpreter?

Whether this is allowable would depend on the exact responsibilities of the translator or interpreter, since Title III funds must only be used to supplement the level of federal, state, and local public funds that, in the absence of such availability, would have been expended for programs for LEP children.

For example, translation of instructional materials or instruction in a language other than English would not be an allowable use of Title III funds, since it falls under the LEA's responsibility, under Lau v. Nichols* (OCR) to offer ELLs services to help them overcome their language barriers and to ensure that ELLs have equal access to education and educational excellence.

This also applies to translation of general information for the LEA (e.g., translating information for the Spanish language version of the LEA website, newsletter, or other communications, translating information related to the LEA data system and to the State's achievement assessments, etc.).

If, however, the translation/interpreting is for a purpose above and beyond the level of other federal (including OCR and Title I, Part A), state, and local requirements, then this may be an allowable use of Title III funds. Possible examples would be to provide interpretation during a Title III parent involvement meeting or event or providing translation of materials to be used for supplemental parent classes, etc.

Such an example may be an allowable use of funds, provided that all supporting conditions were met.

NOTE: These pages are but a small section of the rules and responsibilities of the District and Campus Administrators. Please take time to review all of the Title information located in the TEA Web Site.

Title IV, Part A

Safe and Drug-Free Schools and Communities

The purpose of Title IV, Part A, Safe and Drug-Free Schools and Communities Act (SDFSCA) is to support programs that prevent violence in and around schools; that prevent the illegal use of alcohol, tobacco, and drugs; that involve parents and communities; and that are coordinated with related Federal, State, school, and community efforts and resources to foster a safe and drug-free learning environment that supports student academic achievement. http://tea.texas.gov/About_TEA/Laws_and_Rules/NCLB_and_ESEA/Title_IV_Part_A_-_Safe_and_Drug_Free/Title_IV_Part_A_-_Safe_and_Drug-Free_Schools_and_Communities/

Resource and Topics related to Title IV, Part A:

Alcohol

- stopalcoholabuse.gov – This link gives access to a portal to Federal resources on underage drinking.

Bullying

- http://www.esc14.net/preview.aspx?name=bullying – Provides information to school districts, parents, and students to help prevent, identify, and respond to bullying behavior
- http://www.education.com/topic/school-bullying-teasing – This site includes a list of peer-reviewed articles related to bullying.
- www.stopbullying.gov – This site offers practical advice to students and parents about ways to respond to bullying at school.

Health Education at TEA

- http://www.cdc.gov/HealthyYouth/health_and_academics/index.htm – This site includes resources on the link between healthy students and academics.
- http://www.wholechildeducation.org/about/ – Available at this site is information regarding the Whole Child Approach to Education by the Association for Supervision and Curriculum Development.

Tobacco

- http://www.dshs.state.tx.us/tobacco – This site provides information on tobacco prevention and control.
- http://www.cdc.gov – This site allows access to the weekly Morbidity and Mortality Reports from the Center for Disease Control.

Trauma

- http://www.samhsa.gov/trauma-violence – This Substance Abuse & Mental Health Services Administration web page addresses the impact of trauma on individuals, families, and communities as a behavioral health concern that requires a healing and recovery process.

Violence

- http://www.cdc.gov/mmwr/preview/mmwrhtml/rr5607a1.htm?s_cid=rr5607a1_e – This site contains the most recent (2007) report of the Task Force on Community Prevention Services on "The Effectiveness of Universal School-Based Programs for the Prevention of Violent and Aggressive Behaviors."
- http://www.promoteprevent.org – This site allows access to the National Center for Mental Health Promotion and Youth Violence Prevention.
- http://www.cops.usdoj.gov – This site hosts useful resources on such topics as gangs, school safety, and underage drinking.

Title VII, Part A

It is the purpose of Title VII to support the efforts of local educational agencies, Indian tribes and organizations, postsecondary institutions, and other entities to meet the unique educational and culturally related academic needs of **American Indian and Alaska Native students**, so that such students can meet the same challenging State student academic achievement standards as all other students are expected to meet. http://tea.texas.gov/About_TEA/Laws_and_Rules/NCLB_and_ESEA/Title_VII/Title_VII

When may a district receive funds under Title VII?

A local educational agency shall be eligible for a grant under this subpart for any fiscal year if the number of Indian children eligible under section 7117 who were enrolled in the schools of the agency, and to whom the agency provided free public education, during the preceding fiscal year —

- was at least 10; or
- constituted not less than 25 percent of the total number of individuals enrolled in the schools of such agency.
- EXCLUSION- The requirement of paragraph (1) shall not apply in Alaska, California, or Oklahoma, or with respect to any local educational agency located on, or in proximity to, a reservation.

What budgetary expenditures are possible with Title VII funds?

1. meeting the unique educational and culturally related academic needs of American Indians and Alaska Natives;
2. the education of Indian children and adults;
3. the training of Indian persons as educators and counselors, and in other professions serving Indian people; and
4. research, evaluation, data collection, and technical assistance.

> *"The goal of education is not to increase the amount of knowledge but to create the possibilities for a child to invent and discover, to create men who are capable of doing new things."*
> - Jean Piaget

Title IX

http://www2.ed.gov/about/offices/list/ocr/docs/tix_dis.html

While most people think of Title IX of merely requiring schools to ensure that women have the opportunity to participate in athletics, proportionality has long been at the center of Title IX enforcement at the collegiate level. Developed in 1979 as part of a three-prong test of Title IX compliance, proportionality sets up a rigid quota for schools where the gender ratio of athletes must match the gender ratio of the overall student body. (Allison Kasic, May 5, 2009).

Participation Opportunities

The Opportunities provision concerns the opportunity for a student to become a par- participant in the interscholastic athletics program. The Three-Part Test was developed to assess a school's performance in affording potential athletes chances to participate. The Three-Part Test provides schools with three methods for compliance. Schools achieve compliance in this area by meeting the standard for one of the three tests, known col- collectively as the Three-Part Test. School personnel may choose which one method the school will meet.

- **Test One – Proportionality**: This first test is based on a comparison of the percent of school enrollment for a gender to the percent of participation in sports by that gender.

- **Test Two – Program Expansion**: The second test is designed to judge the school's efforts to expand or increase the number of participants for the under pre- scented sex – nearly always girls. Usually, schools that achieve compliance with test two have added new sports and teams (for example, freshman, junior varsity, and varsity teams) for girls, which has resulted in a significant increase in the number of female participants.

- **Test Three – Full Accommodation**: The third test assesses whether the school's athletic program already offers every team for the underrepresented sex, usually girls for which there are sufficient interest and ability to field a team, and sufficient competition for that team in the area where the school normally competes. A school is required to meet the standard for one of the three tests to comply with this Title IX component.

Test One – Proportionality

Test One - Proportionality is met when the percentage of the school enrollment for one gender is "substantially proportionate" to that gender's percentage of participation opportunities. For example, girls may comprise 49% of a school's enrollment and 47% of the interscholastic participants. There is a two-percentage points difference between girls' rate of participation and rate of enrollment, and this may be close enough to meet Test One. An individual athlete, or participant, may be counted more than once. For example, a female athlete who participated in varsity volleyball, junior varsity basketball, and varsity basketball would be counted as three participants. This is known as a triple count.

In assessing compliance for Test One – Proportionality, the difference between a gender's percent of school enrollment and the percent of participation in sports by that gender is calculated, as shown in the example above. A compliance target (but not a formal standard), is for a gender's rate of participation to be within three (3) percentage of their rate of enrollment. Therefore, in our example, it appears that the standard for Test One is being met and compliance is achieved.

Test Two – Program Expansion

Test Two – Program Expansion enables a school to comply by demonstrating a history and continuing practice of expanding opportunities for the gender that is underrepresented in the interscholastic program (which is nearly always girls). Underrepresented means that Test One – Proportionality is not met, as students of one gender are participating in interscholastic athletics at a rate that is less than their rate of enrollment. Test Two provides a method to comply even though one gender is underrepresented. The expansion of the number of opportunities may be achieved by adding new sports to the program and adding new teams at different levels of sports (for example, freshman, junior varsity and varsity teams). Test Two – Program Expansion can also be achieved or enhanced by adding opportunities to existing teams – however, this scenario may be more likely at the intercollegiate rather than the interscholastic level.

A school meeting Test Two is likely to have increased opportunities for the under rep- resented sex by 25% in the last five years. This is not a formal compliance standard or requirement; rather, this is a more likely scenario for a school to be judged compliant with Test Two. To calculate the increases, the number of participants added for the under-represented gender during the past five years is divided by the total number of participants for that gender. For example, a particular school has a total in all sports, at all levels, of 206 female participants. Of the 206, there are 33 girls who are participating on teams that were added to the athletic program during the past five years. Thirty-three divided by 206 equals .16, or 16%. The target is 25% or greater. In this example, it is unlikely that the school is meeting Test Two.

Test Three – Full Accommodation

Test Three concerns whether the school is fully and effectively accommodating the in- interests and abilities of the underrepresented sex. In effect, does the school offer every team for girls for which there are sufficient interest and ability for a team and sufficient competition for that team in the area where the school normally competes (this assumes that girls are the underrepresented gender). In high schools, an Interscholastic Athletics Survey (form) is administered to students at least every other year. This Survey gathers information about possible athletic interests that are not currently being met through the sports program. After completing an analysis of the students' responses, <u>school personnel may determine whether a meeting with prospective students and parents is appropriate concerning any expressed interest and whether consideration should be given to expanding athletic offerings</u>. **Documentation** of any meeting with students and parents should be kept in the school's Title IX file. If school personnel determine that there may be sufficient interest and ability to field a team, then an analysis should be conducted to determine if there is sufficient competition. For example, if there are not sufficient competitors within a reasonable travel distance, it would not be feasible to field a team. To determine if a school meets Test Three, this manual presents a series of questions to be answered by school personnel. The questions focus on the need for adding new teams or additional levels of a team (which is determined mostly by an analysis of the survey results). A response of "no" to the questions would suggest that the school may be meeting Test Three with its current program.

Practices and events. Include this information in handbooks and on the school's website. Give student-athletes copies of schedules for both practices and events.

- Schedule a like number of events for boys' and girls' teams for like sports.
- Schedule at least 40% of the girls' home basketball games on prime dates.
- Rotate the start times for boys' and girls' basketball doubleheaders.
- Secure contracts with competitors so that there is a balance of home and away games each season.
- Schedule shared facilities on an equitable, rotating basis.
- Include a comparable number of tournaments, clinics, camps and schedules for "like" sports.
- Endeavor to keep travel times and distances similar for boys' and girls' teams.

Travel and Per Diem

This benefit component involves the mode of transportation, distances traveled, and meals and lodging that are provided for teams. Specifically, factors to consider include:

- The mode of transportation - van versus bus, luxury charter versus school bus;

- Out of state or region travel for tournaments, clinics, and camps;
- Meals arranged by school personnel from restaurants or by booster groups; and
- Accommodations for overnight stays.

Suggestions Regarding Travel and Per Diem:
- Develop a written policy for the equitable purchase and provision of meals. The per diem policy may be structured to address the dollar amount and when teams stop for food based on the distance from the school. Consider the role of booster groups in either funding for meals or providing food for athletes.
- Adopt a written policy that delineates the type of lodging that will house teams for away activities and the number of athletes to be assigned to each hotel room. It may be appropriate to identify a range for the dollar amount to be spent for specific locations that teams may visit for out of town events.
- Ensure that the quality of transportation, such as buses and vans, is comparable for girls' and boys' teams. Again, the actual distance to be traveled may serve as a guide in determining the method of transportation.
- Provide similar travel opportunities for like teams for out-of-region and out-of-state experiences, such as tournaments, clinics and camps. Also, consider providing a similar number of special travel opportunities for boys' and girls' teams overall, including girls' and boys' teams in dissimilar sports.

Coaching

Coaches are responsible for the instruction and supervision of student athletes as well as performing a multitude of other duties that are necessary to field a team. It is critical that both girls' and boy's teams are led by competent and caring individuals. The success of many programs can often depend on the quality of the coaching. The foul- lowing factors are considered relative to this component, as adapted for Kentucky:

- compensation, including the dollar amount and the number of extended days;
- levels of experience and qualifications;
- the location of the primary work assignment, and whether it is on campus or off campus;
- the availability of female coaches;
- the number of coaches per team; and
- the number of volunteer coaches.

Suggestions Regarding Coaching:
- Maintain an equitable pay scale for coaches of boys' teams and coaches of girls' teams, and retain a copy of the pay scale in the school's permanent Title IX file.
- Develop strategies that encourage women to seek coaching positions.
- Provide an equal number of coaches for like teams if the number of participants is similar for both the boys' team and girls' team.
- Hire coaches with similar levels of competence and experience for boys' teams and girls' teams.
- Provide opportunities for attendance at clinics, in-service, workshops, etc., for coaches of both girls' and boys' teams.
- Maintain a balance of on-campus/off-campus coaches for teams of both genders.

Principal's responsibilities for Title IX:

- Maintain communication and documentation with the AAO.
- Accumulate and record all needed documentation
- Maintain active communication with the SHAC
- Provide administrative and clerical support that is equitable for both girls' and boys' coaches.
- Provide office space for all coaches and keep a written copy of the assignments with the school's Title IX documents. Assign the same or similar number of girls' and boys' coaches to offices by season if space must be shared.
- Provide office supplies and equipment and access to equipment (copiers, fax machines, etc.) on an equitable basis for girls' and boys' coaches.

Tutoring

This benefit deals with the provision of instructional assistance to ensure that all athletes are achieving satisfactory academic progress. Most often, students attend the Extended School Service Program offered at their respective school.

Suggestions for Tutoring

Encourage an attitude among athletes that academics come first. Provide an appropriate environment for both male and female athletes for receiving additional instructional services.

Housing and Dining Facilities and Services Recruitment of Student-Athletes Athletic Scholarships

It should be noted that these three components – Housing and Dining Facilities and Services, Recruitment of Student Athletes, and Athletic Scholarships do not apply to public high schools as a general rule.

Budgets, Booster Clubs, and Fundraising

Available funding may determine the extent to which opportunities and benefits are provided. However, lack of funds cannot justify more limited opportunities and/or benefits for one gender.

The funding of a school's interscholastic sports program is a matter that receives extensive scrutiny. Title IX does not require that budgets or expenditures be the same for girls' and boys' teams in the same sport or overall programs. Title IX does require that equivalent opportunities and benefits be provided. While budgets suggest intent, expenditures show practices. It is critically important that spending for athletics is closely monitored to avoid establishing a pattern of inequity. The most prudent approach for a school's financial practices is to implement well-defined procedures for fund raising and expenditures that are followed without exception. It is the responsibility of the school's administration to oversee financial matters and ensure that spending is kept in balance for both genders.

Booster organizations are recognized for their contributions in both time and money, and their efforts are often extremely important in maintaining a viable interscholastic sports program. A booster organization is defined as "any individual or agency which provides resources to a school's athletes and/or athletic teams." School personnel must be cognizant of spending by a booster or booster organizations. Benefits provided by boosters are viewed under Title IX as provided by the school, and the school's administration is responsible for ensuring equity. Thus, it is imperative that clear policies and procedures are in place to protect against any one group spending excessive amounts for a particular team. A signed, up-to-date agreement with every booster group is recommended, and a copy of this document should be kept in the school's Title IX file.

Suggestions for Budgets, Booster Clubs, and Fundraising:

- Ensure appropriate administrative oversight of booster activities. Maintain writ- ten agreements with all booster organizations that define the role of the group and its relationship to the school and the school's administration. Ensure that written procedures provide for athletic director/principal/school board approval for booster club fund raising and expenditures that benefit all teams.

- Include representative(s) from booster organization(s) on the Gender Equity Review Committee.

- Meet with booster clubs and other community groups periodically. Provide information for all interested parties that clearly delineate your school's commitment to equitable funding of boys' athletics and girls' athletics.

- Consider establishing one booster club that supports all teams or one booster club for like sports such as boys' basketball and girls' basketball.

- Structure joint fund raising activities that benefit both a girls' team and a boys' team. For example, the boys' basketball and the girls' basketball teams engage in an activity and equitably share the funds collected.

- Evaluate expenditures for athletics over a two-year period.

- Calculate and monitor the amount of money spent per male athlete as compared to the amount spent per female athlete. Identify the cause for any significant differences, and whether those differences may be justified by the nature of sports (for example, providing pants and a jersey, protective padding and a helmet requires a greater expenditure for a football athlete than a uniform for a volleyball athlete). Differences that cannot be explained by sport-specific needs should be carefully reviewed.

Acronyms for Principals

Budget Acronyms

ADA - Average daily attendance

CIC - Campus Improvement Committee CIP - Capital improvement plan

DBP-Decentralized budget process (SBDM and Campus Level Decisions and Recommendations).

ESEA - Elementary and Secondary Education Act ESL - English as a second language

LFA - Local fund assignment NOGA - Notice of grant award

PTA - Parent-Teacher Association PTAD - Property Tax Appraisal District RFP - Request for Proposal

RPG - Resource Planning Group SBDM - Site-based decision making

SEA - Service efforts and accomplishments SSA - Shared services arrangement

TASBO - Texas Association of School Business Officials TEA - Texas Education Agency

LPAC Acronyms

AEP – Alternative Education Program

ARD – Admission Review and Dismissal Committee

AYP – Adequate Yearly Progress

ELL – English Language Learner

ESL – English as a Second Language

ESOL – English Speakers of Other Languages

FERPA – Family Educational Rights and Privacy Act

LEP – Limited English Proficiency

LPAC – Language Proficiency Assessment Committee

MDR – Manifestation Determination Review

NCLB – No Child Left Behind

PDAS – Professional Development and Appraisal System

SBDM – Site Based Decision Making

SBEC – State Board of Educator Certification

SBOE – State Board of Education

STAAR – State of Texas Assessment of Academic Readiness

NCLB Acronyms

Core Academic Subject Areas - English, reading or language arts, mathematics, science, foreign languages (languages other than English), civics and government, economics, arts (includes theater arts, dance, music, art, and other courses approved by SBOE for graduation credit in Fine Arts), history, and geography.

Elementary EC - 6th grades - This definition is based on the degree of rigor and technicality of the subject matter that the teacher will need to know in relation to the Texas' content standards and academic achievement standards for the subjects that will be taught.

Experienced Teacher - For all highly-qualified purposes other than the equity plan requirement: A teacher who has one or more creditable years of teaching experience. For practical purposes, the term "experienced" teacher does not have a different meaning than the term "veteran teacher" or "teacher who is not new to the profession." The term experienced teacher is used rather than veteran teacher in this context only because we do not want to imply that such a teacher must have extensive teaching experience.

Experience is defined as - Employment as a teacher; therefore, documented employment as a teacher—in an accredited public school, charter school, or private school—is required. Experience does not include student teaching or its equivalent or employment as a substitute; however, teachers may count their alternative certification program internship if they were the teacher of record. The time requirement associated with experience is at least one creditable year of employment is defined in the Texas Administrative Code, Chapter 153, Subchapter CC. One year of creditable employment is a minimum of 90 full-time instructional days as a teacher in a school year.

Full State Certification - A person who holds a valid Texas standard teacher's certificate, lifetime teacher's certificate, or Texas temporary teaching certificate is considered to have full state certification.

General Elementary Curriculum - English, language arts, math, science, and social studies courses taught in grades EC-6.

Highly Qualified - As defined in P.L. 107-110, Section 9101(23)—See Appendix A

Highly Qualified - As defined by reauthorized IDEIA statute for special education teachers—See Appendix A

Inexperienced Teacher - For purposes of the equity plan requirement, the state defines as a teacher who has five or less creditable years of teaching experience as reported in the AEIS report categories of first year (beginning) and 1-5 years (inexperienced).

New Teacher - There has been a great deal of confusion concerning the term "new." The term is used in two very different instances:

1. **A new teacher to the district** when the "highly qualified" requirements must be met to be hired on Title I campus; and
2. **A new teacher to the profession** to determine what options are available for demonstration of competency.

New teacher to the district:

- **Regardless of the level of Teaching Experience** - A teacher hired for the first time by the district to teach a core academic subject in a Title I, Part A program must meet the "highly qualified" requirements when hired. This is a teacher who is "new to the district," but not necessarily "new to the profession." This determination is not based on years of experience, simply on when the teacher was hired by the district and whether the teacher teaches in a Title I, Part A program.

- **New teacher to the profession** - A teacher that does not have a creditable year of teaching experience at the elementary, middle school, or high school level. A teacher would only be considered "new to the profession" until they have one year of creditable teaching experience.

- **Secondary Teacher - Grades 7-12** - This definition is based on the degree of rigor and technicality of the subject matter that the teacher will need to know in relation to the Texas' content standards and academic achievement standards for the subjects that will be taught.

Title I, Part A Program - Campuses that receive Title I, Part A funds operate as either Schoolwide Programs or as Targeted Assistance Programs, as indicated in the LEA's current approved Consolidated NCLB Application for Federal Funding (SAS-NCLB-AA).

PDAS Acronyms

(Until TEA choses to start testing over the T-TESS at present PDAS is still used within TExES 068 testing).

Below Expectations - PDAS domain rating - Students in a teacher's classroom are "occasionally" successful in learning. (50-79% of the time).

Continuous Improvement Instructional Planning Process - A tool for teachers to link and align student needs with instruction, staff development, assessment and PDAS.

Creative thinking - Alternative, divergent, cognitive processes which result in solving problems, making products, or posing questions which are initially novel or unconventional

Criteria - Descriptions of behaviors evaluated within the Professional Development and Appraisal System.

Critical Attributes - Words and expressions used in each of the criteria in the appraisal framework which convey the central meaning of the criteria, i.e., that behavior which is to be evaluated.

Documentation - For purposes of PDAS, documentation is data collected by a teacher's appraiser for use in the summative conference. Documentation is obtained from walkthroughs, the observation summary form (OSF), the Teacher Self-Report,

Domain - One of eight broad categories of teaching practice in the Professional Development and Appraisal System which serve to organize the behaviors (criteria) evaluated within the system.

Exceeds Expectations - PDAS domain rating - Students in a teacher's classroom are "consistently" engaged and successful in learning that has great depth and complexity. (90-100% of the time)

Learner Centered - Focused on learning, the learning needs of students and the varied characteristic of students; contributing to student success.

Motivational Strategies - Teacher behaviors which increase the probability that a student will actively and successfully participate in the learning. Elements include level of concern, level of difficulty, stimulus variation, rewards and feeling tone.

PGP – Professional Growth Plan, also Teacher Intervention Plan, or Needs Assessment Plan, or other depending on the district usage.

Proficient - PDAS domain rating – Students in a teacher's classroom are engaged and successful in learning. (80-89% of the time).

TAC – Texas Academic Code

TAKS – Texas Assessment of Knowledge and Skills.

TEC – Texas Education Code

TEKS – Texas Essential Knowledge and Skills is the state curriculum framework established by law. (TEC § 28, Subchapter A. Essential Knowledge and Skills; Curriculum)

Walkthroughs – Informal, unannounced, and unplanned

SBDM Acronyms

CAP – Campus Action Plan

CIP – Campus Improvement Plan

CIT – Campus Improvement Team

CBC – Campus Budget Committee

CCC – Campus Curriculum Committee

CNC – Comprehensive Needs Assessment

CPC – Campus Planning Committee

CSDC – Campus Staff Development Committee

DIP – District Improvement Plans

SCEP – State Compensatory Education Program

RESC – Regional Education Service Centers

SHAC – Site Health Action Committee

References

Agency, T. E. (January 2010). *Site-based decsion making*. Austin, Texas: Texas Education Agency.

Andrews, D., & Lewis, M. (2002). The experience of a professional community: Teachers developing a new image of themselves and their workplace. *Educational Research, 44*, 237-254. Retrieved from http://dx.doi.org/10.1080/00131880210135340

Andrews, R., Soder, R., & Jacoby, F. (1986). *Principal Roles, Other In-School Variables, and Academic Achievement by Ethnicity and SES*. San Francisco: Addison-Wesley.

Ashton, P. T., & Webb, R. B. (1986). *Making a difference: Teachers' sense of efficacy and student achievement*. New York, NY: Longman.

Augustine, C. H., Gonzalez, G., Ikemoto, G. S., Russell, J., Zellman, G. L., Constant, L., . . . Dembosky, J. W. (2009). *Improving School Leadership: The Promise of Cohesive Leadership Systems*. RAND Corporation.

Barth, R. S. (1990). Improving schools from within. In R. S. Barth, *Learning by heart*. San Francisco, CA: Jossey-Bass.

Bennis, W. (1990). Managing the dream: Leadership in the 21st century. *Training: The Magazine of Human Resource Development, 27*(5), 44-46.

Bennis, W., & Nanus, B. (1985). *Leaders: The strategies for taking charge*. New York: Harper & Row.

Blase, J., & Blase, J. (2006). *Teachers bringing out the best in teachers: A guide to peer consultation for administrators and teachers*. Corwin Press: Thousand Oaks, CA.

Bosman, J. (2010, March 30). Retrieved from www.nytimes.com/2010/03/31/nyregion/31cash.html

Brookover, W. B., & Lezotte, L. W. (1979). *Changes in school characteristics coincident with changes in student achievement*. East Lansing, MI: The Institute for Research on Teaching.

Brownell, M. T., Adams, A., Sindelar, P., N., W., & Vanhover, S. (2006). Learning from collaboration: The role of teacher qualities. *Exceptional Children, 72* (2), 169-187.

CASEL Website. (2006). *practice rubric for schoolwide SEL implementation*. Retrieved from Collaborative for Academic, Social, and Emotional Learning: http://casel.org/publications/practice-rubric-for-schoolwide-implementation/

CASEL website. (n.d.). *Climate & Connectedness*. Retrieved from Collaborative for Academic, Social, and Emotional Learning: http://casel.org/why-it-matters/what-is-sel/climate-connectedness

CASEL website. (n.d.). *Collaborating districts initiative*. Retrieved from Collaborative for Academic, Social, and Emotional Learning: http://casel.org/collaborating-districts-initiative

CASEL: The first ten years 1994-2004, Building a foundation for the future. (2004). Retrieved from Collaborative for Academic, Social, and Emotional Learning: http://casel.org/research/publications/?t=casel-annual-event-reports

Cowan, G., Bobby, K., St. Roseman, P., & Echandia, A. (2002). *Evaluation report: The home visit project*. Sacramento, CA: Sacramento City Unified School District. Retrieved from www.eric.ed.gov/PDFS/ED466018.pdf

Cuban, L. (1989). At-risk students: What teachers and principals can do. *Educational Leadership, 46*(5), 29 - 33.

Datnow, A., Park, V., & Wohlstetter, P. (2007). *Achieving with Data: How High-Performing School Systems Use Data to Improve Instruction for Elementary Students.* Los Angeles: University of Southern California, Center on Educational Governance.

De Pree, M. (1989). *Leadership is an art.* New York: Doubleday.

Epstein, J. L., Clark, L., Salinas, K. C., & Sanders, M. G. (1997). Scaling up school-family-community connections in Baltimore: Effects on student achievement and attendance. *annual meeting of the American Education Research Association.* Chicago, IL.

Ferlazzo, L., & Hammond, L. A. (2009). Building parent engagement in schools. Santa Barbara, CA. *Linworth.*

Freedman, S. (2009). Collegiality Matters: How Do We Work with Others? Proceedings of the Charleston Library Conference. Retrieved from http://dx.doi.org/10.5703/1288284314771

Fullan, M. (2001). *Leading in a culture of change.* San Francisco, CA: Jossey-Bass.

Fullan, M. G., & Hargreaves, A. (1991). *What's worth fighting for? Working together for your school.* Ontario, CAN: Ontario Public Schools Teachers' Federation.

Greenfield, W. D. (1987). *Instructional leadership: Concepts, issues, and controversies.* Boston: Allyn and Bacon.

Greenfield, W. D. (1991). *The micro politics of leadership in an urban elementary school.* Chicago.

Hanifan, L. K. (1916, September). The rural school community center. Annals of the American Academy of Political and Social Science. 67, 130–138.

Harris, D. L., & Anthony, H. M. (2001). *Collegiality and its role in teacher development: perspectives from veteran and novice teachers, Teacher Development.*

Haycock, K. (1990). Equity, relevance, and will. In J. G. Bain & J. L. Herman (Eds.). *Making schools work for underachieving minority students: Next steps for research, policy, and practice,* 53-58.

Heck, R. H., Larsen, T. J., & Marcoulides, G. A. (1990). Instructional leadership and school achievement: Validation of a causal model. *Educational Administration Quarterly,* 26, 94-125.

Henderson, A. T., & Mapp, K. L. (2002). *A new wave of evidence: The impact of school, family, and community connections on student achievement.* Austin, TX: National Center for Family and Community Connections with Schools.

Jerald, C. (2006, December). *Issue Brief. School Culture: "The Hidden Curriculum.".* Retrieved from The Center for Comprehensive School Reform and Improvement: www.centerforcsri.org

Killion, J. (2001). *What works in elementary schools: Results-based staff development.* Oxford, OH: National Staff Development Council.

Killion, J., & Harrison, C. (2006). Taking the Lead: New Roles for Teachers and School-Based Coaches. *National Staff Development Council,* MetLife Teacher Survey. Spring 2008.

Kwantes, C. T., & Boglarsky, C. A. (2007). Perceptions of organizational culture, leadership effectiveness and personal effectiveness across six countries. *Journal of International Management.*

Larner, M. (2004). *Pathways: Charting a course for professional learning.* Portsmouth, NH: Heinemann.

Little, J. W. (1982). Norms of collegiality and experimentation: Workplace conditions of school success. *American Educational*

Research Journal, 19 (3), 325-340.

Little, J. W. (1990). The persistence of privacy: Autonomy and initiative in teachers' professional relations. *Teachers College Record*, 91 (4), 509-536.

Little, J. W. (1993). Teachers' professional development in a climate of educational reform. *Educational Evaluation and Policy Analysis 15*, 129-151.

Little, J. W. (1999). Colleagues of choice, colleagues of circumstance: A response to M Fielding. *The Australian Educational Researcher*, 26 (2), 35-43. Retrieved from http://dx.doi.org/10.1007/BF03219693

Mandinach, E., Honey, M., & Light, D. (2006, April). A Theoretical Framework for Data-Driven Decision Making. *American Educational Research Association*. San Francisco, CA.

Marzano, R., Pickering, D., & Pollock, J. (2001). *Classroom instruction that works*. Alexandria, VA: ASCD.

Mediratta, K., Shah, S., McAlister, S., Fruchter, N., Mokhtar, C., & & Lockwood, D. (2008). *Organized communities, stronger schools: A preview of research findings. Providence, RI: Annenberg Institute for School Reform at Brown University*. Retrieved from www.annenberginstitute.org/pdf/OrganizedCommunities.pdf

Moir, E. (1990). *Phases of First Year Teaching*. California New Teacher Project Newsletter.

Murphy, J. A. (1988). Improving the achievement of minority students. *Educational Leadership*, 46(2), 41-42.

Pink, D. (2009). *Drive: The surprising truth about what motivates us*. New York: Riverhead Books.

Plecki, M. L., Knapp, M. S., Castaneda, T., Halverson, T., LaSota, R., & Lochmiller, C. (2009). *How Leaders Invest Staffing Resources for Learning Improvement*. University of Washington.

Portin, B. S., Knapp, M. S., Dareff, S., Feldman, S., Russell, F. A., Samuelson, C., & Yeh., T. L. (2009). *Leadership for Learning Improvement in Urban Schools*. University of Washington.

Reitzug, U. C. (1989). Principal-teacher interactions in instructionally effective and ordinary elementary schools. *Urban Education*, 24, 38-58.

Richardson, J. (2008, April 7). Principals Cultivate Support to Nurture New Teachers. *The Learning Principal Vol. 3*. Retrieved from www.nsdc.org

Rothstein, R. (2010, October 14). *How to fix our schools (Issue brief 286)*. Retrieved from Washington, DC: Economic Policy Institute: www.epi.org/publications/entry/ib286

Sergiovanni, T. J. (1990). In T. J. Sergiovanni, & J. H. (Eds.), *Schooling for tomorrow: Directing reforms to issues that count* (pp. 213-226). Boston: Allyn and Bacon.

Sizemore, B. A., Brossard, C. A., & Harrigan, B. (1983). *An abashing anomaly: The high achieving predominantly black elementary school*. Pittsburgh: Pittsburgh University, Department of Black Community Education.

Slavin, R., Karweit, N. L., & Madden, N. A. (1989). Effective programs for students at risk. *Needham Heights*.

Southwest Educational Development Laboratory. (2002). A new wave of evidence: The impact of school, family, and community connections on student achievement. *Southwest Educational Development Laboratory*.

Texas association of school boards. (2008). *Creating a new vision for public education in texas*. Retrieved from http://www.tasanet.org/cms/lib07/TX01923126/Centricity/Domain/111/workinprogress.pdf

Texas education agency. (2006). *Long-range plan for technology 2006-2020*. Retrieved from tea.texas.gov/WorkArea/DownloadAsset.aspx?id=2147494561

Texas education agency. (2010). *Accountability Update 14*. Retrieved from tea.texas.gov/WorkArea/DownloadAsset.aspx?id=2147491736

Texas education agency. (2010). *Budgeting Update 14*. Retrieved from http://tea.texas.gov/Finance_and_Grants/Financial_Accountability/Financial__Accountability_System_Resource_Guide/

Texas education agency. (2015). *Texas examinations of educator standards program preparation manual principal (068)*. Retrieved from http://cms.texes-ets.org/files/4714/4976/3536/068_principal_prep_manual.pdf

Texas education agency. (2016). *Co-teaching a how-to guide:guidelines for co-teaching in texas*. Retrieved from http://www.esc17.net/users/0209/GuidelinesforCoTeachinginTexas.pdf

Texas education agency. (2016). *Parents Guide to the Admission, Review, and Dismissal Process*. Retrieved from https://framework.esc18.net/Documents/ARD_Guide_ENG.pdf

Texas education agency. (2017). *2017 LPAC decision -making resources*. Retrieved from http://tea.texas.gov/student.assessment/ell/lpac/

Texas education agency. (2017). *ELL assessment documetation forms and related resources*. Retrieved from http://tea.texas.gov/student.assessment/ell/lpac/

Texas education agency. (n.d.). *Site-based decision making*. Retrieved from https://www.google.com/#q=Texas+Education+agency+budget+manual&*

Texas legislature online. (2017). Retrieved from Texs statutes education code: http://www.statutes.legis.state.tx.us/?link=ED

Texas school safety center. (2017). *Emergency managment*. Retrieved from https://txssc.txstate.edu/topics/emergency-management/

Texas school safety center. (2017). *Texas school safety*. Retrieved from https://txssc.txstate.edu/

Tuss, P. (2007). *Evaluation of the CAHSEE Home Visit Pilot Project*. Sacramento, CA: Sacramento County Office of Education, Center for Student Assessment and Program Accountability.

U.S. department of education. (2007). *Practical information on crisis planning: a guide or schools and communities*. Retrieved from http://rems.ed.gov/docs/PracticalInformationonCrisisPlanning.pdf

U.S. department of education. (2012). *FERPA presenation for elementary/secondary school officials*. Retrieved from https://www2.ed.gov/policy/gen/guid/ptac/pdf/slides.pdf

University interscholastic league. (2016). *Academic eligibility basics*. Retrieved from https://www.uiltexas.org/academics/resources/eligibility/

Van Voorhis, F. (2001). Interactive science homework: An experiment in home and school connection. *NAASP Bulletin*, 85(627), 20–32. Retrieved from http://www.sagepub.com/kgrantstudy/articles/10/van%20Voorhis.pdf

Venezky, R. L., & Winfield, L. F. (1979). *Schools that succeed beyond expectations in teaching reading*. Newark: University of Delaware, Studies in Education.

Wyly, C. (2014). *Educator's quick reference for section 504 building on the basics.* Retrieved from http://www.esc20.net/users/0057/docs/New%20Administrator's%20Guide%20to%20Section%20504.pdf